Success
in English
Reading

Barry Scholes
Anita Scholes
Stuart Bell

Series Editor: Jayne de Courcy

Ages 9–11   BOOK **1**

Contents

Collins Educational
An Imprint of HarperCollinsPublishers

The ★3★ Steps to Success ...

Step 1

Key skills practice

★ *Success in English Book 1* provides practice in a number of important English Reading skills. These skills are the ones that your child needs to master in order to achieve a high level in the English National Test at the end of Key Stage 2.

★ Each chapter takes one reading skill and works through it in straightforward steps. At the end of each chapter there is a *Test yourself* section containing questions to answer. This allows you and your child to see how well the skill has been understood.

★ This in-depth teaching and practice ensures that your child achieves real understanding of each skill.

Step 2

Practice with National Test questions

★ At the end of the book there is a Reading Test paper which is similar to the one that your child will have to sit in his/her KS2 English National Test.

★ This Test-style paper allows you to see the sort of passages and questions your child will meet in the Reading Test. The questions require your child to demonstrate all the reading skills taught in the book.

★ Your child can do this Test paper immediately after working on the skills chapters. You might, however, prefer to wait and ask your child to do it a little later to check that the reading skills have been thoroughly mastered.

Step 3

Improving your child's performance

★ The book contains detailed *Answers and Guidance* to both the *Test yourself* sections and the Reading Test paper.

★ The authors, one of whom is a KS2 Test Examiner, provide model answers and also explain what the questions are trying to assess. They show what sort of answers will score high marks in the Reading Test and why.

★ In this way, you can work with your child to help him/her improve his/her performance in the KS2 English National Test.

Help with timing

★ As the English National Test is timed, it is important that your child learns to answer questions within a time limit.

★ Each *Test yourself* section and the Test paper give target times for answering the questions. If you choose to, you can ask your child to time himself/herself when answering the questions. You can then compare his/her time against the target times provided in the *Answers and Guidance*. In this way, you will form a good idea of whether your child is working at the right rate to complete the National Test Reading paper successfully.

Progression

★ *Success in English* is aimed at 9–11 year-olds who are in Years 5 and 6 of primary school. There is in-built progression: each book builds on skills taught in previous books.

★ To get the most out of *Success in English*, it is important that your child works through all four books in sequence. If you are buying this series for your child who is aged 9/10 (Year 5), then buy Books 1 and 2, and Books 3 and 4 at age 10/11 (Year 6). If your child is already in Year 6, then it is still advisable to work through from Book 1 to Book 4, to ensure that your child benefits from the progression built into the series.

Note to teachers

★ This book, and the other four titles in the *Success in English* series, are designed for use at home and in schools in Years 5 and 6. They focus on the key reading and writing skills that will raise children's performance in the English National Test.

★ You can use the books in class or give them to children for homework to ensure that they are fully prepared for their English National Test.

What's it all about?

★ In this chapter you will learn how to find information that the writer gives you in a story.

★ The questions are all multiple choice. You need to choose the word or group of words that fit best with what you have read in the story.

★ Your National Test Reading paper will include several questions like this.

How to find information

Read the passage below carefully.

The Pencil-box

Now Barry Hunter was tormenting Mark, snatching his pencil-box from him as he steeered past.

'Give it back!'

'What?'

'That box. It's mine. Give it back.'

Mark stamped over the playground after Barry. But Barry was quicker on his feet. Prancing and dancing backwards as Mark advanced, he held the box a few inches from Mark's grasping fingers.

'Say please!'

'It's my box. You snatched it. Give it back!'

'Manners! Say please.'

The bell was ringing now.

'Give it back!'

Mr Fairway appeared in the doorway.

'Give it back!'

Mark was almost in tears.

'Say please,' tormented Barry.

'Please,' muttered Mark.

'A bit louder. I can't hear you.'

'Please,' shouted Mark in desperation.

'That's not polite,' said Barry. 'Now say it nicely.'

Mark was about to launch himself on his tormentor when suddenly Barry Hunter let out a scream of pain and swirled about, dropping the pencil-box and clutching the back of his leg.

'Who did *that*?' he yelped.

Celeste was standing right behind, eyeing him steadily.

Mr Fairway was very close now.

'What's going on over here?'

Let's see if you can answer this question:

The pencil-box belonged to:

(Barry) (Celeste) (Mark) (Mr Fairway)

The passage tells us that the pencil-box belonged to Mark. The evidence for this is in the very first sentence: 'Now Barry Hunter was tormenting Mark, <u>snatching his pencil-box from him</u> as he steered past.'

Now let's see if you can work out the answer to this question:

The action took place:

(in the park) (in the playground) (in a doorway) (on the way to school)

The evidence we are looking for here is in the words 'Mark stamped over the <u>playground</u> after Barry'. A doorway is mentioned later in the passage, but this is not where the action took place.

Now read this story by the Brothers Grimm.

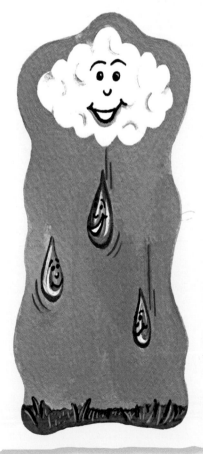

Three raindrops

A raindrop was falling out of a cloud, and it said to the raindrop next to it: 'I'm the biggest and best raindrop in the whole sky!'

'You are indeed a fine raindrop,' said the second, 'but you are not nearly so beautifully shaped as I am. And in my opinion it's shape that counts, and I am therefore the best raindrop in the whole sky.'

The first raindrop replied: 'Let us settle this matter once and for all.' So they asked a third raindrop to decide between them.

But the third raindrop said: 'What nonsense you're both talking! *You* may be a big raindrop, and *you* are certainly well-shaped, but, as everybody knows, it's purity that really counts, and I am purer than either of you. *I* am therefore the best raindrop in the whole sky!'

Well, before either of the other raindrops could reply, they all three hit the ground and became part of a very muddy puddle.

Answer these questions by choosing the word or group of words that best describes what happened in the story.

The Pencil-box

1 Barry wanted Mark to:

| give the pencil-box back | say 'please' | speak politely | say please loudly, but politely |

2 Barry stopped tormenting Mark because:

| Mr Fairview was very close | he felt a pain in his leg | the bell was ringing | Mark made him give the pencil-box back |

Three raindrops

3 The second raindrop thought he was:

| the biggest | the purest | the most beautifully shaped | the biggest and the best |

4 They spoke to the third raindrop because:

| he was the wisest | he was the most pure | they wanted him to settle the argument | they were in a hurry |

5 The argument ended when:

| they fell out of a cloud | they became part of a puddle | the third raindrop gave them his opinion | they fell in some mud |

Answers and Guidance are given on p.31. **How long did you take?**

6

2 Finding facts in information texts

What's it all about?

★ In this chapter you will learn how to find facts in an information text.

★ You will learn how to use key words in the questions to help you find the facts you need.

★ You will also learn how to put these facts in your own words.

★ Your National Test Reading paper may include several questions like this.

How to find information

Read carefully this information text about sharks. Don't forget to study the diagrams and read the captions, as well as the main text.

What is a shark?

Sharks are fish, but they are different from fish like cod or herring because a shark has soft bones.

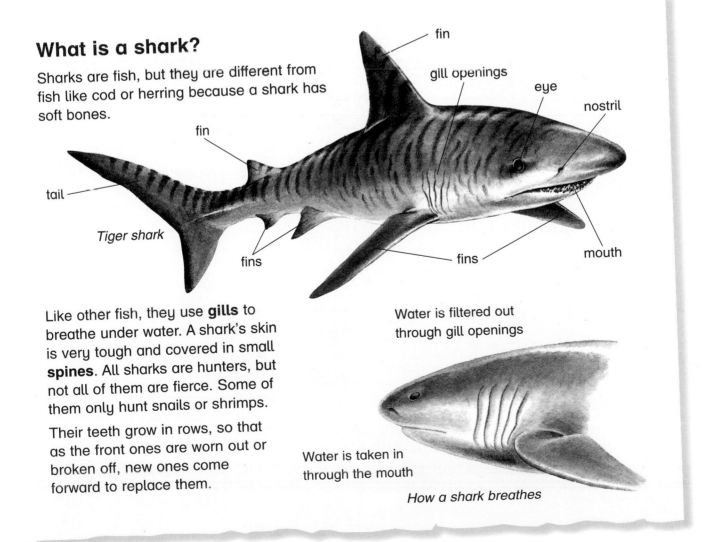

fin

gill openings

eye

nostril

fin

tail

Tiger shark

fins

fins

mouth

Like other fish, they use **gills** to breathe under water. A shark's skin is very tough and covered in small **spines**. All sharks are hunters, but not all of them are fierce. Some of them only hunt snails or shrimps.

Their teeth grow in rows, so that as the front ones are worn out or broken off, new ones come forward to replace them.

Water is filtered out through gill openings

Water is taken in through the mouth

How a shark breathes

Help! Sharks!

Most people are afraid of sharks, because they think that they will attack people who go swimming. In some parts of the world big sharks are dangerous, but there are many different kinds of shark, and most of them are harmless.

Some sharks live at the bottom of the sea. Others live in rivers and can give strong electric shocks.

Some sharks are even good to eat!

Angel shark

Sand Tiger shark

Mako shark

Sharks and people

Great white sharks are not the only ones that are dangerous to people. Hammerheads, blue sharks and sand sharks will all attack if they have the chance.

In warm countries, there is often a net in the sea to keep sharks away from beaches where people swim. A few small sharks, such as dogfish, are good to eat. Some Chinese people use shark fins to make a special soup.

Sharks are being studied by scientists, so that we can learn more about them.

Let's see if you can answer this question:

Why are shark nets used in warm countries?

The key words in this question are 'nets' and 'warm countries'. Look over the text quickly for these key words. When you have found them, read the text carefully to find the information you are looking for.

This kind of reading – looking quickly for key words – is a very important skill called **scanning**. You will need to scan whenever you look for information.

The passage tells us that 'there is often a net in the sea to keep sharks away from beaches where people swim'. With questions such as this, you need to answer in your own words, rather than copying words from the passage.

A good answer to this question is:

In warm countries nets are used in the sea to keep sharks away from people swimming.

Now let's see if you can work out the answer to this question:

> What is unusual about sharks' teeth?

The key word to scan for is 'teeth'. The passage tells us that sharks' 'teeth grow in rows, so that as the front ones are worn out or broken off, new ones come forward to replace them'.

A good answer is:

Sharks' teeth grow in rows and as the front teeth break off new ones take their place by coming forward.

This answer gives all the information needed, but puts it in different words.

Test yourself

Answer these questions by finding the correct information in the text. Pick out the key words in the question to help you.

1 Are all sharks fierce hunters? Give a reason for your answer.

2 We are told of two places where sharks might live. What are they?

3 In what way is a great white shark dangerous? What other sharks are equally dangerous?

4 In what ways are sharks useful to humans?

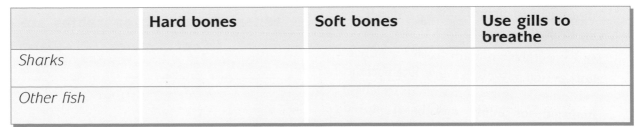

5 How does a shark breathe?

6 Copy this grid. Use facts from the passage to help you put a tick in the right spaces.

	Hard bones	Soft bones	Use gills to breathe
Sharks			
Other fish			

Answers and Guidance are given on p.31. **How long did you take?**

9

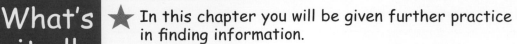

⭐ In this chapter you will be given further practice in finding information.

⭐ You will also learn how to write this information down in a different way.

⭐ Your National Test Reading paper will include questions that expect you to write down, in a different way, information that you have found in a non-fiction passage.

How to find and write down information

Read the passage below carefully.

Fruit and vegetables

Fruit and vegetables are the parts of plants which may be eaten. As you would expect apples, oranges, bananas or pears are the fruits of their plants, but vegetables may be leaves, flowers, stems or even roots.

We eat the leaves of vegetables such as cabbage, lettuce and spinach, but the flower parts of cauliflower and broccoli. With sweetcorn and peas we wait until the flowers turn to seed before we eat them. Celery and asparagus are the stems of plants, while carrots, turnips, beetroots and radishes are roots. Potatoes are the underground tubers of the plant, and leeks and onions are the bases of leaves. Tomatoes are usually considered to be vegetables, but are in fact fruit.

Most vegetables remain fresh for only a short period, although a few, like potatoes and onions, may remain in excellent condition for many months if stored carefully.

Many vegetables are preserved by canning, freezing, or drying. When de-frosted, frozen vegetables are the closest in taste and look to fresh ones.

Fruits are often kept fresh in refrigerated storage rooms. Some, such as dates, figs, prunes and apricots, are usually dried, while fruits that would go rotten quickly, such as strawberries, raspberries and blueberries, are canned or frozen.

Fruit and vegetables are very important for our continued good health, as they are rich in vitamins and minerals and also supply fibre.

Where fruit and vegetables are grown		
	Cool climates	**Warm climates**
Fruit:	apples	apricots
	cherries	bananas
	pears	figs
	raspberries	grapes
	strawberries	pineapples
Vegetables:	cabbage	aubergines
	lettuce	peppers
	onions	sweetcorn
	peas	tomatoes
	spinach	yams

Let's see if you can answer these questions:

> Write **two** facts about figs.

The key word in this question is 'figs'. Scan the passage for this key word. When you have found it, read that part of the text carefully. Then continue scanning the rest of the passage for figs until you have found all the information you need.

Figs are mentioned twice: as fruit growing in a warm climate, and as fruits which are preserved by drying. We can combine these two pieces of information into one sentence:

Figs grow in a warm climate and are usually preserved by drying.

> Write a sentence about each of these, saying what they are and where they are grown: a) tomatoes b) raspberries c) pineapples.

All the information we need is in the chart. Scan for each item and note whether it is in the vegetable or fruit section. Then check if it is in the cool or warm climate column.

Then write out this information in three separate sentences. Notice that each sentence below is slightly different in structure.

Aubergines are vegetables which are grown in warm climates. Raspberries are cool climate fruits. Apricots are fruits from warm climates.

Test yourself

1 Copy and complete this chart about **vegetables**, using information from the text. The first box has been completed for you.

Parts of a plant where vegetables come from						
Leaves	**Flowers**	**Seeds**	**Stems**	**Roots**	**Tubers**	**Bases of leaves**
cabbage						
lettuce						
spinach						

2 Write a sentence containing two facts about tomatoes.

3 Write a sentence containing two facts about potatoes.

4 Write down three ways in which strawberries and raspberries are similar.

Answers and Guidance are given on p.32. *How long did you take?*

11

What's it all about?

★ In this chapter you will learn how to 'read between the lines' of a story.

★ You will be learning how to use clues to read beyond the words that the author has actually used.

★ Your National Test Reading paper will include several questions that expect you to look for clues in a story to work out the answers.

How to read for clues

Read the passage carefully. It is taken from a story by Jamila Gavin.

Aziz and the amazing motorbike ride

Aziz sat in his wheelchair looking out of the window.

In each long day it was the afternoons that seemed the longest part. He would wait and wait, watching for the moment when the children would explode out of school. That was the best time.

But now he just gazed out of the window at other people's back gardens. He could see Mrs Lal hanging out her saris on the washing line; Mr Yates digging his garden, and over there was Masood – tinkering with his motorbike.

Aziz loved that motorbike. He wanted to see Masood jump on the starter and hear the engine catch and turn over. He wanted to hear him open up the throttle and rev up until a great roar filled the neighbourhood. He knew this made Mrs Lal very angry because it woke her baby. She would shake her fist and hold her head. Mr Yates did not like it much either and he would yell at Masood and tell him to be quiet. But Aziz thought the noise of the motorbike was the greatest sound in the world. Whenever he heard it he would push himself up in his chair until his arms were straight – as if the power of the machine could lift him out of his chair.

This afternoon Masood did not look as if he was going to take the bike out. He lay on his back with an oil can at his side, greasing the engine and cleaning the parts. When the job was done he went back indoors to wash. Aziz flopped back, disappointed. The motorbike stood proudly on its stand, its chrome and paintwork gleaming in the sunlight.

Suddenly Aziz heard the kick of the starter and the roar of the engine. He looked up – but too late! The motorbike had gone.

'Oh no! I missed him!' groaned Aziz. 'Masood must have come out so quickly.' He listened to the sound of the engine as it went down the alley that ran between the gardens. But strangely enough, the sound seemed very close. Right next to him! Aziz leaned forward to look out and gave a shout of excitement. There at his window – with the engine running – stood the motorbike!

'Come for a ride,' said the motorbike. 'I'm shiny and oiled and full of petrol.'

'How can I?' cried Aziz. 'Since my accident I cannot move my legs.'

'Just slide on to my seat,' said the motorbike. 'Grip my handlebars and I'll do the rest.'

So Aziz stretched out as far as he could and seemed to float through the window. In a second he was astride the motorbike. Masood's helmet and goggles were hanging from the handlebars. Aziz put them on and felt like a motorcycle champion.

'I'm ready!' he shouted.

'RRRRrrrmmmm ... RRRRrrrmmmm ...RRRrrrmmm ... RRRrrrmmm ...' the motorbike roared. Aziz felt the power rush through him – and then they were off.

Let's see if you can answer this question:

> Do you think Aziz was looking out from the front of the house or the back? What makes you think so?

The author does not tell us where Aziz was sitting, but there are two clues in the story to help us to work out the answer. Since Aziz 'gazed out of the window at people's back gardens' it is more than likely that he was sitting in a room at the back of his house. Also, Aziz saw Mrs Lal hanging out her saris on the washing line and washing lines are usually in back gardens.

A good answer would be:

Aziz was probably sitting in a room at the back of his house because he could see other people's back gardens and he also saw Mrs Lal hanging out some washing on the line.

Now let's see if you can work out the answer to this question:

> How can you tell that Masood spent a lot of time looking after his motorbike?

There are lots of clues in the text which suggest this: 'tinkering', 'greasing the engine and cleaning the parts', 'paintwork gleaming' and 'I'm shiny and oiled and full of petrol'.

A good answer would include some or all of these points:

I can tell that Masood spent a lot of time cleaning his motorbike because the passage says that he was always tinkering with it, greasing the engine and cleaning the parts, and that the bike's paintwork was gleaming.

Test yourself

Answer these questions by using clues in the passage.

1 Why do you think Aziz found that the afternoon seemed the longest part of each day?

2 Why do you think the best time for Aziz was when the children came out of school?

3 Do you think that Aziz was unable to move his arms and his legs, or only his legs? What makes you think so?

4 At the end of the fourth paragraph the author says, '… as if the power of the machine could lift him out of his chair'. What happens later to remind us of these words?

5 Did Aziz expect Masood to take the bike out? What makes you think so?

6 What sort of ride do you think Aziz was about to have? What makes you think so?

Answers and Guidance are given on p.32. **How long did you take?**

14

5 Reading information texts for clues

How to read an information text for clues

Read these information texts carefully.

Make your own yoghurt

You will need:

750 ml longlife milk

2 teaspoons fresh natural yoghurt

2–3 tablespoons dried skimmed milk

chopped fruit or nuts (optional)

1 Mix a little longlife milk and the yoghurt.

2 Stir in the remaining milk and the dried milk.

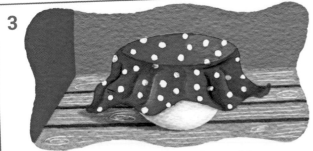

3 Cover with a tea-towel, and leave in a warm place.

4 After about 12 hours, add chopped fruit or nuts.

Eggs

Most of the eggs you eat come from chickens. Sometimes the egg box tells you about the lives of the chickens that laid them.

★ Free range chickens roam around a farmyard, eating whatever they find. You have to hunt for the eggs.
★ Deep litter chickens live in a warm shed with straw on the floor. The farmer gives them special food.
★ Battery chickens are kept in cages and given special food. The eggs are collected from a tray below the cage.

From the farm to the box

Every day, large farms send eggs to a packing station. Here, workers measure them, then shine a bright light on them which shows if any are bad. They then pack them into boxes.

How fresh is your egg?
Place your egg in a glass bowl full of water. Now watch to see what it does.

 Fresh

 Not so fresh

 Bad

There is an airspace inside one end of the egg. The older the egg, the larger the space, and the more likely it is to float.

Let's see if you can answer this question:

If you were making yoghurt, in which order would you do the following two things:
a) leave the mixture in a warm place
b) stir in the remaining milk and dried milk?
From looking at the instructions, how do you know this?

Recipes and instructions are always listed in the order of things to be done, and these steps are usually numbered. 'Leave in a warm place' is part of numbered instruction 3, while 'stir in the remaining milk and the dried milk' is instruction 2.

So the correct answer is:

I would stir in the remaining milk and dried milk before leaving the mixture in a warm place, because in the recipe this instruction comes before the instruction to leave it in a warm place.

Now let's see if you can work out the answer to this question:

> What is wrong with this explanation: 'All chicken farmers have to give their chickens special food'?

Special food is mentioned as being given to deep litter and battery chickens only. The text tells us that 'free range chickens roam around a farmyard, eating whatever they find'.

So the answer is:

Chicken farmers who only have free range chickens do not have to give their chickens special food, as they eat whatever they find in the farmyard.

Test yourself

Answer these questions by using clues in the passage.

1 Why do you think the yoghurt recipe starts with a list?

2 Can the yoghurt be made without chopped fruit or nuts? Give a reason for your answer.

3 Why do you think farm workers measure eggs?

4 Which do you think is the easiest way for a farmer to collect eggs? Give a reason for your answer.

5 Which method of producing eggs do you think is best for the chickens? What makes you think so?

6 Why do you think a glass bowl is suggested for testing how fresh an egg is?

7 The information on yoghurt is arranged differently from that on eggs. What makes the passages different?

8 Copy this grid about the information on eggs. Tick the boxes which you think best describe why it was written.

To inform
To amuse
To increase sales of eggs
To guide
To raise issues about chickens

 Answers and Guidance are given on p.33. **How long did you take?**

What's it all about?

★ In this chapter you will learn how to answer questions which ask you to find and use 'evidence' from a story.

★ Your answers will sometimes need to be completely in your own words. Sometimes they will need to contain words or phrases which you take directly from the story and which you must put in quotation marks.

★ Your National Test Reading paper may include questions that expect you to support your answers with 'evidence'.

How to use evidence from a story

Read the passage carefully.

Ginny's Egg

Ginny picked up the egg. Its gold-speckled shell shimmered very slightly in the dim light that struggled through the dusty windows of the hen house. It was the size and shape of a pear, but more like an oversized tear drop, warm and fragile. In some strange way it seemed strong too.

As Ginny held the egg in her hand, she could feel it throbbing slightly. She took her thumbs away from the shell for a moment to test whether the throbbing came from her own thumb pulses beating onto the egg, but it didn't. The pulsing came from inside the egg. Ginny's tummy beat too and a cold tingle of excitement suddenly swept through her as she recognised what it was that she was feeling.

'You're alive, aren't you!' she said to the egg. 'There's a chick inside you.' Then she looked at the egg again. 'But it can't be a hen chick. You're the wrong sort of egg.'

She held the egg's warmth to her cheek.

'You're the wrong colour and you're too big,' she told it. But what other sort of bird could have got into the hen house and laid the egg? Ginny looked around her at the high fox-proof fence of the hen run. Something could have flown down into the run from above, but it still didn't make much sense that it would lay its egg and then just leave it, did it? There were only Gran's six hens in the run now.

'You *must* be a hen egg, an odd sort of hen egg,' Ginny told it. Ginny often told herself sensible things, though she hardly ever really believed them. And today, however much a part of her wanted the excitement of a mystery egg, what she needed most was ordinary sense. She knew that the baby was about to be born and she didn't want any distractions from that.

'Think sense, Ginny Abbot. Gran's hens lay one egg every morning.' She looked in the egg basket and counted. 'See! Five eggs and the one in your hand makes six, and there are six hens. It's a hen's egg. Put it into the basket with the rest.'

Let's see if you can answer this question:

> Which words in the first paragraph suggest there was something odd about the egg?

The egg is described as 'warm and fragile' but at the same time 'in some strange way it seemed strong too'. 'Strange' is another word for 'odd'.

A good answer is:

The words which suggest the egg is odd are 'in some strange way it seemed strong too'.

Now let's see if you can work out the answer to this question:

> Write down two ways in which the egg was different from an ordinary hen's egg.

The evidence for this is in Ginny's words as she examines the egg: 'You're the wrong colour and you're too big.'

A good answer is:

Ginny's egg was bigger than a hen's egg and a different colour.

Test yourself

Answer these questions by using evidence from the story.

1 Which words describe Ginny's excitement as she held the egg?

2 Explain why she took her thumbs away from the egg as she held it.

3 Explain why she thought it unlikely another bird had laid the egg.

4 Which words tell us that she wanted the egg to be that of another bird?

5 Explain what finally made her believe it was a hen's egg.

6 Do you think the egg really is a hen's egg? Explain your reasons, using parts of the story to help you.

Answers and Guidance are given on p.34.   ***How long did you take?***

7 Using 'evidence' from information texts

What's it all about?

★ In this chapter you will learn how to answer questions using evidence from information texts.

★ Your answers will sometimes need to explain things in your own words, using the evidence you have found in the text. They will sometimes need to include direct quotations (words and phrases which you lift from the text and put quotation marks around).

★ Your National Test Reading paper may include questions that expect you to support your answers with evidence.

How to use evidence from an information text

Read this information text carefully.

What a load of rubbish

Every year, we throw away more rubbish than ever before. The type of rubbish has also changed. Fifty years ago there was far more dust and cinders, and no plastic at all. Nowadays, the average family throws away 600 cans, 2 trees' worth of paper, 120 plastic bottles and 2.4 kg of plastic wrapping, 449 glass bottles and jars and 24 kg of rags.

Contents of an 'average' dustbin

Paper	30%
Food and garden waste	25%
Dust and cinders	17%
Glass	10%
Metals	8%
Plastic	7%
Rags	3%

Litter
Litter is rubbish in the wrong place. It can be dangerous:

• broken glass can cut •

• animals can suffocate eating plastic •

• birds can get trapped •

Why reuse and recycle?

Reducing the rubbish mountain
Almost one third of our rubbish comes from packaging. Think about all the cardboard and plastic that protects the things we buy. Do we need so much packaging, and can we do something other than throw it away?

To reduce waste we can:
Reuse Lots of the objects we throw away can be made into something useful – but remember, always clean your rubbish first.

Recycle Many of the materials found in our dustbins can be sorted, taken to a factory to be cleaned and broken down, and then made into something new.

Think before you throw
Here are 3 good reasons for recycling rubbish:
1 It helps to reduce pollution, because it stops waste being buried (landfilled) or burnt (incinerated).
2 It saves energy and raw materials.
3 It creates jobs and makes money.

Let's see if you can answer these questions:

> Explain how the type of rubbish we throw away is different from that of 50 years ago.

The key words in this question are 'type of rubbish' and '50 years ago'. Scan through the text for those words, and then read that part of the text carefully. The text tells us: 'Fifty years ago there was far more dust and cinders, and no plastic at all.' It then goes on to list the rubbish we throw away today. This is the evidence we need for our answer:

Today people throw away less ashes and cinders than they did 50 years ago. The average family throws away 120 plastic bottles and 2.4 kg of plastic wrapping, but 50 years ago there was no plastic waste at all.

> The passage tells us almost one third of our rubbish comes from packaging. What kind of packaging is this? Which words tell you this?

Look for the key word 'packaging'. It is in the paragraph headed 'Reducing the rubbish mountain'. We are told: 'Think about all the cardboard and plastic that protects the things we buy.' We can now use this evidence in our answer:

The packaging we throw away is made mainly from cardboard and plastic. The words which tell us this are 'the cardboard and plastic that protects the things we buy'.

Test yourself

Answer these questions by using evidence from the text.

1 Write down three ways in which litter is dangerous to animals.

2 Explain the difference between litter and rubbish.

3 What evidence is there in the passage to suggest that lots of families do not reuse or recycle their glass bottles?

4 What would happen to forests if more families recycled their paper rather than throwing it away?

5 Explain how recycling rubbish would help to protect the countryside.

6 What evidence is there that central heating was not so common 50 years ago?

Answers and Guidance are given on p.34. *How long did you take?*

What's it all about?

★ In this chapter you will learn how to develop your understanding of characters – what they feel, what they are thinking and why they behave as they do.

★ In most stories, the writer will give you some information about the characters but will leave you to 'read for clues' in order to find out more.

★ Your National Test Reading paper may include questions which test how well you understand the characters in a story from what they do, think, say and feel.

How to develop your understanding of characters

Read this extract from 'Linda's Lie' by Bernard Ashley. Linda has not admitted at school that her parents cannot afford £1.00 for a school trip to the ballet. She has told her teacher that she is going to a christening on that day, but this is a lie. At home, she dreads anyone talking about the forthcoming trip, especially her father …

Her heart turned over when he came in. It was horrible. She wasn't pleased to see him. She had to act it. Is this what being a liar's like? she thought. This nasty pain all the time, and not being able to look straight at your dad?

And he seemed all full of himself today – taller in the doorway. But he didn't say why, not to her, nor to Michael. He looked at the TV set, hummed a little something deep in his throat and went out to the kitchen.

It was bed-time before Linda found out what it was. And then it wasn't her father who told her. He wasn't a showy man.

"Look!" said her mother as she tucked Linda in on the lumpy mattress. She held out a shiny pound piece. "This is for your outing. Your daddy got it extra today. Did a little job for a man he met. We won't miss it, being extra." She was smiling such a happy smile.

Linda looked up at the coin. It should have looked good and made her smile, but it didn't. It looked like money from another country. Even the Queen looked cross as if she was saying, "We've found you out, Linda Ann Steel. Look where lying leads you...."

Linda's eyes filled with tears. She put her head under the blankets to hide them – and she suddenly felt like their silent canary must feel – covered, and trapped: only she was in a cage of lies.

"Ah – don't cry, Petal." Her mother patted the mound of her head. "It's a happy ending to the story, eh?"

The next day

The cold coin in Linda's sock seemed to stick out like some nasty bite. You could see it if you knew where to look for it, even with white socks on. And you'd see where it had been when she took them off for dance, grazing her all grey where it scratched her ankle.

But she didn't know what else to do with it. She couldn't just give it in and say she was going to the ballet after all. Not really. They didn't cancel christenings just like that, and she'd made it sound much too important to just have changed her mind.

There was nowhere to hide it at home where someone wouldn't come across it – and nobody's place was secret enough in school. The only other thing would be to throw it away. But she shivered at the thought. A picture in her head of her father working for it made the money much too precious for that.

It weighed her down as if it had been in pennies. Why had she had to tell Miss Smith a lie? It had seemed easy at first, but now it was getting harder and harder every minute.

Let's see if you can answer this question:

> Write down two things which show Linda's father was pleased when he arrived home.

The passage tells us that Linda's father 'seemed full of himself today – taller in the doorway'. He also 'hummed a little something deep in his throat'.

We can use this evidence in our answer:

Linda's father looked pleased and hummed to himself.

Now let's see if you can work out the answer to this question:

> How did Linda feel when her father came home?

Linda's feelings are described in the first paragraph. A good answer would include some of the following points, and a very good answer would include them all:

Linda's 'heart turned over' when she saw her father, but she had to pretend she was pleased to see him. She couldn't look directly at him, and her lie was like a pain inside her. She wondered if this was what it was like to be a liar.

It is best to answer a question like this mainly in your own words.

Test yourself

Answer these questions using information and clues in the text.

1 How did Linda's mother feel when she gave Linda the money? Which words tell you this?

2 How did Linda feel when she was given the coin?

3 What did she do with the coin? Why?

4 Explain why she decided not to pay for the trip.

5 Explain why she did not throw the coin away.

Answers and Guidance are given on p.35.　　*How long did you take?*

24

What's it all about?	★ In this chapter you will learn how to read texts in order to find out what the writer's own opinion is on the subject he or she is writing about.

★ In this chapter you will learn how to read texts in order to find out what the writer's own opinion is on the subject he or she is writing about.

★ An opinion is what someone thinks or believes about something. Sometimes writers make their own views very clear. Sometimes you have to read the text carefully for clues about what their opinion is.

★ Your National Test Reading paper may include a question which tests whether you can find out, and explain, what the writer's opinion is about the subject he or she is writing on.

How to find out the writer's opinion

Read this letter from a newspaper carefully.

Dear Editor,

It's nearly Christmas again: the time of the year when puppies and kittens are bought as gifts. Unfortunately many of them are turned out a few months later, when they have become fully grown. Of course, the majority of these pets are loved and cared for, but some children lose interest once the Christmas period has passed. They then neglect their pets, sometimes even turning them out on the streets.

Animal Rescue does wonderful work in taking in pets that have been abandoned, but may I remind all readers to think carefully before buying a pet for Christmas. If readers are considering a pet then it would be much better to wait until early in the new year. In the meantime they might consider contacting our rescue centre and arrange to sponsor a rescue animal over Christmas.

Denise Hallworthy, Upton Animal Rescue Centre

Let's see if you can answer this question:

> **What does the writer of the letter think about buying pets as Christmas gifts?**

You need to read a text all the way through when trying to understand a writer's opinion. In the first paragraph the writer points out that some pets given as Christmas gifts are neglected later. In the second paragraph she suggests what might be done instead. Taking the two together we can see that she is not in favour of giving pets for Christmas.

A good answer is:

> The writer thinks that buying pets as Christmas gifts is not a good idea, as they are often neglected later.

Now let's see if you can work out the answer to this question:

> **Do you think the writer approves of the work of Animal Rescue? How can you tell that the writer has this opinion?**

The clue to the writer's opinion lies in the words 'wonderful work'. This is further supported by the fact she recommends people to help the rescue centre by sponsoring an animal over Christmas.

Your answer could, in part, quote words from the passage but the rest of your answer should use your own words:

> I think the writer approves of the work of Animal Rescue because she refers to their 'wonderful work', and suggests people support the rescue centre by sponsoring an animal over the Christmas holiday.

Answer these questions which ask you about the writer's opinion.

Letter to the editor

1 Which words show that the writer believes that having a pet for Christmas is not always a bad thing?

2 Why do you think the writer believes that it is better to wait until after Christmas before buying a pet?

3 What two things does the writer of the letter want to persuade people to do?

Now read this passage about UFOs:

The number of reports of UFOs (unidentified flying objects) is increasing. The people who see them often believe they have seen an alien spacecraft, yet many such sightings are easily explained, such as a weather balloon reflecting the sun at high altitudes. Just occasionally someone reports seeing something no one can explain: a light moving across the sky at incredible speed, or changing direction so suddenly and quickly that would be impossible for any human-made plane or rocket. Whenever this happens some people claim that the object is a visitor from another world, a flying saucer, but few people take them seriously.

The term 'flying saucer' was first used in the 1940s when sightings of a number of saucer-shaped objects were first reported. The term 'UFO' is now used because sightings report many different shapes.

Some people even claim to have seen a UFO land, and others claim they have been actually inside one and met aliens. Of course, there is never any real evidence which proves such claims. Perhaps these people have seen one sci-fi film too many!

4 Do you think the writer believes that UFOs are visitors from another world? How can you tell that the writer has this opinion?

Answers and Guidance are given on p.35.
 How long did you take?

What's it all about?	★ In this chapter you will learn how to write down what you think about what you have read.
	★ You will need to explain your opinion in a quite long, detailed answer.
	★ Your National Test Reading paper will include at least one question which asks you to express your opinion.

How to write what you think

Before you can form an opinion you will need to read the whole passage very carefully. Sometimes you might be asked to comment on the whole passage, and sometimes not.

Read this extract from 'Truth, Lies and Homework' by Josephine Feeney. Claire's teacher has asked her to write about what her grandfather did during the war. Claire has found out that, owing to a misunderstanding, he was sent to prison. Her mother does not want Claire to take her work to school. She has sent Claire and her brother, Chris, to their rooms so that she can discuss the matter with Claire's father.

I sat on the top stair, trying hard to hear what Mum and Dad were saying. My dressing-gown was wrapped tightly around me against the chill, even though it wasn't a cold night and the heating was on full blast. The computer beeped every few seconds in Chris's room and Dominic played a slow, depressing tape – probably about a fifteen-year-old boy with spots.

'Go to your room, Claire,' Mum had snapped half an hour earlier. 'Get ready for bed.'

'What about Grandad's story?'

'Claire, do as you're told,' Mum snapped again.

'Why? I haven't done anything wrong.'

'Claire.' Mum's tone softened. She massaged her forehead, drawing her hair back from her face. 'Please, Claire. Your dad and I need some time to discuss a few things. Off you go now, like a good girl.'

Chris joined me on the top stair. 'What gets me,' he whispered urgently, 'is that when they're in a bad mood and "need to talk", we get sent to our rooms.'

'Yes,' I said vaguely.

'Why can't they go to their room? We all get sent upstairs, nobody can watch the telly or make toast or do anything downstairs, just so they can talk. They're dead selfish.'

'Just listen, Chris!'

'What's so special about that room? Why do they always have to have their "talks" in that room? Makes me sick.'

'Shut up, Chris, and listen! I can't hear what they're saying. I'm in dead trouble if I don't hand in that project.'

Dad's voice was raised in protest. 'You can't do that, Linda. She's worked so hard on it these last few weeks.' Mum hissed a reply.

'What did she say?' Chris asked. It wasn't real life for him – just another drama he was watching.

'I didn't know anything about it – I'm as surprised as you are!' Dad shouted. Another subdued reply from Mum, then Dad again. 'No! that's totally unfair. You haven't read it properly, you've just skimmed through it looking for the bad parts. I know you were never keen on my father but there's no need to take your prejudice this far!'

'We'd better make ourselves scarce,' Chris whispered. 'I think she's about to make an exit.' At that moment the lounge door was pulled open quickly. I had only just closed my bedroom door when I heard Mum running up the stairs. The whole house seemed to shake for ages after she slammed her door. I didn't hear Dad going upstairs. I must have fallen asleep.

Let's see if you can answer this question:

> **Did you enjoy reading this story? (Yes/No) Explain your opinion.**

Think about why you did or did not enjoy the story. Did you find the story believable? Have you ever felt like the characters in the story? What do you think about the way they behaved? How did the story make you feel? Is there any part you particularly liked or disliked?

This is a good answer for someone who enjoyed the story:

I enjoyed the story because it seemed so real. I have often felt like Claire when I have been sent to my room while my parents discuss things they don't want me to hear. I can understand how Claire felt, and why she was so short-tempered with her brother, who didn't really understand how important their parents' discussion was to her. I would like to read more of the story to see how things work out for her.

Now let's see if you can answer this question:

> Do you think the instructions for making yoghurt are clear for children of your age? (Yes/No) Explain your opinion. (You need to look back at Chapter 5, page 15.)

Recipes should have a list of ingredients and clear instructions set out in the right order. Illustrations can help the reader to understand what they have to do. Sometimes a separate list of equipment is given. Ask yourself: Is the yoghurt recipe organised properly? Is it easy to understand?

Here is a good 'yes' answer:

> I think the recipe is very clear. There is a list of ingredients, the instructions are numbered in the correct order, and they are easy to follow. The illustrations help the reader to understand what they have to do.

Here is a good 'no' answer:

> I think the recipe would be better if there was a separate list of equipment. The reader needs to know from the beginning that a basin and tea-towel are necessary. The illustrations would be more useful if they were photographs. It would be helpful to see what the finished yoghurt should look like.

Test yourself

The following questions are about passages earlier in the book. Before you answer each question read *the whole of the passage* listed for that question.

Chapter 1: *The Pencil-box* (p. 4)

1 Did you enjoy reading this story? (Yes/No) Explain your opinion.

Chapter 4: *Aziz and the amazing motorbike ride* (pp. 12–13)

2 Did you enjoy reading this story? (Yes/No) Explain your opinion.

Chapter 5: *How fresh is your egg?* (p. 16)

3 Do you think the instructions for testing the freshness of an egg are easy to understand? (Yes/No) Explain your opinion.

Chapter 6: *Ginny's Egg* (p. 18)

4 Would you be interested in reading the rest of this story? (Yes/No) Say what you liked or did not like about the story so far.

Chapter 8: *Linda's Lie* (pp. 22–23)

5 Do you think Linda should give the money to the teacher? (Yes/No) Explain your opinion.

Answers and Guidance are given on p.36. **How long did you take?**

Answers and Guidance

Here is a chance for you to check your answers to the questions. Examples are given of possible ways of answering the questions and you should compare your answer with those given.

1 Finding information in stories

These are the points you should have included in your answers.

1 Barry wanted Mark to say 'please' loudly, but politely.

The first answer is wrong because it is Barry, not Mark, who has the pencil-box. The remaining answers are all true, but the last answer is the best because it gives the fullest information about what happened. You know this from what Barry says: 'Say please', 'A bit louder, I can't hear you', and 'That's not polite. Now say it nicely.'

2 Barry stopped tormenting Mark because he felt a pain in his leg.

The passage says 'Barry Hunter *let out a scream of pain* and swirled about, dropping the pencil-box and *clutching the back of his leg*.'

3 The second raindrop thought he was the most beautifully shaped.

The information you needed to find is in the second raindrop's words: '… it's shape that counts, and I am therefore the best raindrop in the whole sky.'

4 They spoke to the third raindrop because they wanted him to settle the argument.

The passage tells us 'they asked a third raindrop to decide between them'.

5 The argument ended when they became part of a puddle.

There was no time for the other raindrops to agree or disagree with the third raindrop, because as he finished speaking 'they all three hit the ground and became part of a very muddy puddle'.

> *Target time for all questions: 10 minutes*

> *Your time for all questions*

2 Finding facts in information texts

1 Not all sharks are fierce hunters. Some sharks eat only snails or shrimps.

The passage tells us 'All sharks are hunters, but not all of them are fierce. Some of them only hunt snails or shrimps.'

2 Some sharks live in the sea, while others live in rivers.

These facts can be found in the second paragraph under 'Help! Sharks!' (page 8).

3 Great white sharks are dangerous because they attack people. Other sharks which will do the same are hammerheads, blue sharks and sand sharks.

These facts can be found under the heading 'Sharks and people'.

4 Some people eat small sharks, such as the dog shark. Sharks' fins are used to make soup by some Chinese people.

The passage tells us this in the next to last paragraph.

5 A shark breathes by taking in water through its mouth and filtering it out through its gill openings.

This information is given in the captions to the diagram 'How a shark breathes'. Remember: information books often use pictures and diagrams to explain things.

6 You should have filled in the spaces like this:

	Hard bones	Soft bones	Use gills to breathe
Sharks		✓	✓
Other fish	✓		✓

The facts are in the first two paragraphs on page 7.

> *Target time for all questions: 12 minutes*

> *Your time for all questions*

Answers and Guidance

3 Writing down information

1 Your completed chart about vegetables should have all this information from the second paragraph:

Leaves: cabbage, lettuce, spinach

Flowers: **cauliflower, broccoli**

Seeds: **sweetcorn, peas**

Stems: **celery, asparagus**

Roots: **carrots, beetroots, radishes, turnips**

Tubers: **potatoes**

Bases of leaves: **leeks, onions**

2 **Tomatoes are considered to be vegetables, but are in fact fruit. They need a warm climate to grow.**

You needed to combine these two facts into one sentence from information in the second and third paragraphs.

3 **Potatoes are underground tubers, and if they are stored carefully they can stay in excellent condition for many months.**

This sentence has two facts which you should have found in paragraphs two and three.

4 **Strawberries and raspberries are fruits which grow in cool climates. As they are perishable, they are often canned or frozen.**

This answer has all the facts about strawberries and raspberries from paragraph five and the chart.

 Target time for all questions: 12 minutes

 Your time for all questions

4 Reading stories for clues

1 **Aziz probably found that the afternoon seemed the longest part of each day because by then he was getting bored.**

The passage tells us that Aziz spent his time watching from his window. By the afternoon he would have been watching for most of the day, and time would be passing very slowly for him.

2 **I think Aziz liked watching the children coming out of school best because then there would be lots to see and hear as they hurried home.**

The phrase 'the children would explode out of school' tells us that the children came racing out and that Aziz found them exciting to watch.

3 **I think Aziz could move his arms, but not his legs, because the story tells us that although he could not move his legs he pushed himself up in his chair using his arms.**

Aziz says to the motorbike 'I cannot move my legs' but he does not mention his arms. Earlier the writer tells us that 'Aziz would push himself up in his chair until his arms were straight'. The motorbike tells him to 'grip the handlebars' which requires strength in his arms. We are also told that Aziz was able to put on the helmet and goggles.

4 **We are reminded of these words when Aziz seemed to float through the window onto the motorbike.**

When the motorbike invited Aziz to go for a ride he 'seemed to float through the window'. This was impossible for Aziz to do by himself, so it must have been 'the power of the machine' which lifted him out of his chair.

5 **Aziz did not expect Masood to take the bike out because the passage tells us that Masood did not look as if he were going to take the bike out.**

The clue is in those first words of the fifth paragraph. Later in the paragraph it says that 'Aziz flopped back, disappointed.' On their own, these words might suggest that Aziz expected Masood to start the bike, but the earlier 'Masood did not look as if he were going to take the bike out' shows that Aziz was hoping, rather than expecting, that Masood would do so.

6 **I think Aziz was about to have an exciting ride, because the motorbike could work magic and would probably take him anywhere he wanted.**

Any answer of yours is acceptable as long as it fits the sense of the passage. The bike is obviously magical in some way, and the ride would be very exciting for Aziz after being inside for so long.

 Target time for all questions: 15 minutes

 Your time for all questions

Answers and Guidance

5 Reading information texts for clues

1 The yoghurt recipe starts with a list because these are the ingredients you must have before you follow the instructions.

All recipes begin with a list of ingredients, and sometimes a list of cooking equipment. This is the part of the recipe which tells you what you need to buy, or collect, before you follow the instructions.

2 The yoghurt can be made without chopped fruit or nuts, because the recipe says they are optional.

The word 'optional' means that these ingredients are not essential for making the yoghurt: they are something you might prefer to add to make the yoghurt more tasty. All the other ingredients are essential.

3 Farm workers measure eggs so that eggs of the same size can be packed together.

The text does not tell us why the eggs are measured, but we know that after this happens they are packed in boxes. It is reasonable to suppose that they are measured so that eggs of the same size can be packed together. If you already knew that eggs are bought by size, then that knowledge will have helped you. Remember: what you already know about a subject can sometimes help you to work out an answer.

4 The easiest way for a farmer to collect eggs is to keep the hens in cages, because it is then easier to collect the eggs.

The writer tells us that free range eggs have to be hunted for. Deep litter hens lay their eggs on straw on the floor of a shed, and though the passage doesn't tell us, it is reasonable to suppose the farmer will still have to look for them all over the shed. Battery hens lay their eggs in trays. The farmer will know exactly where to find them, and so collecting will be easier.

5 I think the method of producing eggs which is best for the chickens is free range. With this method the hens have freedom to move about and find their own food.

The life of free range hens is closest to the natural life of hens. This is because, as the passage tells us, they find food for themselves, and have the freedom to move about the farmyard, instead of being kept in cages or a shed.

6 I think a glass bowl is suggested for testing how fresh an egg is because glass makes it easy to see what happens to the egg.

Think how much easier it is to see how an egg floats if you can look through a glass bowl, instead of just looking down from above.

7 The information on yoghurt is a recipe and is arranged as a list of ingredients and numbered instructions. The information on eggs explains how they are produced and packaged and is arranged in paragraphs. The instructions for testing eggs are not numbered because there are only two steps.

As explained in answer 1 above, recipes are arranged in a special way: a list of ingredients, and a list of instructions in sequence. Most of the information on eggs is an explanation of how they are produced. This, like most explanations, is written in paragraphs. The instructions for testing eggs are different from the recipe instructions because there is no need for a list of ingredients, or for numbered instructions, since there are only two steps: place the egg in the water and watch.

8 You should have filled in your grid like this:

To inform	✓
To amuse	
To increase sales of eggs	
To guide	✓
To raise issues about chickens	

The text about chickens *informs* the reader because it gives information. The instructions guide the reader by explaining how to test for the freshness of an egg.

The writers do not seem to be trying to raise issues about chickens because they describe the different ways they are kept, without saying that any of them are cruel or kind.

Also, the writers do not seem to be trying to increase the sale of eggs because they describe how the eggs are laid and packed but they do not say that people should be eating more eggs – for example, because they are good for you.

There is nothing amusing about the way the information is given. All the artwork is very informative – if the writers had wanted to amuse they might have included a cartoon somewhere.

Your National Test Reading paper may include a question like this that asks you why you think the information text was written. You will need to think carefully about your answer, even if you are only asked to tick a grid as with this question.

Target time for all questions: 25 minutes

Your time for all questions

Answers and Guidance

6 Using 'evidence' from stories

1 The words which describe Ginny's excitement are 'Ginny's tummy beat too and a cold tingle of excitement suddenly swept through her'.

Ginny became excited as she held the egg and realised the pulsing she could feel came from within the egg. The words quoted in the answer above are evidence for this excitement.

2 She took her thumbs away from the egg to tell if the throbbing was coming from the egg or from the pulses in her thumbs beating into the egg.

This question asks you to *explain*, so just using words from the passage will not give a full enough answer, nor show that you have understood what you have read. You need to find the evidence, and then write it out in your own words as an explanation.

3 She thought another bird was unlikely to lay an egg and then leave it.

This question again expects you to find the evidence and then explain in your own words. The evidence for this answer is in the words 'it didn't make much sense that it would lay its egg and then just leave it, did it?'.

4 We know she wanted the egg to be that of another bird from the words 'part of her wanted the excitement of a mystery egg'.

The words quoted in the answer above are evidence to show Ginny wanted the egg to be that of another bird. There is further evidence for this in the words 'Ginny often told herself sensible things, though she hardly ever really believed them'. Ginny often preferred an exciting explanation to a more sensible one!

5 She believed it was a hen's egg because there were six hens and six eggs.

You are again being asked to find the evidence and then explain in your own words. The evidence for this answer is: 'Five eggs and the one in your hand makes six, and there are six hens. It's a hen's egg.'

6 *Either:* **I think the egg really is a hen's egg because it is unlikely another bird would lay its egg there and leave it, and because there was one egg for each hen.**
Or: **I think the egg is not a hen's egg because it is the wrong colour and size, and is fragile, yet strong too.**

You may either believe the egg to be a hen's egg or not, and so there are two possible answers to this question. Either of these may be correct if supported by evidence from the text. Each answer above uses evidence to support it, although there is no direct quote from the story.

 Target time for all questions: 15 minutes

 Your time for all questions

7 Using 'evidence' from information texts

1 Animals may be cut by broken glass. They may be suffocated by eating plastic. Birds may be trapped and be unable to fly or feed.

The evidence for these answers is in the text under the 'Litter' heading. One picture shows a person's foot cut by broken glass, but of course this happens to animals too.

2 Rubbish is what we throw away in dustbins. Litter is 'rubbish in the wrong place'. The correct place for rubbish is in the bin. Dropped anywhere else it becomes litter.

This is a good answer because it quotes from the text and then explains what the writer means.

3 We can tell that lots of families do not reuse or recycle their glass bottles because the passage tells us that the average family throws away 449 bottles, and that 10% of dustbin rubbish is glass.

The evidence for the number of bottles thrown away is in the first paragraph, and the table tells us that 10% of rubbish in a dustbin is glass.

4 If more families recycled paper then fewer trees would need to be cut down.

In the first paragraph it says that the average family throws away '2 trees' worth of paper', so your answer should show that you understand that fewer trees would need to be cut down. You needed to read the text carefully to answer this question as the evidence was hidden away in a long sentence.

5 Recycling rubbish would help to protect the countryside because it would mean the end to litter, which is dangerous to people and animals, and it would reduce pollution by stopping waste being buried or burnt.

Answers and Guidance

You should have found your evidence in the section headed 'Litter', and under the subheading 'Think before you throw' in the section 'Why reuse and recycle?'. You may often need to look for the answer to a question in more than one section of the text.

6 The fact that there was far more dust and cinders thrown away is evidence that central heating was not as common 50 years ago.

The key words to look for here are 'fifty years ago'. The text tells us: 'Fifty years ago there was far more dust and cinders' in the rubbish thrown away. At that time most people had solid fuel fires instead of central heating, and solid fires produce a great deal of dust and cinders.

 Target time for all questions: **20 minutes**

 Your time for all questions

8 Understanding characters

1 Her mother was happy when she gave Linda the money. I know this because it says, 'she was smiling such a happy smile'.

Always find the part of the story the question is asking you about, and look for the evidence you need.

2 Linda felt guilty and trapped by her lies.

We know this because she imagined that the Queen's head on the coin seemed to be saying, 'We've found you out, Linda Ann Steel. Look where lying leads you …'. The text then tells us 'she felt like their silent canary must feel – covered, and trapped: only she was in a cage of lies'.

3 She hid the coin in her sock because she did not know what else to do with it.

The text tells us what she did with it: 'The cold coin in Linda's sock seemed to stick out like some nasty bite.' In the following paragraph it explains: 'But she didn't know what else to do with it.'

4 She decided not to pay for the trip because she said she was going to a christening. Christenings are not usually cancelled, and she had made it sound too important to have changed her mind about going.

The text says: 'They didn't cancel christenings just like that, and she'd made it sound much too important to just have changed her mind.' Notice that the answer above puts this in slightly different words. Always try to answer in your own words, unless the question asks you to use words from the passage.

5 She did not throw the coin away because she knew her father had worked hard for it, and throwing it away would have seemed ungrateful.

The evidence for this is in the words: 'A picture in her head of her father working for it made the money much too precious for that.' When the question says 'explain', always try to give as much detail in your answer as possible. You need to show that you have understood why the character behaves in the way that he or she does.

 Target time for all questions: **15 minutes**

 Your time for all questions

9 Finding out the writer's opinion

Letter to the editor

1 The words 'of course, the majority of these pets are loved and cared for' shows that the writer believes having a pet for Christmas is not always a bad thing.

This evidence can be found in the third sentence of the letter.

2 I think the writer believes that it is better to wait until after Christmas before buying a pet because then people will appreciate it as a pet rather than just a Christmas present. At the same time it gives them the opportunity to sponsor a rescue animal over Christmas.

This question asks what *you* think. The letter does not say why the writer believes this, but the letter provides clues if you 'read between the lines'. Any answer you give which fits the sense of the letter will be acceptable.

3 The writer of the letter wants to persuade people to think carefully about buying a pet for Christmas, and to consider sponsoring a rescue animal.

The evidence for these points is in the words 'may I remind all readers to think carefully before buying a pet for Christmas' and 'in the meantime they might consider contacting our rescue centre and arrange to sponsor a rescue animal over Christmas'.

Answers and Guidance

Passage about UFOs

4 **I think the writer does not believe that UFOs are visitors from another world. I can tell this from the words he uses, such as 'few people take them seriously'. His closing statement is a joke which suggests those who believe in UFOs have got their ideas from science fiction films.**

When answering a question of this type, look for clues to the writer's opinion in the words he or she uses. The answer above refers to 'few people take them seriously', but the words 'others claim' also reveal the writer's opinion. Pay particular attention to closing statements as they often give the biggest clues.

 Target time for all questions: 15 minutes

 Your time for all questions

10 Expressing your opinion

Below are sample 'yes' and 'no' answers, but these may well be different from the ones you wrote. There are as many possible right answers to these questions as there are different opinions. A good answer will state your opinion clearly and explain why you think as you do, based on evidence in the text. Note that it is usually easier to say why you liked a text. If you did not like it, do not simply say you found it boring or uninteresting. You need to give *reasons* why it did not interest you.

1 *(Yes)* **I enjoyed this story because I know children like Mark and Barry. I particularly liked the end of this extract because it looks as if Barry will get told off. I would like to read more to find out why Barry screamed and what Celeste has to do with it.**

(No) **I did not enjoy this story because I think it would be more interesting if Mark had stood up to Barry. He should not have let Barry see how upset he was. It only made the bullying worse. The story made me feel angry.**

2 *(Yes)* **I enjoyed reading about Aziz. I could understand the way he felt, at first bored and unable to leave his wheelchair. Then the whole story changed as he was able to float through the air onto a bike that suddenly came to life. I found that part very exciting and would like to read more about that amazing ride.**

(No) **I did not enjoy the story because although the beginning was real, I could not believe that a motorbike could come to life. If this part is just a dream then I think Aziz will be disappointed in the end. I felt sorry for Aziz.**

3 *(Yes)* **I think the instructions are very clear. They tell the reader clearly what to do, and the diagrams show you exactly what to look for. The explanation makes it easy to understand why the egg floats or doesn't float.**

As these instructions are very clear, it would be difficult to write a 'no' answer.

4 *(Yes)* **I would like to read the rest of the story to find out if the egg really is a hen's egg. I liked the way the writer made me think that the egg might contain something wonderful. I like the way it is described: 'its gold-speckled shell shimmered very slightly' and 'like an oversized tear drop, warm and fragile'. The egg seems magical and mysterious. Like Ginny, I want 'the excitement of a mystery egg'. I was left in suspense at the end of the story.**

(No) **I would not like to read the rest of the story. I think the egg is quite ordinary and that Ginny only thinks it is odd because that is what she wants to believe. It says in the story 'she wanted the excitement of a mystery egg'. I think she is going to be disappointed.**

5 *(Yes)* **I think Linda should give the money to the teacher. She will have to admit her lie, but that is better than waiting until she is found out. If she keeps silent about the money, she will have a big problem on the day of the trip. She won't be able to go to school because she has lied about going to the christening, and she won't be able to stay at home because her parents expect her to go on the trip.**

(No) **I think Linda should tell her mother instead. She is the best person to advise Linda what to do. She might suggest that Linda tells the teacher, but I think her mother will do so herself to make it easier on Linda. Whatever happens, I'm sure Linda will wish she had not lied.**

 Target time for all questions: 40 minutes *(including time to re-read the passages)*

 Your time for all questions

Read this story and the following passage (pages 39–40).
Then answer the questions.

Selwyn the Brave

"Selwyn!", called mother sharply. Her voice cut through the air like an arrow and shot deep into the sleepy haze that he was enjoying. Trouble, he thought to himself, it must be trouble because mother only uses my proper name when something is wrong. The rest of the time she used her pet name for him of Sel.

"Funny", he muttered to himself, "adults only use your name like that when they are about to tell you off for something." When you are called like that it is sensible to respond quickly and he knew it.

With stiff jerking movements Selwyn stretched himself and shook each leg in turn. His ears strained for the slightest sound and his eyes blinked furiously to adjust to the half light.

"Just coming mother", he yelled at the top of his voice as a kind of insurance against being called for a second time. Selwyn's mind raced and flickered trying to seize upon a deed from the day before.

"Ah, there you are", she said with a little laugh in her voice. "You really are a scruffy young spider, no wonder you are always getting up to mischief" she continued. Selwyn waited for it to be mentioned. It might be the adventure with the garage doors, a masterpiece of a web that was. It might be a warning about upsetting the human's cat. It might be all sorts of things. It might be ... but it wasn't.

"Now look, I am going out for a while and I want you to be a good little spider whilst I am gone", mother began. "You could give adventures a rest for a change and do a few things around here, like making your web tidy", she said with a tone that was more an order than a suggestion.

Mother was an elegant spider and Selwyn watched her as she moved purposefully around gathering up a few items. She always looked so smart, with a deep shine to her body and her angular legs effortlessly gliding her around. Selwyn loved to watch his mother at work, but even his natural pride in his beloved parent kept being interrupted by dancing thoughts and delights. These ideas, like flickering images upon a screen, flashed in his brain and just as quickly flashed out again. By the time that his mother was ready to leave, adventurous ideas were growing in his imagination and he hardly heard the concern in her voice when she disappeared under the skirting board with a "Take care, you know how dangerous the world can be".

All alone, Selwyn began to get the flickering images into some sort of order. Even though he had been told many times of the dangers in the outside

world, away from his home, he felt sure that they were stories made up by adults to get their children to do as they were told. After all, he had been under the skirting board before and explored the human world, and absolutely nothing had happened to him. He had even been beyond the human world and seen the colours and smelt the smells that were there to be enjoyed.

"Enough thinking, time for action", shouted the excited spider and Selwyn marched briskly towards the crack in the skirting board. Exploring the human world could not wait for another minute. At the very opening, he paused for a brief moment. He thought that he heard a familiar voice warning him to be careful, but he shrugged all eight shoulders because another adventure called.

Out into the room Selwyn sprang, and felt the soft tickling surface of the carpet. He rolled around giggling for a few moments until an enticing smell drew him towards the door. It was a sweet smell the like of which he had never experienced before. Now that just had to be investigated. As he approached the door, he scanned the scene, looking for the best way through to reach the alluring smell. A loud click sounded and the heavy wooden door swung open and Selwyn flung himself against the skirting board behind it. As he peeped out he saw large feet padding across the carpet pushing a strange mechanical device out in front. A long thin snake unravelled itself and its mouth was pushed with a thud into a white box set in the wall on the other side of the door. The mechanical device began to purr and move up and down the carpet. Selwyn did not like the noise, but that was only a small part of his problem. The carpet began to vibrate and he noticed that tiny particles of dust danced merrily in front of this awful machine. They lept, they twisted and then they were gone, leaving only the next group to pick up where they had left off.

Selwyn knew that he had to get back to his part of the skirting board and began to calculate his best route to safety. If the dreadful machine or the human saw him he knew that he too would join the particles in their feverish dance, and then be just as swiftly gone. Straining every part of his body he edged slowly and silently around the edges of the room. All the time the noise grew louder and louder until all Selwyn's bravery had ebbed away. With a sharp intake of breath, he ran as fast as he could and threw himself into the welcoming gloom of his familiar surroundings.

Selwyn slumped in an exhausted heap and felt the coldness of the perspiration trickle along his body. He was still there when his mother returned, smiling and calm as ever.

"Sel, are you alright?" she asked in a concerned voice. "You look as if you've seen a monster".

"I think I have mother", he whispered faintly.

Spiders everywhere

Different kinds of spiders

The weight of insects eaten by spiders in the world each year is more than the weight of all the people living. This surprising calculation was made by a naturalist who has made a special study of spiders. In a typical English field he found more than two million spiders per acre.

Even if we live in a town we will no doubt have met many kinds of spiders. Big, **dark brown spiders** get themselves trapped in the bath. On still days in late summer tiny **black 'money' spiders** crawl over our face and clothes and hair and tickle our skin. **House spiders** make new cobwebs in the corners of ceilings or on electric light shades only an hour or two after their old ones have been dusted away. On frosty mornings the cartwheel webs of fat-bodied **garden spiders** sparkle in the hedges.

Garden spider

These are only a few examples of the spiders that swarm everywhere. There are well over 23,000 different kinds of spider in the world, more than 600 of them in Britain. They have been in the world for a long time, too. Geologists have found the first traces of spiders in rocks that are well over 300 million years old. There were spiders around before the first flies appeared. Indeed, some experts think that flies and other flying insects developed wings and learned how to fly in order to get out of the way of spiders!

Why spiders are not insects

All insects have **six** legs, but if you count a spider's legs you will find that it always has **eight** – unless it has lost one in a fight or an accident!

Also, insects have **three** parts to their bodies – namely, head, thorax and abdomen – and spiders have only **two**. The head and thorax are merged into one part, known as the **cephalothorax**. The legs are attached to this, not to the abdomen.

Insects pass through four well-defined stages in their life. With spiders the young that emerge from the eggs are just like their parents, only smaller. As they grow, they split their skins and shed them. We may often find the cast skins of house spiders on the floor in the mornings.

How spiders behave

Nearly all spiders are able to spin webs, which they use for many different purposes. As you will know, we ourselves have five senses – those of sight, smell, hearing, taste and touch. Spiders rely chiefly on the **sense of touch**. Those which spin webs lie hidden until some insect or other creature becomes entangled. Then vibrations along the web alert the spider to hurry to the kill. Spiders will react to vibrations caused by other creatures. You can experiment by striking the stick or stone on which a spider is resting with a tuning-fork.

Some spiders, especially jumping spiders, have excellent **sight**. Others are very short-sighted. Wolf spiders are thought to locate their mates by means of **scent**, though this is not certain. Many spiders certainly do have a **sense of taste**, as they reject any insect which has, to them, an unpleasant flavour.

No-one knows whether spiders can **hear**, but some experts think they have senses which react to pressure (like a barometer), heat and humidity.

Palm spider, found in Jamaica

Spiders are **carnivorous**, or flesh-eaters. They do not, however, gnaw or chew the flesh of their victims. First they kill their prey by striking with their fangs, which inject a poison. Then they extract the blood and juices, leaving just a dry, feather-light husk. No British spider has fangs or poison powerful enough to harm a human being, though the bite of some tropical spiders can be painful and even fatal.

Reading Test questions

Here are different types of question for you to answer. Your answers may be:

- **MULTIPLE CHOICE** where you need do no writing at all but choose the best answer and put a ring round it.

- **SHORT ANSWERS** which are usually followed by a short line for you to write a word or phrase.

- **SEVERAL LINE ANSWERS** with a few lines for a sentence or two.

- **LONGER ANSWERS** with a box for you to write in some detail your explanation or opinion.

MARKS The number after each question tells you the maximum marks that you could gain for each question. Remember: for three marks you will need to write a detailed answer to the question.

Selwyn the Brave

Selwyn Spider was sleeping when:

1 (his mother called) (he felt hungry) (the alarm rang) (the door slammed)

1 mark

He expected, judging by the tone in his mother's voice, that he might well:

2 (get a present) (be sent to bed) (be told off) (be going out)

1 mark

Later that day when he was on his own Selwyn decided to explore. This meant that he had to:

3 [get dressed] [eat his breakfast] [squeeze through the skirting board] [face danger]

1 mark

Selwyn liked the feel of the carpet but loud noises frightened him before he could go very far. He raced back to the safety of his home and told his mother that he:

4 [had been good] [had been frightened] [had stayed in bed] [wanted to go out]

1 mark

5 At the beginning of the story how do you know it was quite dark in the place where Selwyn woke up?

1 mark

6 Why was Selwyn surprised that his mother called him using his full name?

_____

_____

2 marks

7 'Selwyn waited for **it** to be mentioned'. Explain as fully as you can what 'it' might have been.

_____

_____

_____

2 marks

8 The author decribes 'flickering images' and 'dancing thoughts and delights'. Describe in your own words what you think Selwyn was doing.

_____

_____

_____

2 marks

9 Selwyn loved the feel of the soft carpet but something drew him to the door. Explain what you think this was and why it was so interesting.

_____

_____

_____

2 marks

10 As the door swung open, Selwyn became frightened. What were the things that caused this and why would they frighten him?

_____

_____

_____

3 marks

11 When Selwyn reached the safety of his home, how does the author try to make the reader understand how frightened he was?

_____

_____

_____

2 marks

12 Write what you think of the story, giving reasons for your opinion. You should include:
- the settings and sequence of events
- the characters
- how you feel about what Selwyn did.

3 marks

Spiders everywhere

1 What surprising facts can you find about the spider population?

_____

_____

1 mark

2 How can you tell a spider is not an insect?

_____

_____

_____

2 marks

3 Spiders rely chiefly on a sense of touch. Explain how they use this sense.

_____

_____

1 mark

4 How do we know that many spiders have a sense of taste?

_____

_____

1 mark

5 If you found a dried-up spider shape, what does the passage tell you that it could possibly be?

_____

_____

_____

2 marks

6 The author believes that we do not know everything about spiders and their lives. In what ways does he tell us this?

3 marks

7 This text was written for children from 8 to 11 years old.
- In what ways do you think the author has tried to help younger children understand the information?
- Do you think that he has succeeded?

3 marks

Answers and Guidance

Reading Test

Here is a chance for you to check your answers to the questions. Examples are given of possible ways of answering the questions and you should compare your answer to those given. Under each one, there is a cross-reference to the relevant skills chapter, so that you can look back at what the question is trying to assess.

Selwyn the Brave

1 his mother called

2 be told off

3 squeeze through the skirting board

4 had been frightened

This type of multiple-choice question gives you the chance to show that you can find information in a story. Always look back at the text when answering this sort of question rather than relying on your memory.

CROSS-CHECK CHAPTER 1 Finding information in stories

5 His eyes blinked in the half light. or
Half light means that it was gloomy and dull. or
He needed to adjust his eyes to the light.

If you put any of these answers then you have shown that you have understood the clues in the story about the half light and Selwyn blinking. This question is only worth 1 mark which indicates that you are only expected to write a short answer, rewording the information you have found in the text.

CROSS-CHECK CHAPTER 4 Reading stories for clues

6 She usually used a pet name. or
She did not often call him Selwyn. or
She normally called him Sel.

1 mark for a simple direct answer.

Adults often use your full name when you are in trouble. or
It wasn't something she usually did and it told him that she was not pleased.

2 marks for an answer that links the use of his full name with the possibility of his being told off.

This question is asking you to read for clues and it is worth 2 marks because it is expecting you to link two pieces of evidence: the unusual use of Selwyn's first name with the possibility that it might not be good news.

CROSS-CHECK CHAPTER 4 Reading stories for clues

7 'It' might have been to do with the garage doors. or
'It' might have been to do with the cat.

1 mark for a single idea.

'It' might have been the web on the garage doors or to do with the cat. or
Selwyn got up to all sorts of things and 'it' could have been any of them.

2 marks for a full answer.

This question asks you to 'explain as fully as you can' which tells you two things:
- you need to use evidence from the text to support your ideas on what 'it' might have been;
- you need to make your answer as full as possible to be sure of being awarded both the possible marks.

CROSS-CHECK CHAPTER 6 Using 'evidence' from stories

8 He wasn't really listening. or
He was planning things.

1 mark for a single idea.

Lots of ideas were racing around in his head. or
He was getting excited at the thought of the things he could do.

2 marks for a full answer.

A more than one mark question gives you an immediate clue that you need to give a full answer. This question is expecting you to read the story for clues and to use the evidence in your answer. Because the question says 'describe in your own words' you know that the examiners do not want you to quote words or phrases directly from the text.

CROSS-CHECK CHAPTER 4 Reading stories for clues
CHAPTER 6 Using 'evidence' from stories

9 He could smell something in the kitchen. or
Smells from the kitchen made him want to go to the next room.

1 mark

He could smell things that he had never come across before and wanted to investigate. or
It was all new to him and he wanted to investigate the new smell.

2 marks for an answer that links the smell and the fact that it was new to him.

This question is expecting you to use evidence in the story but it is also trying to find out if you have understood Selwyn's lively, inquisitive character.

CROSS-CHECK CHAPTER 6 Using 'evidence' from stories
CHAPTER 8 Understanding characters

Answers and Guidance

10 **The large feet; the machine; the noise; the long thin snake (power cable); the vibration.**

1 mark for finding two of the things that might have frightened him.
2 marks for finding four or more.
3 marks for a detailed explanation of why they might have frightened him:

Selwyn became frightened because he did not know that humans have large feet. As he had never seen or heard a vacuum cleaner before, he was frightened of the long thin power cable and the noise and thought that the machine would injure or kill him.

This question is asking you to show that you have understood Selwyn's character: the full of mischief spider is not as brave as he thinks he is. There are lots of clues in the story about the things that frightened him and it is reasonable to suppose that he had never met these things before.

CROSS-CHECK | **CHAPTER 4** Reading stories for clues
CHAPTER 8 Understanding characters

11 **He fell in a heap.** or
He stayed there until his mother returned.

1 mark for a simple explanation.

The author lets the reader know how frightened Selwyn was because he says that Selwyn did not move before his mother came back, that he was exhausted and covered in sweat, and that when he spoke his voice was faint.

2 marks for a full explanation that draws evidence from several different places.

This question expects you to find several different pieces of evidence. You needed to include both the fact that the author described Selwyn's physical state (perspiration, exhaustion, faint voice) and the fact that he was still lying there when his mother returned.

CROSS-CHECK | **CHAPTER 6** Using 'evidence' from stories
CHAPTER 8 Understanding characters

12 **I liked this story. It was set in a house. Selwyn was a spider who did not do what his mother told him to do. I think he was badly behaved.**

1 mark for a basic answer to each prompt.

I liked this story because the setting seemed real. The story told of the events of one day in Selwyn's life. Selwyn was naughty because he went exploring and did not do as he was told. He nearly lost his life because of it.

2 marks for a more detailed response to all the prompts.

I think this story has a moral to it which is that you should do as your mother tells you. Because the story is set in and around a normal house, you can easily imagine what is happening even though the story is all about a spider. The spider is made to seem almost human and when Selwyn does not behave himself he acts like a small child. Selwyn's mother is very calm, but Selwyn is very excitable and full of mischief. The story starts off quite slowly but once Selwyn goes into the room exploring, lots of things start to happen. I think the writer is very clever because he makes us realise how frightening a vacuum cleaner might be to a spider.

3 marks for an answer that addresses all the prompts and turns them into a well-thought out opinion on the story.

This question is asking your opinion on the story and you are expected to give reasons for your opinion using evidence from the text. The prompts act as a guide about what you need to include in your answer but if you only write three sentences you will not score the full 3 marks.

Your answer may not be exactly like the 3-mark answer given above, but award yourself the 3 marks if you have addressed all the prompts and written a paragraph that is interesting and gives reasons why you like or don't like the story.

CROSS-CHECK | **CHAPTER 10** Expressing your opinion

Spiders everywhere

1 **There are more than two million spiders per acre in a typical English field.**

1 mark for an answer that uses this fact.

Make sure you always read the question carefully. The question is asking about the spider population. If you wrote '23,000 kinds with 600 in Britain' you would not be awarded the mark as this is not a population statistic.

CROSS-CHECK | **CHAPTER 2** Finding facts in information texts

2 **Spiders have eight legs, insects have six. Spiders have two parts to their bodies, insects have three. Spiders emerge from eggs as young spiders, insects pass through four stages in their lives.**

1 mark for an answer that only states one of these facts.
2 marks for an answer that states two or three of these facts.

Answers and Guidance

This question is asking you to find information. The fact that this question is worth 2 marks gives you a clue that you are expected to find more than one piece of information from the text.

CROSS-CHECK **CHAPTER 2** Finding facts in information texts

3 Spiders feel vibrations through the web when an insect gets tangled in it and this is like touching.

1 mark for an answer that links the feeling of vibrations with touch.

This question is asking you to use information and give an answer in your own words. The key word is 'vibrations' which links directly to 'touch'.

CROSS-CHECK **CHAPTER 3** Writing down information

4 They do not eat things that they find unpleasant so they must be able to taste them.

1 mark for an answer that refers to spiders choosing what to eat.

This question is testing your skills at finding information by using clues in the text. The clue here is that spiders find some things unpleasant and therefore do not eat them. This means they must be able to taste.

CROSS-CHECK **CHAPTER 5** Reading information texts for clues

5 Spiders drop their skins on the floor.

1 mark for correctly identifying the information in the passage.

Spiders split their skins as they grow and the passage says that the old skins can be found on the floor. This means that if you found a dried-up spider shape, you would probably have found an old skin rather than a dead spider.

2 marks for a full answer.

This question is testing your ability to use evidence in the text to support your answer. As 2 marks are available you should realise that the examiners are expecting a full answer which shows you have read the text carefully and can refer to it in your answer.

CROSS-CHECK **CHAPTER 7** Using 'evidence' from information texts

6 You can tell that the author believes that we do not know everything about spiders and their lives because of the expressions he uses in the text. He says 'some experts think that ...' , 'Wolf spiders are thought to ...' and 'No-one knows whether spiders can hear'.

1 mark for referring to each of these expressions, making up a total of 3 marks if you have correctly identified all three.

This question is testing your ability to use evidence from the text and it is also testing whether you understand how the writer shows his opinion.

CROSS-CHECK **CHAPTER 7** Using 'evidence' from information texts
CHAPTER 9 Finding out the writer's opinion

7 He has used big headings and put in pictures. The writing is spaced out to make it easy to read and the names of the spiders and some of the difficult words are in bold type.

1 mark for a simple response covering the text but not giving an opinion on whether the author has been successful.

The author has used headings and some bold print to help younger children to find the information but many of the words would be too difficult for some of them to read. The pictures would help young children to get information and parents could read the hard bits and explain it all to them.

2 marks for an answer that mentions the ways that young readers can be helped and gives some indication of whether the author has succeeded.

He uses headings and bold print which makes it easier to find the information. The pictures and captions also give some help. In this way the author has done quite a lot to help children. Even though there are headings and pictures, there are lots of difficult words to read in the text and younger children would have a problem with that. It is suitable for 11-year-olds but eight-year-olds would be put off by the amount of text and would probably want more pictures.

3 marks for an answer that fully covers the print style, the illustrations and the language, and gives a personal opinion on whether the author has been successful.

This question has two prompts and you need to respond to both of them. The question is testing whether you can write your own personal opinion on the text. You may or may not feel that the author has been successful, but whichever you feel, you must support your opinion with detailed reasons, referring closely to the text.

CROSS-CHECK **CHAPTER 10** Expressing your opinion

FOCUS ON
BIOLOGY

HABITATS AND
THE ENVIRONMENT

HABITATS AND THE ENVIRONMENT

Peter Freeland

Hodder & Stoughton

LONDON SYDNEY AUCKLAND

British Library Cataloguing in Publication Data
Freeland Peter
   Habitats and the environment. – (Focus on biology)
   I. Title   II. Series
   574.5

ISBN 0–340–53267X

First published 1991

© 1991 Peter Freeland

Typeset by Litho Link Ltd, Welshpool, Powys.
Printed in Great Britain for the educational publishing division of
Hodder and Stoughton Ltd, Mill Road, Dunton Green, Sevenoaks,
Kent by Thomson Litho Ltd.

CONTENTS

PREFACE

This book is mostly about ecology and its relevance to human populations. There is currently much public concern about environmental issues, especially about wildlife habitats that are threatened by pollution and species that are in danger of extinction. Indeed, the Earth itself may be under threat, as global temperatures warm, causing unpredictable changes in climate, sea levels and the distribution of plants and animals. Fortunately a further decline is not inevitable, providing the right steps are taken to reverse current trends. Such actions however, including conservation and anti-pollution measures, need to be based on firm scientific principles, the cornerstones of ecology.

The broad purpose of this book is to provide A level biologists with a modern account of applied ecology and its relevance to the human situation. It describes a number of common habitats, their structure and function, productivity, environmental factors, population dynamics and evolution. The ecological problems associated with escalating human populations are then reviewed. From an ecological viewpoint, humans are a remarkably successful species, numerically dominant in most parts of the world, a large omnivore at the apex of many terrestrial and aquatic food webs. As human populations have spread, there has been widespread destruction of natural habitats and the wildlife that lived in them. Human populations are often selfish, destructive and dirty, causing waste lands to form and pollution to spread. Ecology gives a broad overview of these processes. Its ultimate aim of course is to find a better balance between human demands and wildlife preservation, so that future generations can also enjoy, and use, these natural resources.

The following titles are also available in the *FOCUS ON BIOLOGY* series:

Habitats and the Environment Investigations (pack)
    ISBN 0 340 554339

Micro-organisms in Action
    ISBN 0 340 532688

Micro-organisms in Action Investigations (pack)
    ISBN 0 340 539224

Genetics and Evolution
    ISBN 0 340 532661

1 WILDLIFE HABITATS

Anyone who travels across the UK passes through uplands, lowlands, wetlands and coastlands. Each of these regions may contain a range of habitat types, where characteristic, and sometimes unique, groups of plants and animals live. Indeed, the UK is fortunate in having such a wide range of habitats (Table 1) which, in turn, support a varied, and relatively prolific, flora and fauna. Every native species has its own habitat, or habitats, where it feeds, grows, produces offspring and interacts with its living (**biotic**) and non-living (**abiotic**) surroundings. The swallowtail butterfly, for example, occurs only in one or two low-lying fens in Norfolk and Cambridgeshire. This insect is limited in its distribution by the availability of its food plants; these are milk parsley, angelica, wild carrot and fennel during its larval stage. In contrast, the frog, is very widely distributed, with populations in almost every type of wetland. Apart from requiring water to keep its skin moist and for rearing its young, this amphibian is not restricted to any particular locality because it will feed on a very wide range of invertebrates, including arthropods and annelids.

Coniferous forest in Rothiemurchus, Scotland

Back water and marsh, Kent

Dry heathland on Thursley Common, Surrey

Cuckmere Haven, Sussex

Table 1   Wildlife habitats in the UK

	HABITAT	EXAMPLES
UPLANDS	coniferous woodland	
	broadleaved woodland	Torrachilty (Scotland)
	mixed woodland	
	upland heath	
	limestone pavement	Shap fells, Ingleborough
	pastures (e.g. chalk grassland)	
LOWLANDS	broadleaved woodland	Epping Forest, Forest of Dean
	mixed woodland	New Forest (Hampshire)
	lowland heath	Frensham Common (Surrey)
	pastures (e.g. chalk grassland)	North and South Downs, Chilterns
	roadside verges	
WETLANDS	moorland (upland peat bog)	North York Moors
	peat bog (lowland)	Somerset Levels, Fens
	fen	Norfolk Broads
	wet heath	
	ponds/lakes	Windermere, Loch Ness
	rivers/streams	
COASTLANDS	coastal cliffs and scarps	South and West Wales, West and North Scotland
	shingle beach	Chesil beach, Dungeness
	sandy shore	
	rocky shore	
	sand dunes	Culbin sands (Scotland), Braunton burrows (North Devon)
	estuaries	The Wash

The human population, like that of the frog, is widely distributed throughout the UK, although concentrated mostly in population centres. Many of these places, towns and villages, have developed around sites that originally provided basic human necessities in the form of water, fertile soil, shelter and food. Today, the success of human populations is self-evident. Increases in the human population, combined with ingenuity in exploiting nature for human purposes, have led to the growth of villages and towns. As the human environment has spread, so it has destroyed many former wildlife habitats, reduced their size, or diminished their diversity. If this trend is allowed to continue, many more wildlife habitats may be destroyed as human population spreads. Clearly, a primary aim of ecologists is to reverse this trend and to conserve habitats and the species they contain. Success in such an enterprise depends on an intimate knowledge of the interrelationships that exist between wildlife, humans and environmental factors. These interrelationships are the subject of this book. We shall begin by taking a closer look at three common habitats: broadleaved woodlands, ponds and rocky sea shores.

1.1 BROADLEAVED WOODLANDS

In prehistoric times, before the Neolithic clearances that took place around 4000 BC, broadleaved woodland covered much of lowland Britain. Today it covers only about 9%. Typically, large ancient woodlands can contain about 60 species of trees and shrubs, several hundred herbaceous plants, and several thousand different animals, mostly invertebrates. Tables 2a and 2b opposite list some of the most widely distributed and common woodland species.

As a very broad generalisation, oak-dominated woodlands grow on acid soils, both sand and clay, while beech is the dominant tree over limestone and chalk. Woodland is distinguished from other habitats by the height of its vegetation. Typically, the plants are stratified into four horizontal zones (Table 3 and Figure 1), ranged one above another from ground level.

Table 3   The four horizontal zones

ZONES	APPROXIMATE HEIGHT
Ground (or moss) layer	< 5 cm
Herbaceous (or field) layer	< 2 m
Shrub (or under-storey) layer	< 20 m
Tree (or canopy) layer	< 30 m

The **ground layer**, covering the floor of the wood, consists of small plants, chiefly mosses, and fungi. Bare soil, between these organisms, is covered by a deep layer of decomposing leaf litter.

The **herbaceous layer** contains shade-tolerant, moisture-requiring species, such as ferns and flowering plants. Spring flowering herbaceous plants, storing food reserves in underground storage organs, are abundant. Perennials such as primrose and bluebell belong to this group. These plants form leaves and flowers during the **pre-vernal period**, from February to April when

Table 2a Some common plants and fungi in broadleaved woodlands

KINGDOM or PHYLUM	SPECIES	COMMENTS
ALGAE	*Pleurococcus*	Green powder on tree trunks
BRYOPHYTES	Common cord moss	On ground
	Swan's neck thread moss	On ground
	Flat feather moss	On tree stumps, trunks
PTERIDOPHYTES	Male fern	
	Hard fern	
	Bracken	On acid soil
ANGIOSPERMS		
Herbs	Bluebell	
	Bugle	
	Dog's mercury	
	Enchanter's nightshade	
	Foxglove	On acid soil
	Lesser burdock	
	Primrose	
	Wild strawberry	
	Wood avens	
	Wood spurge	
Shrubs	Bramble	
	Dog rose	
	Honeysuckle	
	Ivy	Epiphytic on trees
Sub-canopy trees	Birch	On acid soil
	Hazel	
	Holly	On well drained soil
	Willow	On wet soil
Canopy trees	Ash	
	Beech	
	Lime	
	Oak	
	Sweet chestnut	
	Sycamore	
FUNGI	Fly agaric	
	Honey fungus	
	Wood blewits	

Table 2b Some common animals in broadleaved woodlands

GROUP	SPECIES	COMMENTS
ARTHROPODS		
Insects	Bark beetles	
	Fritillary butterflies	Several species represented
	Longhorn beetles	
	Gall wasps	Form galls on oak
Crustaceans	Woodlice	
Arachnids	Spiders	Eat either litter or invertebrates in litter
	Mites	
Myriapods	Centipedes	
	Millipedes	
ANNELIDS	Earthworms	
	Leeches	In wet soil
MOLLUSCS	Slugs	
	Snails	
CHORDATES		
Amphibians	Frog	Eats worms
	Toad	Eats worms
Reptiles	Grass snake	Eats frogs
	Adder	On acid soil
Birds	Lesser spotted woodpecker	Eats insects and berries
	Nightingale	Eats insects and berries
	Nuthatch	Eats nuts and seeds
	Sparrowhawk	Eats small birds and frogs and large insects
	Tree creeper	Eats insects
	Wren	Eats insects
Mammals	Badger	Eats small mammals and birds and large insects and bulbs and acorns
	Bank vole	Eats nuts, seeds, fruits
	Fallow deer	
	Fox	Eats small mammals and birds and snails and large insects
	Grey squirrel	Eats nuts, acorns
	Roe deer	
	Wood mouse	Eats nuts, fruits, bulbs

light intensity at ground level is relatively high, before buds on the overhanging trees have opened to produce leaves.

The **shrub layer** consists of a complex, close undergrowth of shrubs and young trees, that grow in a sheltered, dimly lit, humid part of the wood. Several plants from this layer have long, trailing stems, inadequate for support in a more windy, exposed habitat. In order to obtain light, plants such as ivy have evolved climbing roots so that they can adhere to, and be supported by, the trunks of trees. Others, including honeysuckle, climb with their stems. The large stem thorns of bramble and dog rose can act as hooks, enabling the plants to scramble over other vegetation. The

Ivy, an epiphyte, on the trunk of a tree

Zoned vegetation in broadleaved woodland

they resemble a complete 'mosaic', with layer after layer of leaves, effectively absorbing most of the light that falls on them. Conversely, the leaves of trees growing in full sunlight are small, yellow-green and irregularly arranged. **Shade** and **sun leaves** tend to show special anatomical features. Those grown in deep shade are thin, with a single layer of photosynthetic parenchyma above the spongy mesophyll (Figure 2). Sun leaves are much thicker, with a deeper cuticle, several layers of palisade parenchyma, and a sub-epidermis, in which water may be stored. The major difference between shade and sun leaves may be quantified by comparing their **specific leaf area (SLA):**

$$SLA = \frac{\text{leaf area (cm)}}{\text{leaf mass (g)}}$$

A sun leaf will have a much *lower* SLA than a shade leaf. Further differences may be evident in pigmented plants such as copper beech, which produces more pigment in full sunlight than in shade. Other effects of shading may be seen in the anatomy of honeysuckle and bramble stems. The internodes of honeysuckle plants grown in shade are much longer than those grown in full sunlight. Bramble stems grown in shade are covered by numerous small, soft stem thorns, barely sharp enough to pierce human skin. Stems grown in full sunlight however have fewer stem thorns which are much larger and harder, with needle-like tips.

To some extent the fauna of a wood, like its flora, is also zoned; animals such as birds are confined mostly to the tree and shrub layers. Similarly, litter-feeders (**detritivores**) are confined to the litter layer. Also present are housefly and blowfly maggots, feeding on the flesh of dead

distribution of plants in this layer is determined largely by the dappled pattern of sunlight that penetrates through the overhanging branches. Where trees are absent, plants such as bramble and ivy spread outwards, providing ground cover.

The **tree layer** of mature trees, mainly oak, beech and ash, casts a pattern of light and shade over the other zones of vegetation. This pattern determines the distribution and density of plants in the lower zones. Wherever light penetrates through the canopy, small trees, saplings or shrubs grow in the gaps. A number of smaller shrubs are shade-tolerant, growing in dimly lit surroundings, beneath the larger branches of trees. At the margins of woods, where there is more light, the largest numbers of annual and perennial herbs are to be found.

The effect of shading throughout the summer is most readily observed in young saplings such as beech, silver birch and hazel, which can grow in full sunlight and in dense shade. These trees show adaptations according to the amount of light they receive. The leaves of shaded plants are typically large, dark green and orientated towards the brightest sunlight. The orientation of shaded beech leaves, for example, is often so marked that

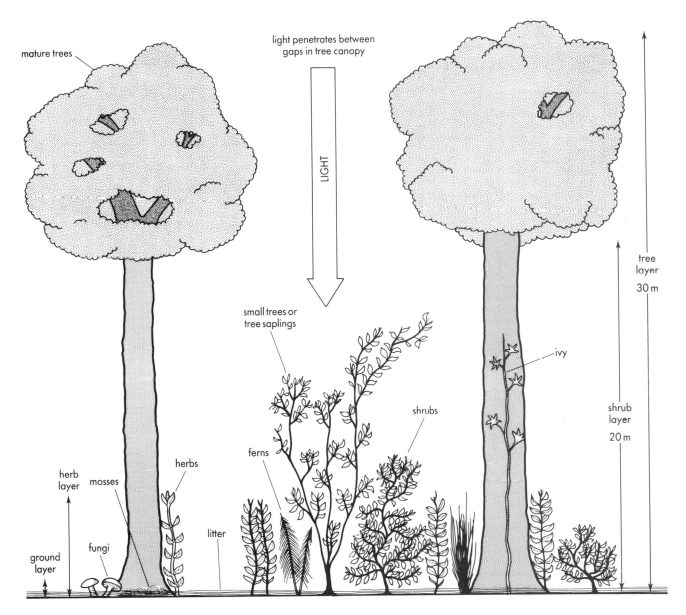

light penetrates between
gaps in tree canopy

LIGHT

mature trees

small trees or
tree saplings

shrubs

ivy

tree
layer
30 m

shrub
layer
20 m

herb
layer

mosses

herbs

ferns

litter

ground
layer

fungi

Figure 1   Plant profile of broadleaved wood

birds and mammals. Plant-eating invertebrates such as earthworms, woodlice, millipedes and slugs, shred whole leaves, stems and roots. Shredded material that has passed through the alimentary canals of these animals forms an ideal growth medium for microscopic decomposers, mostly bacteria and fungi. Woodland **herbivores** belong to many different groups. Herbivore-based and detritus-based food chains are linked by small carnivores (Figure 1, chapter 2), living both at ground level and in the trees. The largest **carnivores**, however, are ground-dwelling species, such as the fox and stoat.

Each horizontal layer of vegetation in a wood is subjected to different climatic conditions. The wind blown, brightly lit, relatively dry and warm conditions at the top of the tree canopy are a marked contrast to the sheltered, shaded, moist conditions that exist lower down in the shrub and herbaceous layers. A majority of woodland trees are wind-pollinated, and may make use of their height, or the wind, to disperse their seeds. Ripe acorns, the fruits of the oak, are blown out of their cupules by the wind. On hitting the ground they bounce and roll, rather like rugby footballs, so that some come to rest beyond the margin of the parent tree. Here, beyond the influence of a germination inhibitor produced by the roots, they

SHADE LEAF   SUN LEAF

(a) *External morphology*

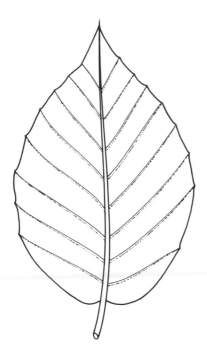

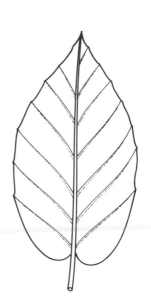

(b) *Internal anatomy*

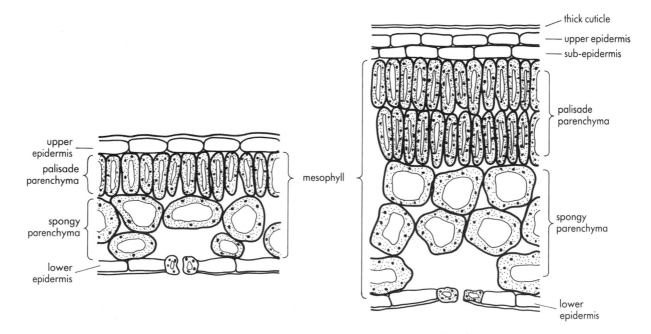

***Figure 2   Shade and sun leaves in beech
(Fagus sylvatica)***

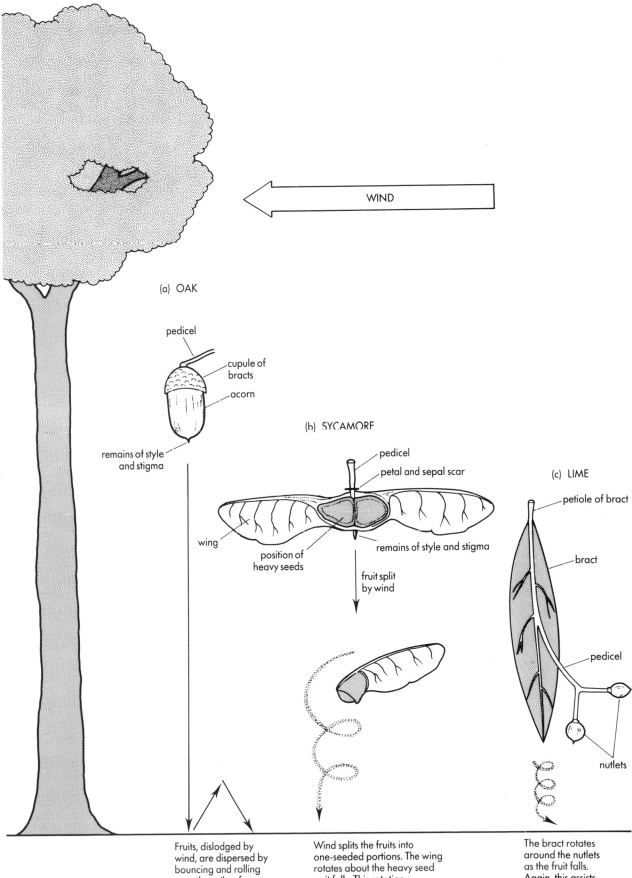

WIND

(a) OAK

pedicel

cupule of bracts

acorn

remains of style and stigma

(b) SYCAMORE

pedicel

petal and sepal scar

wing

remains of style and stigma

position of heavy seeds

fruit split by wind

(c) LIME

petiole of bract

bract

pedicel

nutlets

Fruits, dislodged by wind, are dispersed by bouncing and rolling over the soil surface

Wind splits the fruits into one-seeded portions. The wing rotates about the heavy seed as it falls. This rotation slows its descent and aids its dispersal

The bract rotates around the nutlets as the fruit falls. Again, this assists dispersal by slowing descent

Figure 3   Dispersal of fruits and seeds by wind

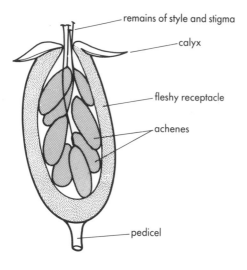

(a) *V.S. (vertical section) rose hip*

remains of style and stigma

calyx

fleshy receptacle

achenes

pedicel

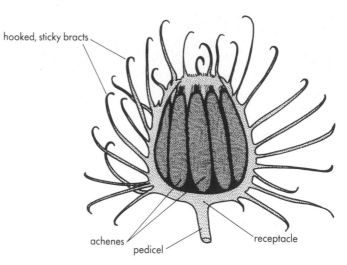

(c) *V.S. fruit of burdock*

hooked, sticky bracts

achenes

pedicel

receptacle

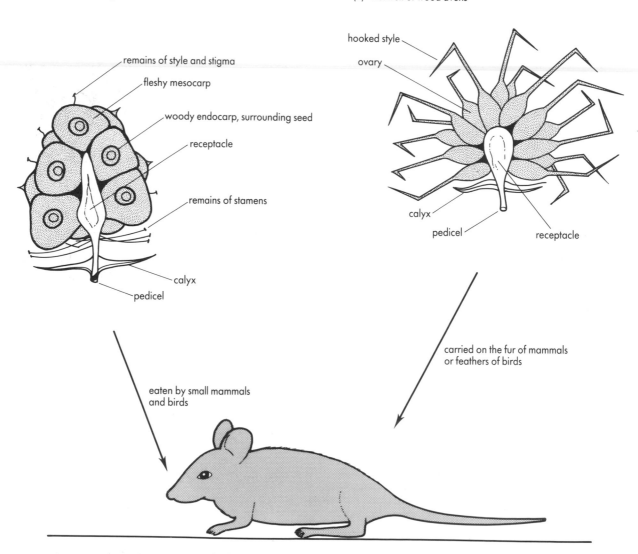

(b) *V.S. fruit of blackberry*

remains of style and stigma

fleshy mesocarp

woody endocarp, surrounding seed

receptacle

remains of stamens

calyx

pedicel

eaten by small mammals and birds

(d) *V.S. fruit of wood avens*

hooked style

ovary

calyx

pedicel

receptacle

carried on the fur of mammals or feathers of birds

Figure 4 Dispersal of fruits and seeds by animals

Wind-dispersed fruits of the creeping thistle

  (i) fallen tree trunks/branches;
 (ii) cut tree stumps;
(iii) holes in trees;
 (iv) wood piles;
  (v) animal droppings;
 (vi) carcases of dead animals;
(vii) animal burrows;
(viii) bird's nests;
 (ix) muddy puddles;
  (x) streams;
 (xi) waterlogged areas;
(xii) ditches.

Each micro-habitat is characterised by its own typical range of light intensity, temperature, relative humidity and wind velocity. In addition, a micro-habitat may provide a particular type of nutrient or a physical condition required by a plant or animal. In other words, each micro-habitat provides the most suitable conditions for one or more vertebrate, invertebrate, fungus, alga, lichen, moss or fern. The trunk of a fallen tree, for example, rotting on the floor of a wood, may offer as many as seven different micro-habitats, as shown in Figure 5.

can germinate to produce saplings. Trees such as sycamore, ash, lime and hornbeam produce **winged fruits** which rotate as they fall. This rotation slows the descent of fruits, allowing the wind to disperse them further from the parent plant. In poplars, the seeds resemble parachutes, floating in the air until they eventually settle under gravity or are brought to earth by rain.

Large numbers of shrubs and herbs produce fruits that are succulent, sticky or burred (Figure 4). **Succulent fruits** provide food for animals. The animals, in turn, disperse the seeds of plants such as dog rose, bramble and holly, which are hard-coated and resistant to digestive enzymes. These seeds are often carried for considerable distances from the parent plant before being voided in the animal's faeces. Alternatively, burred fruits may be carried on the fur or feathers of woodland animals. As the animals move through the wood any vigorous movements dislodge a few seeds, which are slowly released from the burr along the track of the animal. These two modes of seed dispersal by animals illustrate just one example of the interdependence of the plants and animals living in woodland.

A micro-habitat – the nesting hole of an owl

Micro-habitats in woodland

Within the complex structure of woodlands there are smaller areas, or **micro-habitats**, providing organisms with particular combinations of environmental conditions suited to their mode of life. Any of the following woodland features provides one or more micro-habitats:

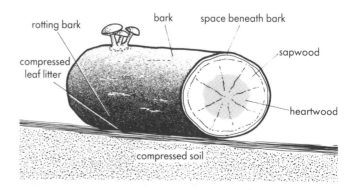

Figure 5   Micro-habitats provided by a fallen tree trunk

1.2 PONDS

Many ponds are man made, originally dug for watering farm animals or for keeping ducks and fish. They were often made water tight by trampling or 'puddling' the clay bed. Such ponds are rarely more than 2–3 metres deep, so that light and oxygen readily penetrate to all levels. Ponds normally support a profusion of herbaceous plants but few, if any, shrubs or trees. In an established pond, the aquatic herbaceous plants (**hydrophytes**) occur in three distinct groupings:

  (i) marginal plants in shallow mud around the edge;
 (ii) rooted plants in open water;
(iii) free-floating, unrooted plants at the surface.

Common duckweed, covering the surface of a pond

and mammals. Plants that are rooted in open water either have their leaves completely submerged, or produce some leaves that float at the surface. Canadian pondweed, water starwort and water milfoil belong to the first of these groups. In contrast, amphibious bisort, water crowfoot, waterlily and broadleaved pondweed normally produce some floating leaves. A third group of macroscopic pond plants, represented by the duckweeds, frog bit, bladderworts and water fern (*Azolla*), float at the surface. This region may also be covered by green filamentous algae, forming a scum, while other free-swimming microscopic algae may colour water beneath the surface.

Floating and rooted pond plants

Water crowfoot, a plant with entire and dissected leaves

Among those commonly found in the marginal zone are soft rush, branched bur-reed, yellow flag, greater water plantain and water cress. The presence of common reed, bulrush or reedmace often creates tall **marginal reedswamp**, a sheltered and well camouflaged habitat for birds

Plant adaptations

In general, the roots of plants growing in open water serve mainly to anchor them to the mud, not primarily for water or mineral salt absorption. These functions may be taken over by the leaves, which lack a cuticle and are therefore able to absorb substances from the water. As water buoys up plants, few submerged species have leaves with supporting petioles. Floating leaves often have their stomata confined to the upper epidermis. Large internal spaces (lacunae), used for storing air, are a common anatomical feature of the stems, leaves and roots of many water plants. Rooted species, with leaves that float at the surface, often show an interesting adaptation known as **heterophylly** (Figure 6), i.e. two different types of leaf are produced on the same plant. Those leaves that float at the surface are generally large, dark green and adapted for carrying out photosynthesis. Submerged leaves are either long and narrow (linear) like blades of grass, or branching (dissected), paler green and sometimes cylindrical. By dividing the leaf into many smaller pieces, the surface area : volume ratio is increased, thereby increasing the efficiency of gaseous exchange. Furthermore, linear and branched leaves offer less resistance to water flow and so are less likely to be damaged by waves and water currents.

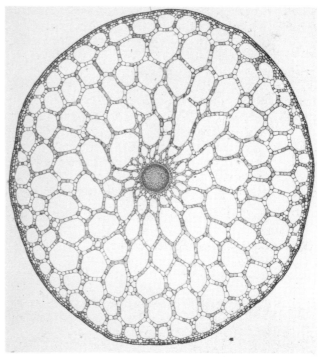

Transverse section of a water plant (Hippuris) showing the large air spaces (lacunae)

(a) *Water-crowfoot*

floating leaf

submerged leaf

(b) *Arrowhead*

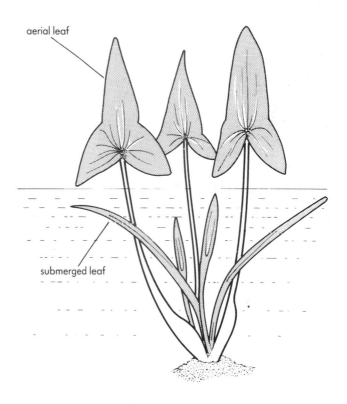

aerial leaf

submerged leaf

Figure 6 Heterophylly in pond plants

Ponds support many different species of insects, in all or some of the stages of their life cycles (Figure 7). Some pond-dwelling insects live on the surface film of the water. Others live in midwater, among plants, or in the thick organic mud that covers the bottom of the pond. Some of the best known surface dwellers are the pond skaters, water measurers and whirligig beetles. Supported by the water's surface tension, these insects walk or swim on the surface film, and feed mainly on flying insects that fall into the water. In contrast, mosquito larvae 'hang' under the surface film, breathing air from above the surface via respiratory **siphons**. Active swimmers such as diving beetles, water boatmen, saucer bugs and the phantom midge fly larva occur in midwater. Dragonfly and damselfly nymphs, together with mayfly larvae and water stick insects, live among the plants. At the bottom of the pond, caddisfly larvae feed at the surface of the mud, while bloodworms (the larvae of *Chironomus* midges) burrow into it, constructing protective mud tubes.

Common pond skater, an insect that lives on the surface of water

Common frog, a carnivore in and around ponds

Apart from insects, ponds may support large populations of other invertebrates. These include herbivorous pond snails, carnivorous leeches and detritus-feeding *Tubifex* worms. Crustaceans, notably water fleas and fresh water shrimps, may also occur in very large numbers. Small chordates are well represented. The coarse fish may include sticklebacks, roach, eels, perch and pike. Large numbers of common frogs, common toads and newts attract grass snakes, a major predator on these amphibians. Dense strands of marginal reedswamp provide nesting sites for the moorhen, coot and mallard duck. Reed warblers and sedge warblers also make their nests in these plants, but build at higher levels well above the water line. If a pond is surrounded by a firm sloping bank, it provides a suitable nesting site for water shrews and water voles.

Reed warbler, feeding chicks

Great diving beetle, a carnivore

Animal adaptations

Effective camouflage is an adaption used by many pond insects to protect them from chordate predators. The larvae of mosquitoes and the phantom midge, both midwater dwellers, are colourless and therefore difficult to see. Larger active insects tend to be brown-black above, and white-grey underneath. Viewed from above they are camouflaged against the dead, brown-black leaves at the bottom of the pond, while their lighter underparts provide effective camouflage against a cloud-covered sky. Caddisfly larvae take their camouflage to an extreme by building their cases of materials such as leaves, twigs and stones that occur naturally in pond mud.

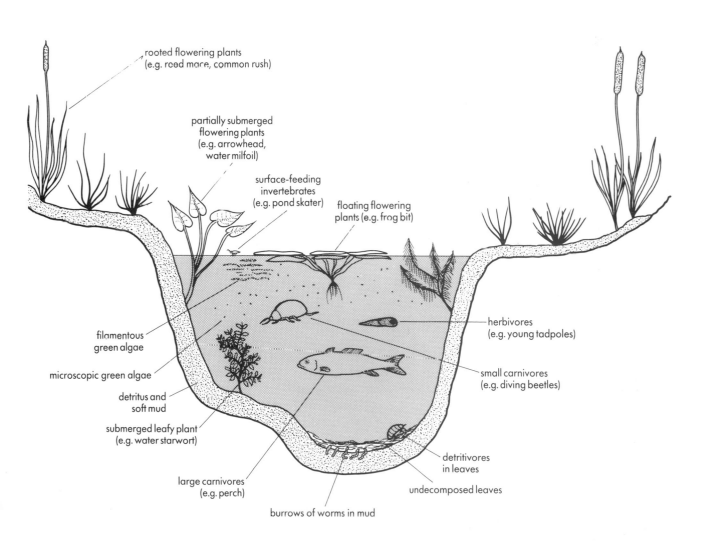

rooted flowering plants
(e.g. reed mace, common rush)

partially submerged
flowering plants
(e.g. arrowhead,
water milfoil)

surface-feeding
invertebrates
(e.g. pond skater)

floating flowering
plants (e.g. frog bit)

herbivores
(e.g. young tadpoles)

small carnivores
(e.g. diving beetles)

detritivores
in leaves

undecomposed leaves

burrows of worms in mud

large carnivores
(e.g. perch)

submerged leafy plant
(e.g. water starwort)

detritus and
soft mud

microscopic green algae

filamentous
green algae

Figure 7   Profile of a pond

Active swimmers have a streamlined body, either with a hard, polished surface, or covered by slimy mucus. This streamlining, with a bluntly rounded head and tapering tail, helped by a smooth body surface, reduces drag as the animal propels itself through the water. Highly active pond animals require high concentrations of oxygen. Insects such as diving beetles, water boatmen and mosquito larvae frequently rise to the surface to replenish their oxygen supply. Insects that remain permanently submerged, such as dragonfly nymphs and alder fly larvae, have external gills to increase the 'surface area : volume' ratio of their gas exchange surfaces. The body fluids of pond animals contain more solutes than the surrounding water. This means that water will flood into their tissues unless it is either kept out or pumped out. Many pond insects have an impermeable, wax-coated cuticle, through which water cannot penetrate. Fresh water fish use a more complex system of osmoregulation: water that enters through their skin and gills is pumped out again by highly efficient kidneys. Salts are retained and concentrated.

Tables 4a and 4b show animals, plants and fungi that commonly occur in ponds.

Table 4a   *Some common animals of ponds*

PHYLUM		SPECIES	COMMENTS
Arthropods	Insects	Caddisfly (larva)	Bottom-dweller
		Dragonfly (larva)	Carnivore
		Great diving beetle	Carnivore
		Mosquito (larva)	Eats microscopic algae etc.
		Phantom midge (larva)	Eats microscopic algae etc.
		Water boatman	Carnivore
		Water skater	Surface-dweller
		Water stick insect	Herbivore
	Crustaceans	Hoglouse	Eats detritus
		Fresh water shrimp	Eats detritus
		Water flea	Eats microscopic algae
	Arachnids	Raft spider	Carnivore
		Water mite	
		Water spider	
Annelids		Leeches	Non-parasitic and parasitic species
		Tubifex worms	In mud, feeding on particles
Molluscs		Pond snails	Herbivores
Chordates	Fish	Carp	Secondary and tertiary consumers
		Perch	
		Pike	
		Roach	
		Stickleback	
	Amphibians	Frog	Animals with aquatic larvae, feeding on plants, then animals
		Toad	
		Newt	
	Reptiles	Grass snake	Eats frogs, toads and newts
	Birds	Coot	Nest in reeds etc.
		Mallard duck	Nest in reeds etc.
		Moorhen	Nest in reeds etc.
		Reed bunting	Nest in reeds etc.
	Mammals	Brown rat	
		Water shrew	Nest in banks
		Water vole	Nest in banks

Table 4b   Some common plants and fungi in ponds

KINGDOM or PHYLUM		SPECIES	COMMENTS
Algae		*Chlamydomonas*	Unicellular type
		Spirogyra	Filamentous type
		Volvox	Colonial type
Pteridophytes		Water fern	Floating, carpet-forming
Angiosperms	Marginal plants	Branched bur-reed	
		Bulrush	
		Common reed	
		Greater water plantain	
		Lesser spearwort	
		Marsh marigold	
		Rush	
		Water cress	
		Yellow flag	
	Submerged or with floating leaves	Amphibious bisort	
		Arrowhead	
		Canadian pondweed	
		Water-crowfoot	
		Waterlily	
		Water milfoil	
		Water starwort	
	Floating	Bladderworts	
		Duckweeds	Floating, carpet-forming
		Frog-bit	
Fungi		*Saprolegnia*	Saprophyte

1.3 ROCKY SEA SHORES

Rocky sea shore near Start Point, South Devon

Approximately 6000 kilometres (3700 miles) of the UK coastline is cliffed, with rocky shores between the cliffs and the sea. Most of these shores are formed by the continuous erosion of limestone and chalk, worn down to sea level by the ebb and flow of the tides. Other rocky shores are formed from sandstone or granite. All rocky shores can be divided up into specific vertical zones, each zone having its own characteristic species of seaweeds and animals able to withstand the conditions imposed by the tide. The four principal regions are show in Figure 8:

   (i) splash zone
  (ii) upper shore
 (iii) middle shore
 (iv) lower shore

   (i) **The splash zone** is the highest zone, furthest from the sea. Composed of a sloping rock face, it is inhospitable, buffeted by strong winds, and subsequently exposed to salt sea spray. This region is only covered by sea water during spring tides. The plants and animals of this region are found mostly in rock crevices where there is some protection. Yellow and black lichens grow on the exposed rocks. Isolated groups of flowering plants, such as rock samphire, thrift and sea campion, grow wherever there are deposits of soil or detritus. Small periwinkles and sea slaters (woodlouse-like

15

scavengers) are the only invertebrates commonly found in this zone.

(ii) **The upper shore** is covered by the sea during extreme high tides. This means that the plants and animals that live there must tolerate long periods of exposure. Two brown algae, the channelled wrack and the spiral wrack, are the most abundant species in this zone. Both are firmly attached to rocks by means of a 'holdfast' (**hapteron**), and both are covered by a slimy moisture-retaining mucilage. The green alga *Enteromorpha* is another mucilage-coated plant commonly found in this zone. Acorn barnacles, cemented to rocks to prevent their removal by waves, use chalky plates to close the opening into their shells when the tide is out. Rough periwinkles have a thick shell, resistant to wave action, and avoid desiccation by retaining sea water. Limpets adhere to rock surfaces by means of a sucking foot, and pull down the edges of their shells to make close contact with rocks, thus preventing water loss by evaporation.

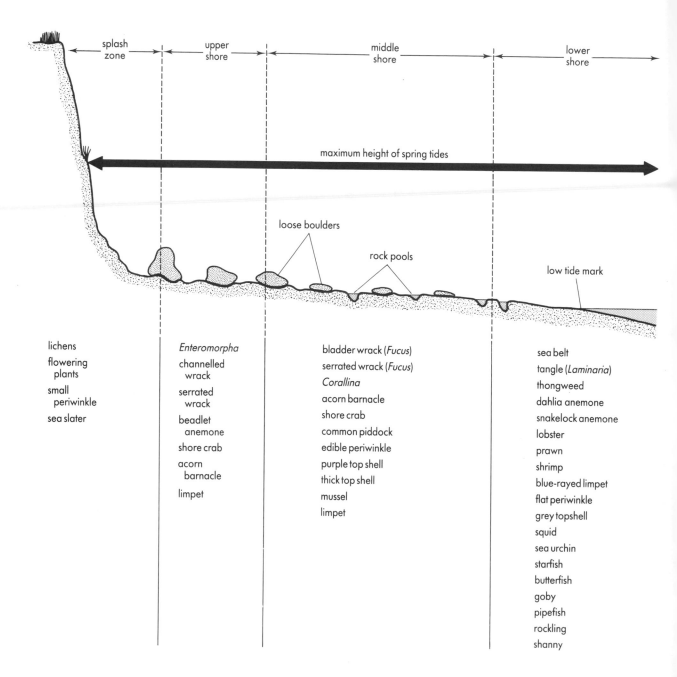

Figure 8   Profile of a rocky shore, and the principal occupants of each zone

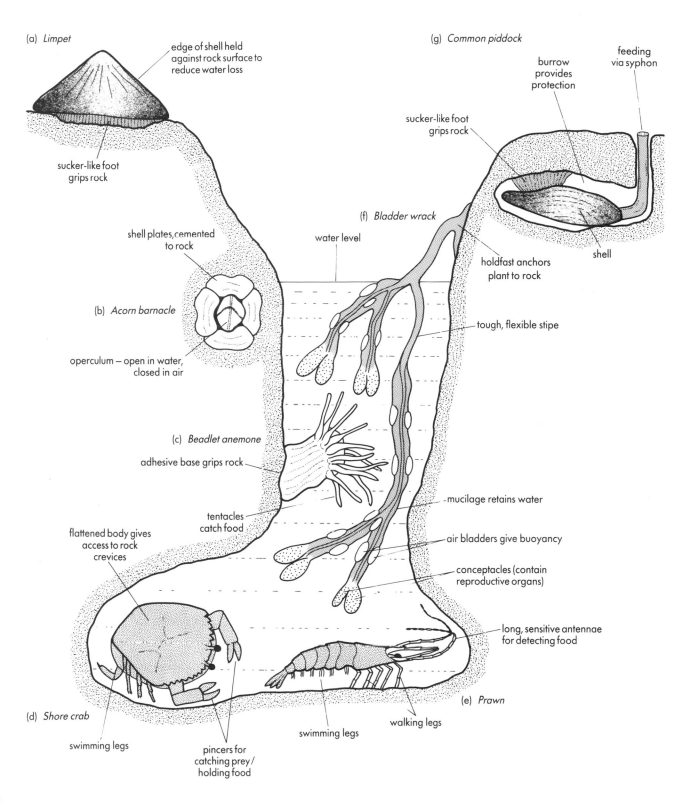

(a) *Limpet*

edge of shell held against rock surface to reduce water loss

sucker-like foot grips rock

(g) *Common piddock*

burrow provides protection

feeding via syphon

sucker-like foot grips rock

shell

shell plates, cemented to rock

(b) *Acorn barnacle*

operculum – open in water, closed in air

(f) *Bladder wrack*

water level

holdfast anchors plant to rock

tough, flexible stipe

(c) *Beadlet anemone*

adhesive base grips rock

tentacles catch food

mucilage retains water

air bladders give buoyancy

conceptacles (contain reproductive organs)

flattened body gives access to rock crevices

long, sensitive antennae for detecting food

(e) *Prawn*

(d) *Shore crab*

swimming legs

pincers for catching prey / holding food

swimming legs

walking legs

Figure 9   Adaptations to middle shore conditions

(iii) **The middle shore** (Figure 9) is the region that is most affected by the ebb and flow of the tides. Characteristically, this region has loose boulders, and shallow rocks pools in which animals seek refuge at low tide. Brown algae, notably the bladder wrack, serrated wrack and knotted wrack, are often abundant in this zone, as well as the red alga *(Corallina officinalis)*. Animal life is more varied, including coelenterates, crustaceans and molluscs. Barnacles, mussels and limpets are attached to the surface of rocks. Crabs and shrimps hide beneath stones, or burrow into the sand. Piddocks and flask shells bore into soft rocks, and feed from their burrows via siphons. Edible periwinkles, dog whelks, purple top shells and thick top shells litter the surface of rocks at low tide. Beadlet anemones line the sides of rock pools and water channels.

(iv) **The lower shore** is mostly covered by the sea, and is exposed to air for relatively short periods during low tide. Within this region, the plant and animal life is abundant and varied. Large stalked brown algae, notably tangle *(Laminaria)*, sea belt and thong weed grow in profusion. Their fronds provide the food and shelter for the blue-rayed limpet, flat periwinkle, grey top shell, tubeworms and crustaceans. Stalked jelly fish, dahlia anemones, snakelock anemones, sea urchins, starfish and brittle stars feed in the deeper rock pools. Among the fish frequenting these pools are rockling, pipe fish, shanny, gobies and butterfish. During high tide larger fish, lobsters and squid enter the lower shore zone to feed.

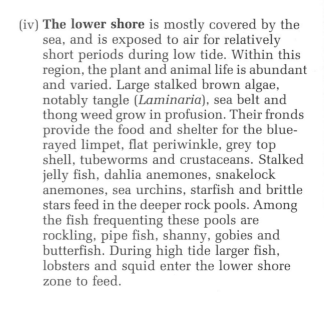

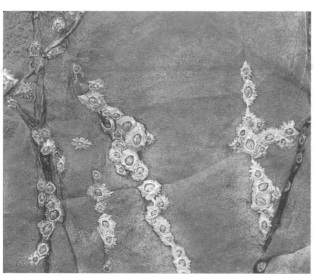

Acorn barnacles on rocks

Oyster catcher, a wader

Serrated wrack, bladder wrack and egg wrack on rocks

Many birds visit rocky shores during low tide to feed on the crustaceans, molluscs or the detritus. Mussels are eaten by oystercatchers, which prise them open with their beaks, and by herring gulls, which drop them onto rocks. Rock pipets turn over seaweeds in search of periwinkles and insect larvae; turnstones lift pebbles to feed on crustaceans; purple sandpipers forage at the water's edge, moving with the tide. Two mammals, the brown rat and the fox, roam the shore at night in their search for food.

1.4 SUCCESSION

If a habitat is stripped of its original vegetation (e.g. by tree-felling, fire, flood or drainage), the area is rapidly recolonised by a succession of different plants and animals. **Primary succession** refers to the introduction of organisms into areas that have not previously been colonised. Such potential habitats might include mud deposits in river deltas, cooled volcanic larva and man made ponds. Conversely, **secondary succession** refers to the reintroduction of organisms into a denuded habitat previously occupied by plants and animals.

All successions usually involve changes in community structure and function, until the community reaches a **climax of succession**, such as mature mixed woodland (Figure 1). The **climax community** stabilises in a persistent structure that appears to undergo little, if any, further change. As Figure 10 shows, the same climax community may be reached from different starting points, along **convergent** routes.

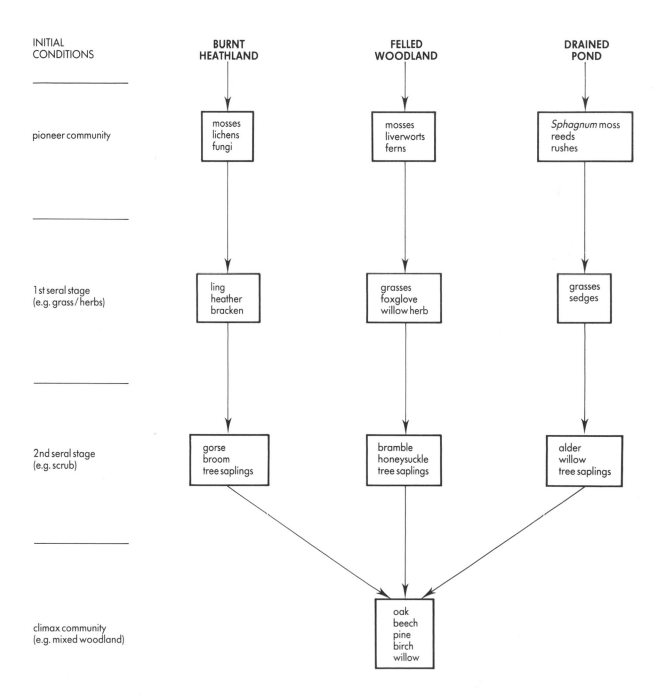

Figure 10   Seral succession leading to mixed woodland from different starting points

The initial colonisers form the **pioneer community**. They are followed by a number of **seral communities (seral stages)**, leading to the climax community. All of these stages taken together constitute a **sere**. Ecologists refer to an **autogenic succession** if the driving force for change is the organisms themselves, for example, on heathland. Here, plants of each seral community create the conditions that favour the growth of plants in the next seral community. Once established, these plants take over from those that prepared the ground for them. The process continues until the climax community is established, with self-perpetuation of climax vegetation over several generations.

A different type of succession may occur in aquatic habitats. **Allogenic succession** is driven by abiotic changes in the environment, such as the gradual filling of a pond by deposition of a layer of detritus from overhanging vegetation. As the detritus accumulates, bacteria release nutrients into the water, making it a more fertile habitat for vascular plants. Rooted plants become established around the edge of the pond and a floating mass of vegetation forms at the centre. This mat is composed mostly of sphagnum moss; as it broadens and thickens, it is colonised by sedges and grasses. Soon, tree saplings become established. The detritus layer increases in depth and begins to dry out. Firm, dry land forms, supporting a climax community of broadleaved trees, dominated by oak and beech (Figure 11).

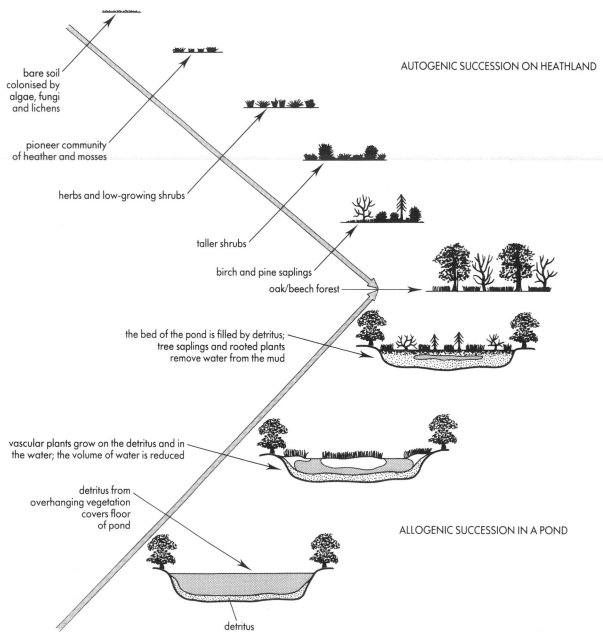

AUTOGENIC SUCCESSION ON HEATHLAND

bare soil colonised by algae, fungi and lichens

pioneer community of heather and mosses

herbs and low-growing shrubs

taller shrubs

birch and pine saplings

oak/beech forest

the bed of the pond is filled by detritus; tree saplings and rooted plants remove water from the mud

vascular plants grow on the detritus and in the water; the volume of water is reduced

detritus from overhanging vegetation covers floor of pond

ALLOGENIC SUCCESSION IN A POND

detritus

Figure 11 Autogenic and allogenic successions leading to oak/beech woodland

Regardless of the climax communities to which they lead, seral successions are characterised by the following general features:

(i) An increase in **species diversity** as the succession progresses. Climax communities always support more species of plants and animals than pioneer communities. As a direct result of increasing species diversity, animal feeding relationships become more complex at each stage of the succession.

(ii) A progressive increase in the total organic matter (**biomass**) per unit area of the community. As biomass accumulates, the number and relative importance of organisms that decompose dead organic matter increases.

(iii) Succession stops when energy input as **community photosynthesis (CP)** equals energy loss as **community respiration (CR)**. In the early seral stages, CP > CR. Later, CR increases relative to CP. The succession stabilises at its climax when CP = CR.

QUESTIONS

1 The table below gives the leaf area and mass of ten leaves collected from beech twigs growing in (i) full sunlight and (ii) partial shade.

| LEAF | LOCATION | | | |
| | Full sunlight | | Partial shade | |
LEAF NUMBER	Leaf area (cm)	Leaf mass (g)	Leaf area (cm)	Leaf mass (g)
1	11.2	0.8	14.2	0.8
2	12.6	0.9	16.3	0.9
3	13.4	0.9	18.4	1.1
4	9.3	0.6	14.1	0.8
5	8.6	0.5	11.6	0.6
6	13.4	0.9	14.6	0.9
7	14.4	1.1	19.2	1.3
8	15.1	1.3	13.9	0.7
9	9.6	0.7	14.6	0.9
10	11.2	0.8	16.2	1.0

a) Calculate the mean (average) leaf area and mass of the leaves collected in (i) and (ii).

b) Specific leaf area (SLA)= $\dfrac{\text{leaf area (cm)}}{\text{leaf mass (g)}}$.

Calculate the mean SLA for those leaves growing in (i) and (ii).

c) Why are SLA measurements of value in ecological studies?

d) Write a brief summary of your conclusions. What further tests, if any, would be required to confirm your conclusions?

e) Devise and describe two different methods for estimating the surface area of leaves.

2 a) What do you understand by the term ''ecological succession'?

b) Distinguish between:
(i) primary and secondary succession;
(ii) autogenic and allogenic succession.

c) The diagram below represents a succession of plant communities colonising bare earth.

BARE EARTH $\longrightarrow$ A → B → C → D → E

(i) What name is given to the complete succession?
(ii) Which of these stages represents the climax community?
(iii) In which community would you find least species diversity?
(iv) What name is given to the community at stage A?
(v) Which community is likely to be most stable?
(vi) Which group of heterotrophic organisms would always be more numerous at stage E than at stage A?
(vii) Why does the succession stop at stage E?

d) How may natural plant succession affect land used for (i) agriculture, and (ii) coniferous forests?

e) Does succession occur on a rocky sea shore? Explain your answer.

3 Imagine that you have been asked to carry out an ecological survey of a small area of broadleaved woodland, not previously studied. Describe how you would:
a) catch and identify the invertebrate animals;
b) estimate the density of plants in the herb layer;
c) make a record of all the plants and animals in the area.

4 Review the variety and distribution of plants and animals in a named terrestrial or aquatic habitat.

5 a) From your own investigations, name three plants and three animals that were collected from one of the following habitats:
(i) deciduous or coniferous woodland;
(ii) pond or lake;
(iii) rocky or sandy sea shore.

b) Describe how each of the organisms you have named is adapted for life in its habitat.

c) Explain how any two of the organisms you have described were (i) collected, and (ii) identified.

6 a) Describe the typical zonation (stratification) of plants that occur (i) in a broadleaved wood, and (ii) on a rocky sea shore.

b) Explain, for each of these habitats, the reasons for this plant zonation.

c) How does the zonation of plants affect the distribution of animals in each habitat?

7 Write illustrated notes on any three of the following topics: micro-habitats; fruit and seed dispersal; aquatic plants (hydrophytes); seashore invertebrates; sun and shade leaves; the decomposition of leaf litter.

8 What do you understand by plant succession? Illustrate your answer by reference to (i) one terrestrial habitat, and (ii) one aquatic habitat which you have studied.

BIBLIOGRAPHY

Ashby, M (1969) *Introduction to Plant Ecology* Macmillan

Bishop, O N (1973) *Natural Communities* John Murray

Clegg, J (1974) *Fresh water Life* Warne

Emberlin, J C (1983) *Introduction to Ecology* Macdonald and Evans

Jenkins, M (1983) *Sea shore Studies* George Allen and Unwin

Leadley Brown, A (1987) *Fresh water Ecology* Heinemann

Macan, T T (1974) *Fresh water Ecology* Longman

Macan, T T and Worthington, E B (1951) *Life in Lakes and Rivers* Collins

2 ECOSYSTEMS

The scientific study of habitats, the organisms that live there, and their interrelationships with one another and the physical environment, has led to a unifying ecological concept known as the **ecosystem**. An ecosystem is a community of living organisms and their non-living environment. Woods, ponds and rocky shores are all ecosystems, driven by solar energy and maintained from generation to generation by the recycling of nutrients. Every ecosystem has both living (biotic) and non-living (abiotic) components. The biotic components consist of producers that synthesise food, consumers that eat it, and decomposers that break down dead organic materials into simpler compounds such as gases, salts and water, for recycling. Among the most important abiotic components are soil and climate, which together determine the global distribution of plants and the animals that depend on them.

2.1 THE BIOTIC COMPONENT

Woods, ponds and rocky shores support populations of plants and animals. A **population** is a group of organisms of the same species occupying a particular place at a given time. The place where a population lives is called its **habitat**. The habitat of squirrels, for example, is woodland; for newts it is ponds; for mussels it is the sea shore. **Terrestrial habitats** are land based; **aquatic habitats** are water based. Within both types, materials such as water, mineral salts and gases are exchanged between organisms and their surroundings. Most habitats contain more than one species. The populations of all the species that occupy a habitat form a **community**. In all large communities the species play different roles, acting as producers, consumers or decomposers.

Producers are the synthetic (**autotrophic**) organisms in a habitat. They include chemosynthetic bacteria, photosynthetic bacteria, algae, bryophytes and green vascular plants. They produce complex organic molecules, including carbohydrates, fats and proteins, from simple organic substances using energy from the sun or from inorganic substances. The essential

ecological function of the produce... the food on which the other types ...sm (**heterotrophs**), which are unable to synthesise their own food depend. Within a defined area, the total mass of an organism is called its **biomass**. Plant biomass is usually expressed as dry mass per unit area, g/m^2 or kg/ha. Alternatively, plant biomass may be expressed in terms of **ash content**: plant material from a given area is burned and the ash is weighed. **Plant productivity** is the rate at which energy accumulates in a unit area per unit of time. It may be expressed as $kJ/m^2/yr^{-1}$, but is more usually expressed as dry mass of assimilated material, e.g. $g/m^2/day^{-1}$ or $kg/ha/yr^{-1}$. Measurement of **photosynthetic efficiency** also provides a useful way of comparing energy accumulation in different habitats.

Photosynthetic efficiency =

$$\frac{\text{energy of plant assimilate per unit area and time}}{\text{energy received from sunlight per unit area and time}}$$

Most vascular plants have a photosynthetic efficiency within the range 0.5–2.5%, but values vary between species, rarely exceeding 5–6%. Clearly the photosynthetic efficiency of producers in an ecosystem influences the amount of energy that is available to its consumers, detritus-feeders and decomposers. This, in turn, determines the number of consumers a habitat can support.

Consumers are the animals in a habitat, feeding on some of the organic material originally made by the producers. As many as four different types of consumer, grouped according to the nature of their diet, may occur in a large habitat. These are:

(i) **herbivores**, feeding from living plants
(ii) **carnivores**, feeding from living animals
(iii) **omnivores**, feeding from living plants and animals
(iv) **detritivores**, feeding on dead plant and animal material.

Animal biomass is the total mass of any given species per unit area of land, or per unit volume of water. **Gross secondary productivity (GSP)** is the rate of production of new animal biomass. **Decomposers** are micro-organisms, mostly saprophytic fungi and bacteria. In general, the fungi break down particles of dead organic material into large molecules. The bacteria then continue the process of breakdown, releasing carbon dioxide and ions such as NO_2^-, NO_3^-,

23

...ach of these compounds, released ...vironment, can be used by green plants ...ilt up once again into plant carbohydrates, ...s and proteins.

Food chains and food webs

Feeding interactions between the different organisms in a community are represented by the use of both food chains and food webs. Food chains indicate the sequence in which organisms feed on each other. They describe the order of eating and being eaten, as in the generalised sequence:

plants → herbivores → carnivores

death ⇄ detritivores

In most large ecosystems, the food chains are of three main types. The first, a **herbivore chain**, is based on fresh primary production, with a herbivore occupying the second position in the sequence:

grass → rabbit → fox

The second, a **detritus chain**, is based on dead organic matter. An example is:

detritus → woodlouse → centipede

In the third type, a **parasitic chain**, animals at the end of the sequence are smaller than those on which they feed. An example, incorporating two different parasites is:

grass → rabbit → rabbit flea

↓

gut flagellates (of flea)

In a herbivore chain each organism occupies a different **trophic level** (*trophos* – is the Greek word for feeding). The first trophic level is always occupied by a **producer**, usually a green plant, and the second by a herbivore, the **primary consumer**. The higher trophic levels are occupied by carnivores, described as **secondary** and **tertiary consumers**, depending on their position in the chain. Hence a chain with four trophic levels has primary, secondary and tertiary consumers:

carnivore 2 (tertiary consumer)

↑

carnivore 1 (secondary consumer)

↑

herbivore (primary consumer)

↑

plant (producer)

Feeding relationships in most ecosystems are often more complex than linear food chains imply. Herbivores may feed off a variety of plants; carnivores may feed off more than one animal.

This means that a **food web**, showing interconnections between different food chains, provides a more accurate picture of feeding relationships between organisms. **Food webs** carry the description of animal feeding one stage further by linking together different food chains into a web, describing both the food sources and predators of most of the animals in an ecosystem. In general, there are clear herbivore-based and detritus-based food chains, linked together at higher trophic levels by carnivores that feed on herbivores from both types of chain. This general pattern is shown in Figure 1. A part of the food web in oak-dominated woodland is illustrated in Figure 2.

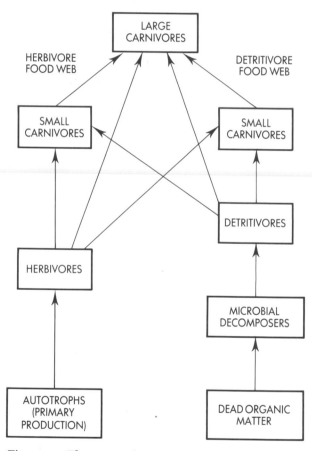

Figure 1 *The general pattern of a food web in a large habitat, with herbivore and detritus-based chains*

The pioneer British ecologist Charles Elton produced effective generalisations to summarise the relationships between organisms in food chains and webs. The simplest and oldest of these is the **pyramid of numbers**, shown in Figure 3a. The pyramid represents the numerical relationships between organisms feeding at different trophic levels. At the bottom of the pyramid, primary consumers are numerous, small and short-lived. The top of the pyramid is occupied by sparse, large and long-lived

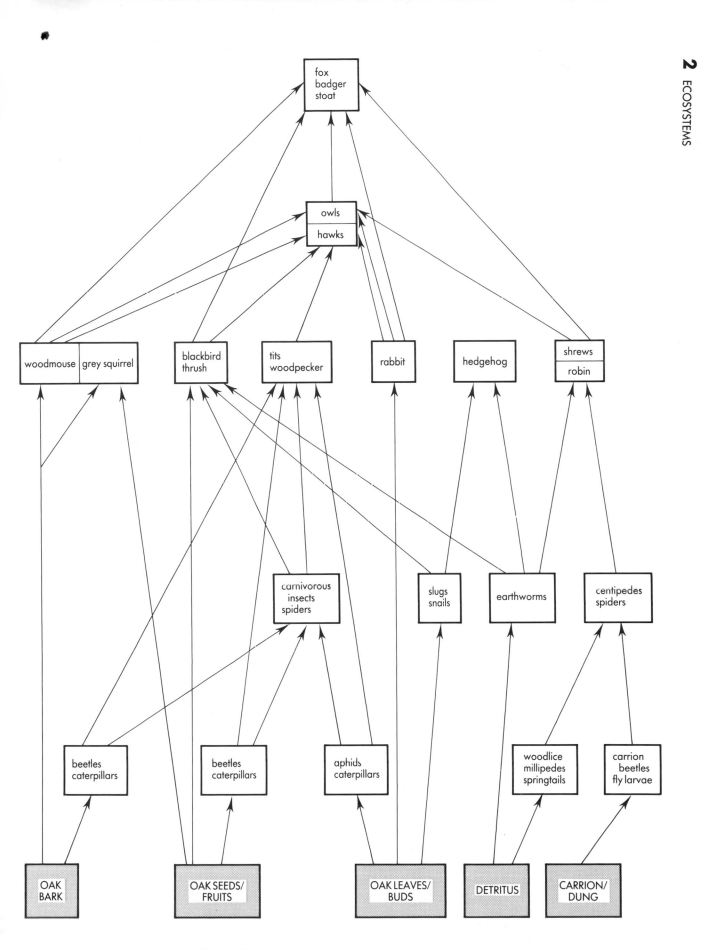

Figure 2   A part of the food web in oak-dominated woodland

carnivores. Applied to actual food chains based on individual herbs or shrubs, the pyramid of numbers often translates into meaningful results (Figure 3b). It is less than ideal, however, when applied to large trees and the insect populations that feed on them, because it gives no indication of size or mass. For these reasons, today's ecologists prefer to use pyramids of biomass and energy, described in section 2.3.

(a) *A generalised pyramid*

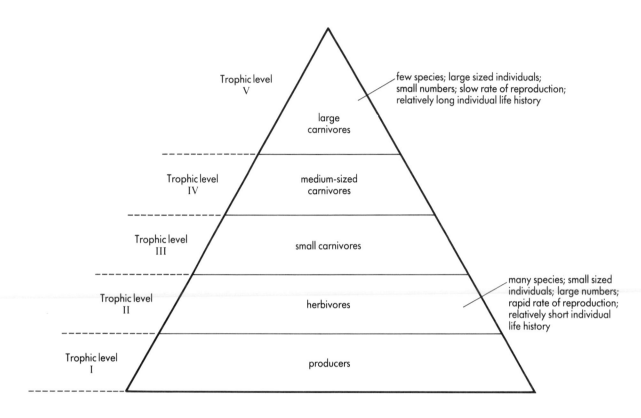

few species; large sized individuals; small numbers; slow rate of reproduction; relatively long individual life history

many species; small sized individuals; large numbers; rapid rate of reproduction; relatively short individual life history

(b) *Some examples of actual pyramids* (not drawn to scale)

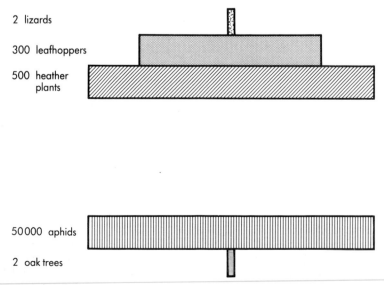

Figure 3   Trophic pyramids

Ecological niches

The term **niche** is used to describe the way in which a species population is specialised within a community. The term not only describes the space occupied by a species (i.e. where it lives, the **niche space**) but also its 'occupation', as a producer, herbivore, carnivore or decomposer (**trophic niche**). The niche space occupied by an organism is determined by at least five different factors.

   (i) Type of food, e.g. plants, animals or a mixture of both.
  (ii) Limit of tolerance to environmental variables, such as temperature, relative humidity, light intensity and pH.
 (iii) Time of activity, e.g. day or night.
 (iv) Method of locomotion, e.g. walking, swimming, flying etc.
  (v) Body size, shape, and (in the case of animals) colour.

The trophic (or feeding) niche of an animal describes its food source and the proportions of each food in its diet. Suppose, for example, that a carnivore's diet consists of:

x% species X
y% species Y
z% species Z

If x = 50, y = 40 and z = 10, then the breadth of its feeding niche (B) may be quantified by the following equation:

$$B = \frac{1}{x^2 + y^2 + z^2} = \frac{1}{(0.5)^2 + (0.4)^2 + (0.1)^2} = 2.43$$

In general, the *higher* the value of B, the *larger* the number of species consumed, and the *broader* the feeding niche of the carnivore.

An organism's **environmental niche** may be defined in terms of its range of tolerance to temperature, humidity and pH for example. Plotted as a graph, this niche may be given one, two or three dimensions (Figure 4). These diagrams represent the organism's idealised or **fundamental niche**, a range of conditions within which it is capable of living and reproducing. In actual habitats however, an organism lives only in a part of its fundamental niche space, a fraction called its **realised niche**. This occurs because competitors and predators prevent it from being equally successful over the complete range of each environmental variable. From an evolutionary standpoint, competition between members of the same species broadens niche space because individuals are forced to explore new food sources, micro-habitats and so on to the limits of their tolerance. Conversely, competition between different species narrows niche space, since one species is likely to be more successful than another in exploiting available resources.

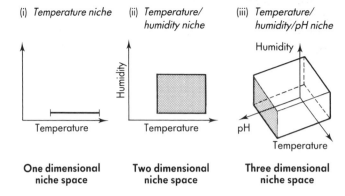

(a) *Range of tolerance to one, two or three environmental variables*

(i) *Temperature niche*
One dimensional niche space

(ii) *Temperature/ humidity niche*
Two dimensional niche space

(iii) *Temperature/ humidity/pH niche*
Three dimensional niche space

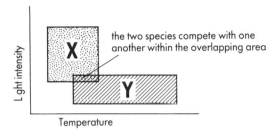

(b) *The effect of interspecific competition between two species, X and Y, on niche space; competition reduces the fundamental niche of both species*

the two species compete with one another within the overlapping area

Figure 4   The ecological niche of a species

2.2 THE ABIOTIC COMPONENT

The most widely important abiotic factors which have ecological effects on organisms are temperature, light, humidity, oxygen concentration, pH and the physical and chemical nature of soil. In this account, only the most important effects of each abiotic factor is discussed, with particular reference to conditions that occur in northern Europe.

Temperature

Throughout northern Europe there is a seasonal variation in temperature, closely linked to changes in light intensity (Figure 5). There are also daily (**diurnal**) temperature and light cycles. **Temperature profiles** at different heights of vegetation above ground level are of considerable practical importance. Investigations have shown that at midday the foliage, together with bare soil between plants, are the warmest places (Figure 6). At night, these exposed regions cool most rapidly. This means that if the vegetation cover is removed, temperature at ground level usually shows more marked fluctuations, a factor that affects the rate of recolonisation. It also means that the central part of woody shrubs and trees provide animals with an approximately uniform temperature for most of the year.

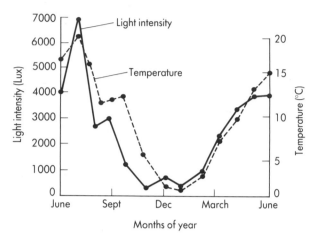

Figure 5   Mean monthly temperatures and light intensities at ground level, Ashdown Forest

Most plants in northern latitudes photosynthesise in the period April to September, when mean air temperature is above 8°C. For the rest of the year they undergo changes that assist survival at low temperatures. Annual plants produce cold-resistant seeds. Perennials either shed their leaves and form winter buds, or survive in winter in some other cold-resistant, dormant condition.

The winter survival strategies shown by animals include cold avoidance and cold tolerance. **Cold avoidance** is shown by migratory birds and butterflies, whose annual migration to warmer countries ensures they never experience adverse winter conditions. As winter approaches, mice and voles avoid the cold by burrowing deeply into the soil, lining their winter nests with good insulating materials such as grass and leaves. **Cold tolerance** is shown by many insects after they have entered a quiescent, non-feeding stage known as **diapause**. This phase may be spent as an egg, nymph, larva, pupa or adult, depending on the species. Hedgehogs and dormice **hibernate** during the winter. They retreat to their nests, curl

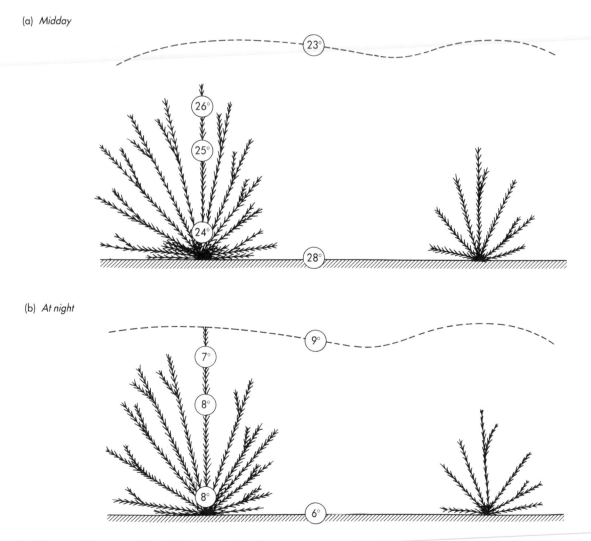

Figure 6   Temperature profiles (°C) in heathland at midday and at night during the summer

up to reduce their surface area : volume ratio, and become physiologically less active, with a marked fall in body temperature and metabolic rate.

Temperature gradients, or **thermoclines**, are an important feature of deep ponds and lakes, especially in summer. Such gradients exist because warm water floats on cold water. Furthermore, as water cools it sinks, reaching its maximum density at 4°C. Below that temperature it becomes less dense and rises again, an unusual physical property that causes ice to form only at the surface. These annual changes in the viscosity of water are of considerable importance to aquatic plants and animals, not least to those organisms that live on the surface film. In summer, the waters of a deep lake are divisible into three horizontal temperature zones (Figure 7):

(i) The **epilimnion**, the upper layer of warm water. Wind causes the water in this layer to circulate.

(ii) The **thermocline**, the middle layer of water where temperature changes rapidly with depth.

(iii) The **hypolimnion**, the lower layer of relatively cold water where daily and

seasonal temperature changes are less marked than in other zones.

As the seasons change there are corresponding changes in the depths of these three layers. By midwinter for instance, the zonation may have disappeared altogether, or both the epilimnion and thermocline may have narrowed while the hypolimnion has extended upward.

Light

Sunlight is the ultimate source of energy that drives all terrestrial and aquatic ecosystems. Seasonal variations in **light intensity**, shown in Figure 5, affect plant productivity, the primary food source in habitats. In most habitats however, less than 0.25% of the total incident radiation of sunlight is utilised by plants in photosynthesis. Furthermore, relatively few plants grow well in full sunlight. A majority show some degree of **shade tolerance**, the ability to achieve optimal growth at relatively low light intensities. Animals respond to changes in light intensity by modifying their behaviour, often by moving into or away from light of a given intensity.

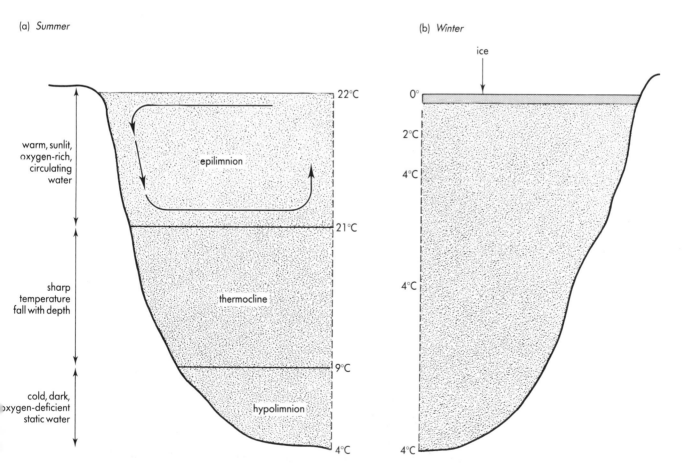

(a) *Summer*

warm, sunlit, oxygen-rich, circulating water

epilimnion

22°C

21°C

sharp temperature fall with depth

thermocline

9°C

cold, dark, oxygen-deficient static water

hypolimnion

4°C

(b) *Winter*

ice

0°

2°C

4°C

4°C

4°C

Figure 7 Thermoclines in a lake during summer and winter

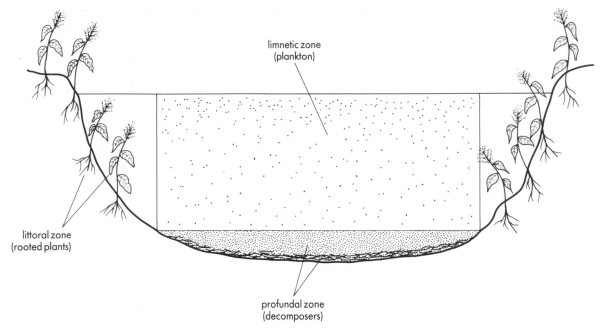

limnetic zone
(plankton)

littoral zone
(rooted plants)

profundal zone
(decomposers)

*Figure 8   Regions of productivity in a pond,
determined by light penetration*

Light penetrates the waters of large ponds and lakes to a depth of about 10–12 m in summer, but only 3–5 m in winter because of lower light intensities. Differential light penetration may create three distinct zones in these aquatic habitats (Figure 8):

(i) The **littoral zone**, surrounding the shore. This is an area with rooted plants, where there is effective light penetration for photosynthesis.

(ii) The **limnetic zone**, of open sunlit water, with small free-swimming organisms, collectively called **plankton**.

(iii) The **profundal zone**, below the level of effective light penetration, where bacterial decomposers dominate.

Photoperiodism refers to the length of the light and dark portions of the 24 hour day. As the earth's axis is tilted, the length of day and night changes seasonally everywhere except at the equator. In the UK, June 21 is the longest day and December 21 the shortest. Spring is characterised by increasing photoperiod, autumn by decreasing photoperiod. **Long day plants** flower in the spring and early summer, stimulated to produce flower buds by increasing photoperiod **short day plants** flower in the late summer or autumn. Animals also respond to photoperiod; diapause in insects is probably induced by photoperiod. Among vertebrates, most song birds and many small mammals breed in the period April to September, brought to reproductive activity by **increasing** daylength. Conversely, sheep and goats respond to **shortening** daylength, becoming sexually active in late summer and early autumn.

Humidity

The amount of water vapour in the atmosphere is called the **humidity**. It is an important ecological factor in terrestrial habitats. **Absolute humidity** is the actual mass of water in a given volume of air. **Relative humidity** is the unit most favoured by ecologists. This is the ratio of the mass of water vapour per unit volume of air to that of a similar volume of saturated air at the same temperature and pressure, expressed as a percentage. The amount of water vapour that air can hold increases with temperature. For instance, at −34°C, one cubic metre of air can hold about 3 g water, at nearly 4°C nearly 90 g, and at 38°C around 600 g. At its point of saturation, water vapour is precipitated from the atmosphere as water droplets and falls as rain, snow hail or fog, depending on air temperatures.

Plants contribute to the relative humidity of the air through **transpiration**, the loss of water, as vapour, from their leaves and stems. Another contributory factor is **evaporation** as the liquid water on the surface of soil and plants vaporises. If plants are removed from a habitat there is a subsequent fall in the relative humidity above ground level. This happens because evaporation is generally less efficient than transpiration in returning water to the atmosphere. Figure 9 shows relative humidity measurements taken at 10 cm and 1 m above ground level in four-year-old stands of heather. During the winter months of October to March, the air was rarely less than 90% saturated at both levels, while in summer the air beneath the leaf cover was invariably moister.

This occurred because plant foliage trapped some of the transpired water vapour. Indeed, this trapped water vapour appears to be an important ecological factor in determining the size and distribution of insect and other invertebrate populations in heathlands, grasslands and woodlands. In the very dry summers of 1976, 1989 and 1990, populations of some heathland insects, spiders and snails fell to very low levels.

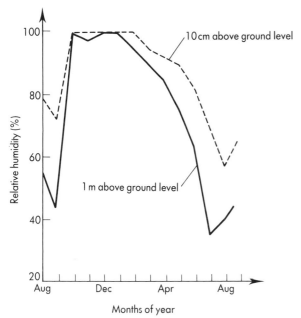

Figure 9   The relationship between relative humidity at 10 cm and 1 m above ground level in four-year-old stands of heather

Oxygen concentration

Humidity determines the distribution and size of many animal populations in terrestrial habitats, but oxygen concentration has a similar decisive effect on animal populations throughout northern European wetlands. Oxygen concentration in water is a limiting factor for most aquatic species, both plant and animal. Water always contains much less oxygen than atmospheric air. For instance, at 0°C, one litre of water contains no more than around 10 cm³ dissolved oxygen when fully saturated. Oxygen concentrations fall as temperature rises. For example, at 30°C, the volume of dissolved oxygen falls to about 5 cm³ per litre (Figure 10). Considering that an animal's rate of metabolism, and therefore its oxygen requirement, increases as temperature rises, it is not difficult to understand why aquatic animals may experience respiratory stress during hot weather. Similar stress may follow water pollution as the addition of solutes, or large volumes of aerobic micro-organisms in sewage, deplete water of its dissolved oxygen.

Oxygen gradients exist in large ponds and lakes for most of the year. Surface water, 100% saturated (or even supersaturated if plants are

actively photosynthesising), contrasts markedly with water at the bottom of the pond or lake which may be only 25% saturated with oxygen. **Oxygen depletion** in ponds and lakes may occur at any of the following times, for these reasons:

(i) In the winter, when the water is covered by layers of ice and snow.

(ii) In late summer, when plants die back, and micro-organisms decompose dead leaves.

(iii) At almost any time of the year if sewage or organic effluents pollute the water.

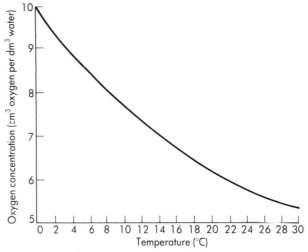

Figure 10   The oxygen content of water saturated with air at normal pressure (760mmHg), (from Leadley Brown, Freshwater Biology, Heinemann Publishers)

pH

The **pH** of a solution is a measure of its acidity or alkalinity and is defined as the negative logarithm of the hydrogen ion concentration. In practical terms, acidity and alkalinity are expressed on a pH scale from 1–14. Neutral solutions have a pH value of 7.0. Acid solutions have a value between 1 and 7; alkaline solutions between 7 and 14. Both in water and in soil, pH affects plant growth. Each species grows best at a certain pH. Any departure from that optimal pH, towards greater acidity or greater alkalinity, has an adverse effect and may even kill the plant. Plants such as bracken, gorse and heather grow only on acid soils, where pH lies within the range 4.0–6.5. Such plants are now known to be intolerant of calcium ions in the soil and called **calcifuges** ('lime haters'). Conversely, many plants found only on limestone and chalk where pH lies within the range 7.5–9.0 and calcium ions are abundant, are **calcicoles** (''lime tolerators'). Certain aquatic animals, such as the fresh water shrimp and hoglouse, can tolerate a very wide range of pH. Others such as white planarian flatworms, caddisfly larvae and some damselfly nymphs, are more abundant in alkaline, calcium-rich waters.

Marked changes in pH are an ecological feature in some habitats. Heathland fires for example may significantly alter the surface pH by adding ash from the burnt stems and leaves of heather and other plants. This ash is extremely alkaline, at pH 10.0–11.5. Its deposition causes an immediate change in soil pH from around 4.5 to 9.0 or more. Over the next six to eight weeks, pH slowly falls as alkaline salts are leached from the soil, stabilising at pH 5.0–5.5 about eight weeks after a burn. Among other effects, this change in pH is believed to inhibit the germination of heather seeds until soil pH has stabilised.

Soil

Soil is the uppermost layer of the earth's crust. It is a mixture of **inorganic material** (sand, silt and clay particles), **non-living organic matter** and living organisms (biomass). Furthermore, the arrangement of inorganic particles and organic matter gives the soil **structure**, with spaces between the solid particles which contain air and solution.

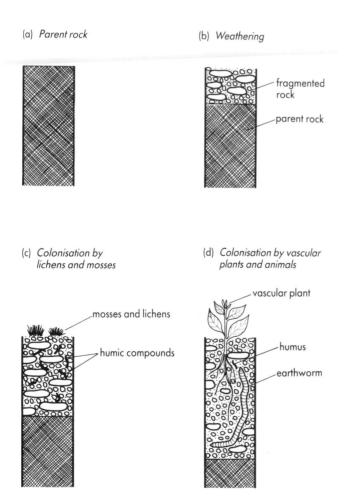

(a) *Parent rock*

(b) *Weathering*

fragmented rock

parent rock

(c) *Colonisation by lichens and mosses*

(d) *Colonisation by vascular plants and animals*

vascular plant

mosses and lichens

humic compounds

humus

earthworm

Figure 11 Stages in the formation of an idealised soil

Soil formation

Natural soils may be formed by weathering, sedimentation, erosion, the activities of living organisms, or a combination of all of them.

(i) **Weathering** is the action of frost, heat, wind and water on a rocky surface. The surface layer of bedrock is broken down into smaller fragments.

(ii) **Erosion** is the removal of soil particles by wind or water.

(iii) **Sedimentation** is the deposition of these particles, in a new location, after transportation through water. Sediments may form on the beds of ponds and lakes, or where a river meets the sea.

Living organisms such as bacteria, fungi, lichens and mosses are the first colonisers of these virgin soils. When they die, these organisms contribute organic matter. Both water and mineral salts are retained by this decomposing organic matter. Its presence allows the soil to support small flowering plants, with roots that penetrate into the rocks and split them into smaller fragments. Finally, the plants attract earthworms and other invertebrates which move in, mixing and circulating the inorganic and organic components as they do so.

Inorganic material

Inorganic material in the soil takes the form of:

(i) insoluble mineral particles, and

(ii) soluble mineral salts.

Both are normally derived from underlying bedrocks. In the UK, calcareous and siliceous bedrocks are fairly widely distributed. The **calcareous rocks**, of which chalk and limestone are examples, weather to produce alkaline soils which are dark in colour, shallow and rich in organic materials. Decomposers operate effectively at the relatively high pH, breaking down organic matter to release mineral salts and carbon dioxide. As a result, these soils often support a luxuriant and varied flora. The **siliceous rocks**, including sandstones and granites, weather to produce light coloured acidic soils, deficient in calcium. Water, falling mostly as rain, dissolves carbon dioxide as it passes through the atmosphere. On reaching the soil, the water contains a solution of dilute carbonic acid containing both H^+ and HCO_3^- ions. Positively charged mineral ions, loosely bound to negatively charged clay particles, are leached lower into the soil. This makes the upper soil particles acidic and often deficient of positive ions. (Figure 12). Under these conditions, organic matter tends to accumulate, decompose slowly and incompletely, yielding acidic end products such as organic acids.

Typically, the weathering process breaks bedrocks into particles of different sizes. In

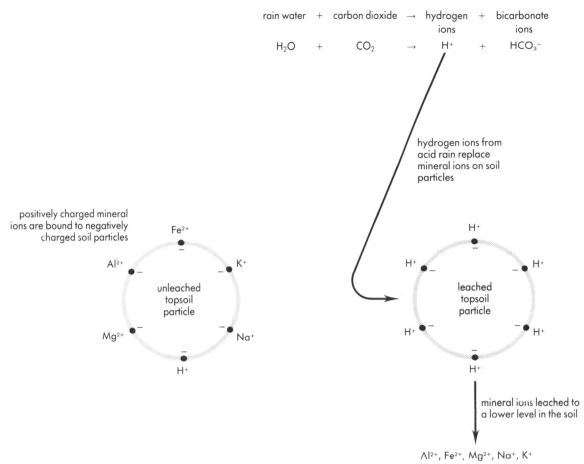

$$\text{rain water} + \text{carbon dioxide} \rightarrow \underset{\text{ions}}{\text{hydrogen}} + \underset{\text{ions}}{\text{bicarbonate}}$$

$$H_2O + CO_2 \rightarrow H^+ + HCO_3^-$$

Figure 12   Sequence of events leading to leaching of mineral ions from topsoil

siliceous soils for example, different names are given to those particles depending on their size (Table 1). Sand and silt particles are mostly quartz, and chemically relatively inert. Clay particles are much smaller but more complex and chemically active, consisting of minute quartz crystals, calcium carbonate and oxides of iron and aluminium. These particles carry a predominantly negative charge on their surface and so attract positively charged ions (cations). The proportions of sand, silt and clay determine the texture of a soil.

Table 1   The approximate size, percentage of air and field capacity of soil particles

TYPE OF PARTICLE	DIAMETER (mm)	% AIR CONTENT OF DRY SOIL	FIELD CAPACITY CAPACITY (%, by mass, of water retained)
gravel	2.0	60	5
coarse sand	2.0–0.2	50	10
fine sand	0.2–0.02	40	15
silt	0.02–0.002	25	20
clay	0.002 or less	15	40

Soluble mineral salts in a soil consist of positive charge cations, such as K^+, Ca^{2+}, Mg^{2+} etc., and negatively charged anions such as NO_3^-, SO_4^{2-}, HCO_3^- etc. The concentrations and availability of these ions is of primary importance in determining the type of flora that a natural soil can support.

Non-living organic matter

Soil organic matter is derived from the organisms which live in or on soil. A major component is **leaf litter**. Large accumulations of litter in various stages of decomposition are known as **detritus**. As detritus decomposes it forms a gelatinous brown material, **humus**, in which the identity of the organic material is lost. Humus is a colloidal brown acid substance, an immediate product in the decomposition of dead plants and animals, probably formed principally from lignin and proteins. The presence of humus in the soil encourages plant growth for a number of reasons:

(i) The moist, sticky humic particles bind mineral fragments together, forming a crumbly, less compacted soil, with a higher percentage of air. Roots can penetrate these soils, without being restricted by densely packed solid material and pressure from all sides.

(ii) Humic particles retain moisture and provide food for many soil invertebrates, including earthworms. On passing through the digestive systems of these animals, the humus is broken down, moistened and softened. This makes it more readily accessible to bacteria and fungi. These organisms break down organic molecules in the humus to obtain energy, while at the same time releasing nitrogen, phosphorus and sulphur, essential elements for plant growth.

(iii) Humus absorbs solar radiation because of its black colour. This enables humus-rich soils to warm up quickly, promoting the germination of seeds and growth of seedlings.

Structure

The arrangement of insoluble mineral particles and organic matter in soil gives the soil its **structure**. This arrangement is often reached as a result of complex physical, chemical and biological interactions taking place over many years. Every mature natural soil consists of several different layers, lying on top of each other, forming a **soil profile**. In each profile there are usually three **horizons**. The top, or **A horizon**, consists of organic material in various stages of decomposition. Below that, the **B horizon** contains a mixture of decomposed rock and humus. Amounts of humus decrease with depth. At the bottom of the profile is the **C horizon**, consisting of undecomposed bedrock. Each of these horizons may be subdivided further into **layers**. The A horizon, in which most plant roots grow, may have an A_0 (undecomposed litter), A_1 (decomposing litter) and A_2 (humus) layer. A similar subdivision of the B horizon recognises B_1 (mineral particles and humus) and B_2 (mineral particles and materials leached from the upper layers) zones.

The soil profile of chalk grassland provides a fairly simple example. A relatively shallow A horizon overlies a B horizon of roughly equal depth (Figure 13). Some leached calcium salts accumulate at the bottom of the B horizon, immediately above chalk bedrock. In these soils however, the top soil never becomes deficient in calcium. By contrast, much more complex soil profiles, with many different layers, may be seen in the soils of heathlands that have formed above soft sandstones. Deep A_0, A_1 and A_2 horizons are generally present, as acidity slows litter decomposition. The B_1 layer is often stained brown by humic and iron (Fe^{3+}) salts which are red and insoluble. Below that is a B_2 layer of

ash-grey leached sand. At the bottom of this layer, where conditions are anaerobic, leached materials are deposited above the bedrock. Such deposits include highly acid humic compounds and clay, frequently stained dull grey/green by reduced iron (Fe^{2+}) salts. These soils are usually calcium-deficient.

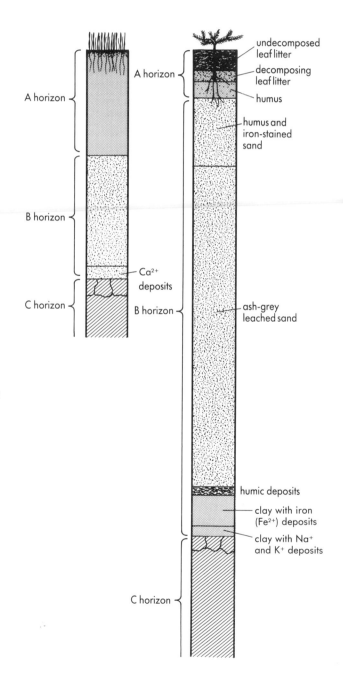

(a) *Beneath chalk grasslands* (b) *Beneath heathlands*

Figure 13   Soil profiles

Two other important features of natural soils, closely related to their structure, are pore space and water retaining capacity. **Air** occupies spaces between soil particles, and the amount of air present is influenced by the size, shape and arrangement of mineral particles, the presence of humus and the amount of water present. Nitrogen in air is required for nitrogen-fixing soil organisms. Carbon dioxide, released by all soil organisms, tends to be more abundant in the soil atmosphere than in air, chiefly because it is more soluble in water than oxygen. **Water** in the soil surrounds solid mineral particles and is absorbed by colloids in humus. Mineral salts, oxygen and carbon dioxide dissolve in this water to form the soil solution. Water is removed from the soil by drainage, evaporation and absorption by plant roots. Plants reach their **temporary wilting point** when their rate of water loss exceeds their rate of water uptake. Recovery from this condition is possible if more water becomes available to the roots. Further water loss, maintained over a longer period, leads to a **permanent wilting point**, at which damage caused by lack of water leads to death. Extremely dry soils still retain some water, either as **non-available capillary water** occupying very small soil spaces, or as **hygroscopic water** held firmly by soil colloids. All of this water is **unavailable** to plants because they cannot extract it against the adhesive forces that bind it to mineral particles. Following saturation of the soil after continuous rain, **gravitational water** drains from the soil. The spaces between soil particles, occupied by air in a dry doil, become filled with **available capillary water**.

2.3 BIOGEOCHEMICAL CYCLES

Water, carbon and some elements that are essential for life tend to move in cycles between the physical environment and living organisms. These cyclic movements are called **biogeochemical cycles**. This recycling is absolutely essential. If it did not occur, shortages of mineral salts would limit the growth of plants, and that would impose a limit on the size of dependent animal populations. Furthermore, there would be a never-ending build up of dead organisms. Biogeochemical cycles are of two types:

(i) **Gaseous cycles** in which the element or its oxide is a gas, drawn from and eventually returned to the atsmosphere (e.g. carbon, nitrogen).

(ii) **Sedimentary cycles** in which the element is a mineral ion, drawn from and eventually returned to the earth's crust (e.g. sulphur, potassium).

The micro-organisms responsible for the breakdown of organic material, notably bacteria and fungi, are called **saprotrophs**. These organisms possess enzymes which catalyse catabolic reactions, oxidations or reductions. The catabolic reactions often lead, via several intermediate stages, to the formation of simpler molecules from more complex ones.

The carbon cycle

The organic molecules from which living organisms are composed are in a continuous state of formation, flux and decomposition (Figure 14). The reservoir or pool of carbon is formed by carbon dioxide in the atmosphere, which makes up approximately 0.03% (320 parts per million) of the air by volume. Although this may seem to be a relatively small amount, the total mass of carbon dioxide in the atmosphere is enormous, generally estimated at something in excess of 2×10^{13} tonnes. In addition, carbon is available in aquatic habitats, either as bicarbonate (HCO_3^-) or carbonate (CO_3^{2-}) ions, dissolved in water.

Carbon fixation from the atmospheric pool is an anabolic process, or one that produces complex organic molecules from small, simpler ones. Two distinct groups of synthesising (autotrophic) organisms carry out this process:

(i) **Photosynthetic organisms**, such as green plants, use light energy to reduce carbon dioxide in the formation of carbohydrates, fats and proteins.

(ii) **Chemosynthetic organisms**, such as nitrifying bacteria, employ energy stored in inorganic chemical bonds, such as nitrate and nitrite, to reduce carbon dioxide.

In both cases, carbon dioxide is reduced by hydrogen from a donor (HA), and carbohydrate is formed:

$$CO_2 + 2H_2A \rightarrow CH_2O + H_2O + 2A + energy$$

($2H_2A$ is the hydrogen donor; CH_2O is the carbohydrate.)

A considerable amount of the organic matter synthesised by autotrophs may be broken down in respiration to provide energy for growth and movement. Respiration is a catabolic process. Complex organic molecules are broken down by a series of oxidations. In **aerobic respiration**, oxidation is complete and may be summarised by the equation:

$$C_6H_{12}O_6 + 6O_2 \rightarrow 6CO_2 + 6H_2O + energy$$

In **anaerobic respiration**, oxidation is incomplete, resulting in the formation of various partially oxidised molecules, such as ethanol in plants and lactic acid in animals.

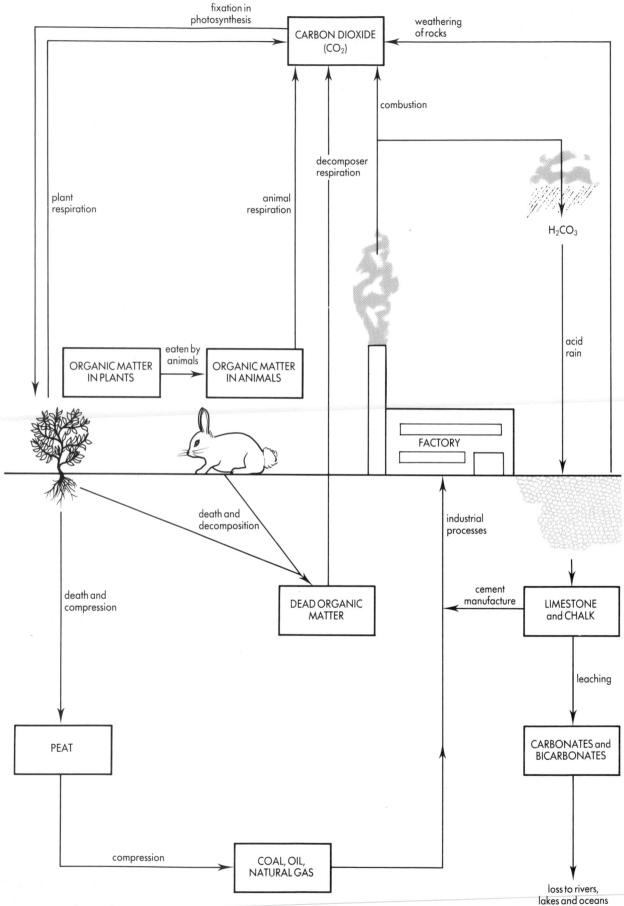

Figure 14   The carbon cycle

If the dead remains of plants and animals accumulate without undergoing oxidation, **fossil fuels** may eventually be formed. Under acid conditions, in the absence of decomposers, plant debris accumulates, layer upon layer, to form deposits many metres in thickness. As pressure increases on the lower layers of debris, slow changes may occur, resulting in the successive formation of the following materials:

peat $\nearrow$ methane and other gases $\rightarrow$ oil
$\searrow$ coal $\rightarrow$ anthracite $\rightarrow$ diamond

Combustion of most of these materials, as in the burning of coal and oil, returns carbon dioxide to the atmospheric pool. Heavy consumption of fossil fuels since the beginning of the industrial revolution has released large amounts of carbon dioxide to the atmospheric pool, slowly increasing concentrations of the gas in the atmosphere. As this carbon dioxide can exert a '**greenhouse effect**' by radiating back to earth heat that would otherwise escape into space, it is causing annual increases in mean temperature which may eventually melt the ice caps. This could cause disastrous flooding by raising the level of the seas (see section 7.3).

Carbon dioxide is also produced by the effects of acid rain and combustion on calcareous rocks, such as chalk and limestone. These rocks were originally formed on the floor of the seas some 70 million years ago, from the skeletons of microscopic organisms that combined calcium with carbon dioxide.

The nitrogen cycle

Nitrogen forms a large part of all organisms. It is a component of proteins, amino acids and nucleic acids. Like carbon, it undergoes a cycle of changes which include formation, transformation and degradation. Nitrogen forms 79% by volume of the Earth's atmosphere, so there is plenty available. It is, however, an extremely stable gas that cannot be utilised by living organisms unless micro-organisms have first combined it with hydrogen to form ammonia NH_3, or with oxygen to form nitrate NO_3^-. The nitrogen cycle (Figure 16) is characterised by four distinct processes:

(i) nitrogen fixation
(ii) nitrification
(iii) denitrification
(iv) assimilation

Nitrogen fixation, which occurs in bacteria, and assimilation, which occurs in green plants, are **anabolic** processes, resulting in the synthesis of more complex molecules. Nitrification occurs through a series of chemical oxidations and denitrification through a series of chemical reductions; both are brought about principally by bacteria.

Nitrogen fixation

Nitrogen fixation is the formation of ammonia, NH_3, when atmospheric nitrogen N_2 is reduced by hydrogen ions H^+. It can be represented by the following equation:

$$N_2 + 6H^+ + 6\,e^- \rightarrow 2NH_3$$

A number of free-living bacteria can fix nitrogen, e.g. species of *Azotobacter* and *Clostridium*. Some nitrogen fixing bacteria, belonging to the genus *Rhizobium*, live only in the roots of legumes, where they stimulate the formation of swellings called **root nodules**. Fixation of nitrogen in root nodules involves the transfer of hydrogen atoms from carbohydrates such as glucose to nitrogen. The site of transfer is the enzyme **nitrogenase** in the cytoplasm of the root nodule. This enzyme

Root nodules on a sweet pea plant

breaks the N=N bond, to form unstable nitrogen atoms. These would immediately react with oxygen were it not for a protective layer of red pigment, **leghaemoglobin**, a product of the legume that surrounds the bacteria. It is believed that this pigment binds oxygen, enabling the enzyme to operate in an oxygen-reduced environment. With oxygen excluded, ammonia is the initial product, produced in a reaction that uses up 12–15 molecules of ATP. In temperate legumes such as clovers, the ammonia rapidly combines with glutamate to form amines such as glutamine and asparagine. These are exported from the nodule. (Interestingly, tropical legumes such as soy bean export ureides, notably allantoin and allantoic acid.) The process is summarised by the following equation:

$$N_2 \xrightarrow[\text{12–15 ATP} \quad \text{12–15 ADP}]{\text{nitrogenase}} NH_3 \xrightarrow{\text{glutamate}} \textbf{amines} \xrightarrow{\substack{\text{transport to} \\ \text{leaves}}} \textbf{amino acids}$$

Widespread interest in nitrogen fixation in legumes has been stimulated by the hope that the genes responsible can be transferred to cereals. Work has shown that nodule formation and nitrogen fixation are controlled by the following groups of genes.

(i) *Nod*-genes control infection of legume root hairs by host-specific *Rhizobium* species. The first phase is adhesion of the rhizobia to the cell wall of a root hair. In response, the hair coils into a semi-circle. One or more tubular structures, called **infection threads**, then carry the rhizobia, often in single file, from the point of entry to a position near the inner root cortex. Once in position, the bacteria degenerate by losing their cell walls. They are then known as **bacteroids** (Figure 15).

(ii) *Nif*-genes regulate nitrogenase formation. Two nitrogenases are produced: one is a molybdenum-containing compound (Mo-nitrogenase), the other contains vanadium (V-nitrogenase). It would appear that having both enzyme systems enables the bacteria to fix nitrogen over a wide range of temperatures.

(iii) *Fix*-genes regulate nitrogen fixation. An enzyme called **dinitrogenase** binds N_2, and a second enzyme, **dinitrogenase reductase**, converts N_2 to NH_3.

In view of the complexity of these genetic systems, it may be some time before we can produce cereals and other crops with a built in capacity for nitrogen fixation.

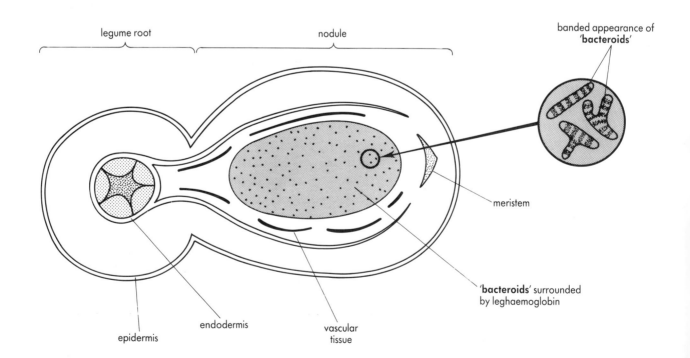

Figure 15 Transverse section of a root nodule, showing the appearance of the degenerate bacteria, known as 'bacteroids'

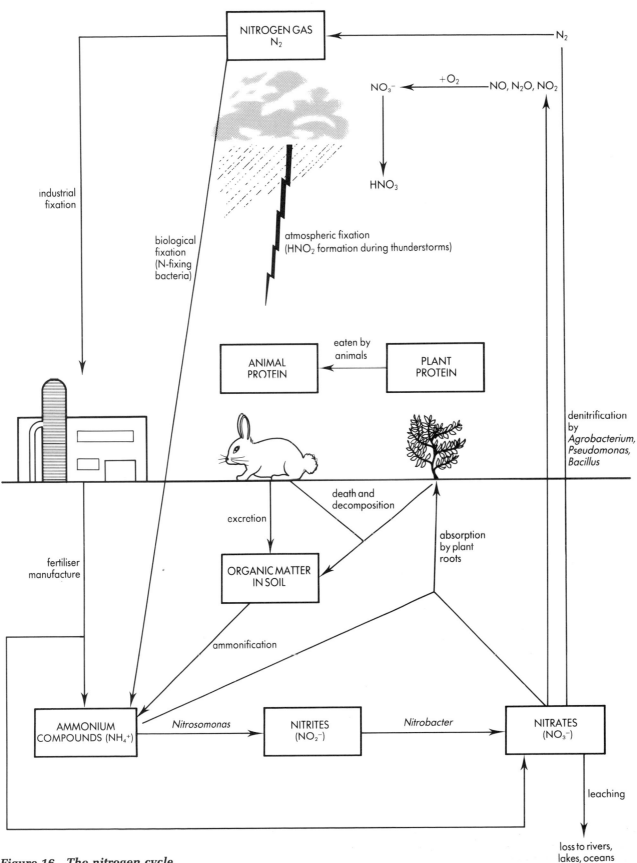

Figure 16   The nitrogen cycle

Nitrification

The oxidation of ammonia (NH_3) to form oxygen-containing compounds is called **nitrification**. It can be represented by the following equation:

$$NH_4^+ \longrightarrow NO_2^- \longrightarrow NO_3^-$$

ammonium   nitrite   nitrate
ions   ions   ions

Ammonium ions are formed in the soil when the structural proteins of dead plants and animals undergo **decomposition**, a breakdown brought about by proteolytic enzymes released by soil micro-organisms. The process is also known as **ammonification** or **mineralisation**. Bacteria and fungi, the principal agents of decomposition, degrade the proteins of dead organisms firstly to amino acids, then to ammonia. Animal excretory products are another source of ammonia. In mammals, any excess dietary amino acids are converted to ammonia or urea. Once the urea has been excreted in urine, **urease** from micro-organisms in the soil catalyses its decomposition into ammonia and carbon dioxide:

$$(NH_2)_2\,CO + H_2O \rightarrow NH_3 + CO_2$$

In well aerated soils ammonia is oxidised first to nitrite (NO_2^-), then to nitrate (NO_3^+). The primary ammonium oxidisers are bacteria belonging to the genera *Nitrosomonas* and *Nitrococcus*. These bacteria obtain energy for growth and reproduction chiefly from the oxidation of ammonia:

$$2NH_3 + 3CO_2 \rightarrow 2\,HNO_2 + 2H_2O + \text{energy}$$

The secondary nitrite oxidisers belong to the general *Nitrobacter* and *Nitrocystis*. These bacteria obtain energy from the oxidation of nitrite:

$$HNO_2 + O_2 \rightarrow HNO_3 + \text{energy}$$

Therefore, in well ventilated soils where oxygen is abundant, ammonium ions tend to undergo oxidation to nitrite, especially in the period March to September when there is increased microbial activity. Throughout the summer, a reserve of nitrate may build up in the soil, especially if no plants are present. Some however may be lost during prolonged spells of wet weather when nitrate ions are leached from around soil particles and carried to a depth in the sub-soil that is out of the range of plant roots. Even though some HNO_2 and HNO_3 may be formed during thunderstorms, when lightning passes through the atmosphere, these small additions often fail to compensate for losses resulting from leaching caused by torrential rain.

Denitrification

Denitrification is a series of chemical reactions in which nitrates are reduced to gaseous nitrogen via a number of intermediate compounds. The following generalised reaction sequence may stop at any stage:

$$NO_3^- \rightarrow NO_2^- \rightarrow NO \rightarrow N_2O \rightarrow N_2$$

Denitrification occurs in poorly aerated soil which has a high nitrogen content, e.g. following waterlogging or trampling. Some 13 genera of bacteria, including species of *Agrobacterium*, *Pseudomonas* and *Bacillus*, are known to be denitrifying agents. The chemical reactions of dentrifiction, which are anaerobic or partly anaerobic in nature, are often complex, driven by energy supplied by glucose and other compounds. The following reactions can be carried out by *Pseudomonas* bacteria :

(i) $C_6H_{12}O_6 + KNO_3 \rightarrow 6CO_2 + 6KOH + 3N_2O + 3H_2O$

(ii) $C_6H_{12}O_6 + 24KNO_3 \rightarrow 3CO_2 + 24KOH + 12N_2 + 18H_2O$

Interestingly, the sulphur-oxidising bacterium *Thiobacillus denitrificans* is also capable of reducing nitrate to nitrogen. The reaction is:

$$6KNO_3 + 5S + 2CaCO_3 \rightarrow 2K_2SO_4 + 2CO_2 + 3N_2$$

As a result of denitrification, nitrates are lost from the soil or converted into a form that cannot be utilised by green plants.

Assimilation

After absorbing nitrogen-containing compounds from the soil, either as NO_3^- or NH_4^+, green plants carry out an important stage in the nitrogen cycle, **nitrogen assimilation**. This process, involving the formation of organic nitrogen-containing compounds, usually begins in the roots where the enzyme nitrate reductase catalyses the reduction of nitrate to nitrite:

(i) $NO_3^- \xrightarrow{\text{nitrate reductase}} NO_2^-$
      NADH $\longrightarrow$ NAD

Following transport of the nitrite via xylem vessels to the leaves, a second enzyme, nitrite reductase, catalyses the reduction of nitrite to ammonia:

(ii) $NO_2^- \xrightarrow{\text{nitrite reductase}} NH_4^+$
      NADPH $\longrightarrow$ NADP

Reaction (i) involves the oxidation of reduced nicotinamide adenine dinucleotide (NADH) while reaction (ii) uses reduced nicotinamide adenine dinucleotide phosphate (NADPH). Most of the ammonia produced from the second reaction combines with α-ketoglutaric acid, a product of the Krebs' cycle, to form glutamic acid, an amino acid from which other amino acids were formed. Polymerisation of these amino acids to form proteins, the principal nitrogen-containing compounds in plants, completes assimilation.

All animals, including humans, are ultimately dependent on plant proteins as a source of the amino acids from which animal proteins are formed. Animals however cannot store protein (as a result of pH and other problems) and they remove any excess dietary proteins either through excretion or defaecation. Herbivores, feeding directly on plants, ingest plant proteins. These proteins are digested by proteolytic enzymes to form amino acids as they pass through the alimentary canal. Some of these amino acids are absorbed from the alimentary canal, transported to cells throughout the animal and used as the building blocks of animal proteins. When herbivores are eaten by carnivores a similar process occurs with new proteins in the carnivore being formed from the amino acids that originate in plants. This means that green plants, along with certain micro-organisms, are the only living organisms capable of synthesising organic forms of nitrogen from NO_3^- and NH_4^+ ions.

The sulphur cycle

Sulphur, like carbon and nitrogen, cycles in nature (Figure 17). The pool consists of elemental sulphur, sulphates and sulphides in rocks and soils. Green plants and micro-organisms absorb sulphate ions (SO_4^{2-}) which they metabolise into cysteine and methionine. Mammals use these sulphur-containing amino acids in the construction of their own proteins. Deamination of the sulphur-containing amino acids in the liver leads to the formation of sulphate ions which are excreted in the urine.

Sulphur oxidation, in well aerated soil, is used by the bacterium *Thiobacillus* to obtain energy. It can be represented by the following reaction:

$$S^2 \rightarrow SO_3^{2-} \rightarrow SO_4^{2-}$$

The bacterium *T. thiooxidans*, for example, can oxidise elemental sulphur to sulphuric acid:

$$2S + 3O_2 + 2H_2O \rightarrow 2H_2SO_4$$

T. ferrooxidans can oxidise reduced sulphur compounds or ferrous (Fe^{2+}) ions, again with sulphuric acid as an end product:

$$2FeS_2 + 7O_2 + 2H_2O \rightarrow 2FeSO_4 + 2H_2SO_4$$

Bacteria belonging to the genera *Beggiatoa* and *Thiothrix* can oxidise hydrogen sulphide (H_2S), either to elemental sulphur or to sulphuric acid:

(i) $2H_2S + O_2 \rightarrow 2H_2O + 2S$
(ii) $H_2S + 2O_2 \rightarrow H_2SO_4$

Photoautotrophic bacteria of the genera *Chlorobium* and *Chromatium* use H_2S as an electron donor for the reduction of CO_2, in reactions similar to photolysis in higher plants.

Elemental sulphur is a waste product of this reaction, which can be represented as follows:

$$H_2S \xrightarrow{\text{light}} 2H^+ + S$$

Therefore, under aerobic conditions sulphate ions accumulate in the soil, forming a reserve of inorganic sulphur that can be absorbed and assimilated by green plants. Some of this reserve however may be leached from soils by heavy rain.

Sulphur reduction, in watelogged or trampled soils, can be represented by the following reaction:

$$SO_4^{2-} \rightarrow SO_3^{2-} \rightarrow S_3O_6^{2-} \rightarrow S_2O_3^{2-} \rightarrow S^2$$

The sulphate-reducing bacterium *Desulfovibrio desulfuricans*, an obligate anaerobe, has received most attention. This bacterium produces hydrogen sulphide gas as one of its waste products; hydrogen sulphide is toxic to most aerobic organisms, including green plants. In soils it may cause precipitation of metal sulphides, notably iron sulphide, which gives a black colour to anaerobic muds at the bottom of ponds, lakes and river estuaries. Other bacteria capable of reducing sulphates, and so leading to their removal from soils, include species of *Clostridium* and *Desulfotomaculum*.

Combustion of coal releases both sulphur dioxide (SO_2) and hydrogen sulphide into the atmosphere. In a light-catalysed reaction that takes place several kilometres above the earth's surface, sulphur dioxide combines with oxygen to form sulphur trioxide SO_3. This gas dissolves in water to form a dilute solution of sulphuric acid which returns to earth as a component of acid rain.

The potassium and phosphorus cycles

The recycling of potassium and phosphorus occurs by sedimentary cycles (Figure 18), without the formation of any natural gaseous compounds. The main source of **potassium (K)** for plants growing under natural conditions comes from the weathering of potassium-containing minerals, especially feldspars and micas. Potassium is taken up by plants from the soil solution as the cation K^+. One of the main functions of the element is activation of various enzyme systems. It is involved in a number of steps in protein synthesis and, for this reason, the rate of nitrogen turnover and protein synthesis in plants depends on their potassium content. The element therefore influences crop production by enhancing growth and synthetic processes.

Phosphorus (P) in soil occurs almost exclusively in the form of orthophosphates. The most important orthophosphates are HPO_4^{2-} and $H_2PO_4^-$. High H^+ concentrations shift the

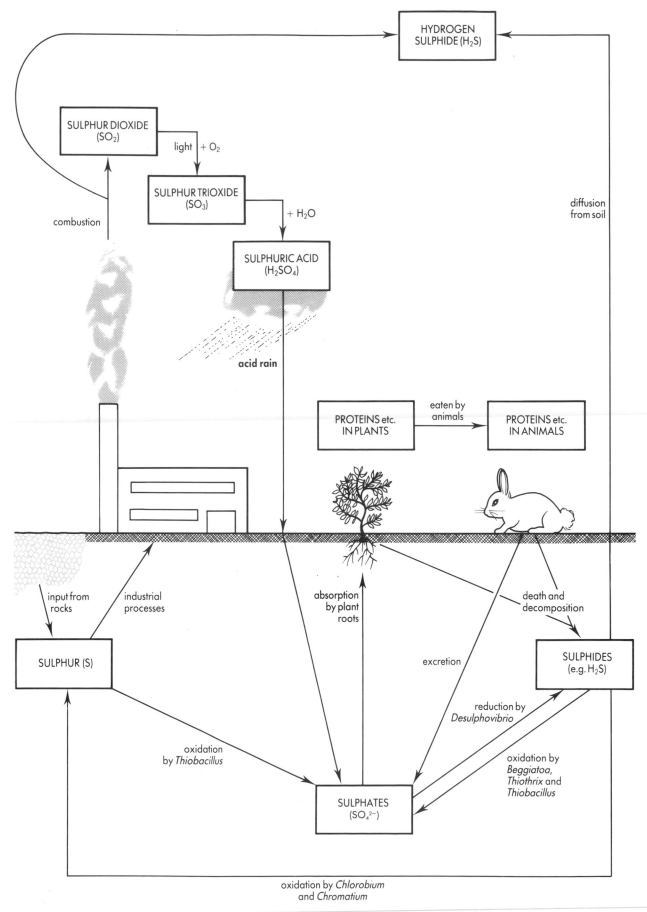

Figure 17 The sulphur cycle

equilibirum to the monovalent form, according to the following equation:

$$HPO_4{}^{2-} + H^+ \underset{\text{high pH}}{\overset{\text{low pH}}{\rightleftarrows}} H_2PO_4{}^-$$

Phosphorus is a constituent atom of many organic compounds, including phosphorylated sugars (e.g. fructose-6-phosphate), phospholipids, nucleotides (e.g. ATP) and nucleic acids (e.g. DNA and RNA). Following the death of plants and animals, their decomposition by micro-organisms releases phosphorus in the form of orthophosphates.

2.4 ENERGY FLOW

Sunlight is the ultimate source of energy on earth. The flow of this energy through an ecosystem is a linear or one-way process. All of the energy flows and transformations are governed by the **first and second laws of thermodynamics**.

(i) The **first law** states that energy is never created or destroyed, only transformed from one form to another. Chlorophyll-containing plants, for example, transform the radiant energy (light) of the sun into chemical (potential) energy.

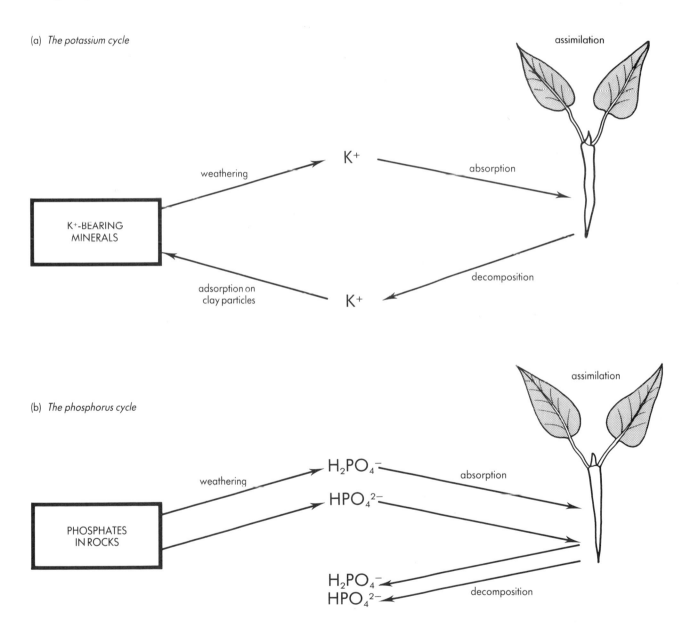

(a) *The potassium cycle*

(b) *The phosphorus cycle*

Figure 18 Potassium and phosphorus cycles (heterotrophic organisms have been omitted)

(ii) The **second law** states that some energy is lost, in the form of heat, at each transformation. As energy, for example, contained in food passes from one trophic level to another, organisms are less than 100% efficient in converting this into their own biomass. At each trophic level there is some loss of heat to the environment as a result of respiration.

The total amount of solar radiation reaching the earth has been estimated at 3×10^{24} J/yr. The radiant energy that falls on the UK is approximately 1×10^6 kJ/m/yr. Green plants may absorb up to 50% of the radiant energy falling on them, but convert no more than about 1% into chemical energy; the remaining 49% is lost as heat. This is added to the heat generated by the absorption of light by abiotic components of ecosystems such as soil. All this heat is subsequently radiated from the earth into space so that as much as 99% of the radiant energy falling on a plant may not be utilised in photosynthesis. This means that most of the energy associated with solar radiaton is lost as heat from ecosystems without ever being trapped by plants or passing through food webs.

The light that a plant absorbs is used to build up organic molecules in photosynthesis. From its total synthesised biomass, each plant then respires some of its own photosynthetic products, dissipating heat in the process. The remainder passes directly to herbivores, then to carnivores or detritivores. Respiration in all of these organisms dissipates more heat. The process continues until all of the original biomass, after transformations by heterotrophs, has been broken down and its potential energy dissipated as heat. Some authors have likened this energy flow to a bank account that does not allow overdraft. Input from plants, the producers of biomass, determines the amount of food available to other organisms (heterotrophs), who can draw on it until it becomes exhausted. In fact, biomass decreases at each trophic level of a food chain, because each organism in the chain disperses some of its potential energy as heat. It follows from the first law of thermodynamics that the flow of energy through an ecosystem can be quantified, providing we can measure the energy input. The output will balance the input in the long term, even if they are sometimes out of balance in the short term. Quantifying the flow of energy within an ecosystem is a difficult process. It involves collecting all the energy-containing material from each trophic level, burning it in a calorimeter, and measuring the amount of heat produced. Plant roots, for example, must be harvested as well as their stems and leaves. In addition to the standing biomass of an animal population (again measured by burning in a calorimeter), consideration must

also be given to heat losses through excretion and defecation. Results show that as potential energy in the form of food is transferred through the trophic levels, a large proportion of its is lost at each step, some as heat for instance. This loss is largely through respiration but there is also some loss via excretion of nitrogenous excretory products, or in the faeces which contain undigested material. It is not until this material is acted on by decomposers that heat is released from it into the atmosphere.

One way of representing energy flow through an ecosystem is to construct a pyramid of biomass. After identifying the organisms in a food chain, the dry mass of each organism, measured over a defined area (e.g. m^2 or ha), or volume (e.g. cm^3 or m^3) of the ecosystem is recorded. In a herbivore and detritus-based chain, this pyramid usually takes the form of a triangle, with the apex directed upwards. Figure 19 shows a typical pyramid of biomass for a heathland food chain, expressed as $g/m^2/yr$. (It should be noted that a pyramid of biomass, based on phytoplankton in aquatic ecosystems, may be wide at the middle and narrower above and below. This is because there is a rapid turnover of short lived unicellular algae that support populations of large, long lived consumers.)

A more fundamental way of representing the energy relationships between organisms is by a **pyramid of energy**. The dry mass of organisms collected from a defined area is burned in a calorimeter, so that biomass is converted into heat. In this type of pyramid, productivity is expressed as $kJ/m^2/day$, or $kJ/ha/yr$, and each bar of the pyramid represents the amount of energy per unit area or volume that flows through each trophic level per unit of time. Such pyramids are always broadest at their base.

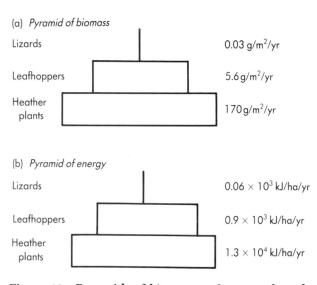

(a) *Pyramid of biomass*

Lizards	0.03 g/m²/yr
Leafhoppers	5.6 g/m²/yr
Heather plants	170 g/m²/yr

(b) *Pyramid of energy*

Lizards	0.06 × 10³ kJ/ha/yr
Leafhoppers	0.9 × 10³ kJ/ha/yr
Heather plants	1.3 × 10⁴ kJ/ha/yr

Figure 19 Pyramids of biomass and energy, based on a heathland food chain

From quantitative measurements of energy flow in different ecosystems of the world, certain general principles have emerged. Firstly, within a defined space, all the organisms occupying a particular trophic level incorporate roughly 10% of the potential energy, as biomass, of all the organisms at a lower trophic level. Therefore, the standing biomass of the herbivores is approximately 1/10 that of the standing biomass of the producers. Similarly, the carnivores that eat the herbivores store approximately 1/10 × 1/10 = 1/100 of the biomass stored in plants. These figures are of course only very rough approximations. They are more applicable to some ecosystems than to others and useful only as a means of conveying the principles of biomass and energy flow. A conventional general diagram for representing this information is illustrated in Figure 20. The diagram maps the flow of energy through an ecosystem, showing the routes of transmission from one trophic level to another. If figures were to be added to this diagram, the energy input from photosynthesis would exactly belance the energy output from respiration. Other generalisations relating to energy flow may be summarised as follows:

(i) Respiration causes a loss of potential energy at each trophic level.

(ii) There is a further loss of energy between trophic levels, partly because animals are inefficient in extracting all of the nutrients from their food.

(iii) Successively smaller amounts of food are available to organisms feeding at higher trophic levels in a food chain. This means that least energy is available to carnivores, occupying the terminal position.

(iv) Decomposers complete the process of releasing energy from organic material. In breaking down dead organic material, heat is released as a result of respiration.

In summary, potential energy in the form of

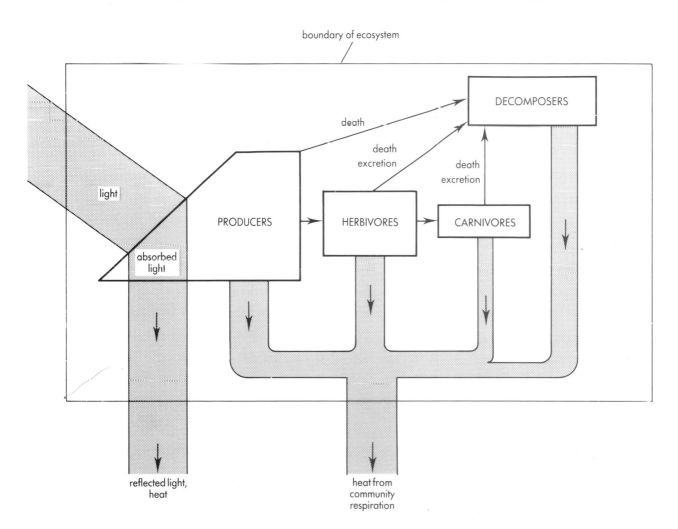

Figure 20 A generalised diagram of an ecosystem, showing the flow of energy. In the long term, the amount of energy, dissipated as heat by community respiration, exactly balances that fixed in photosynthesis by the producers

carbohydrates, fats and proteins, is synthesised in green plants, temporarily stored by them, and then dissipated along food chains. In the long term, no energy is gained and none is lost. Living organisms make effective short term use of solar energy, but in the long term they serve only to delay the transformation of solar radiation into heat.

2.5 ACCUMULATED BIOMASS

If ecosystem productivity exceeds the rate of decompositon, or if decomposers are absent from an ecosystem, dead biomass accumulates. This undecomposed biomass is a store of energy. **Fossil fuels** such as coal, oil and natural gas are the valuable products of this material, deposited in swamps or shallow seas between 70 million and 150 million years ago. Today, worldwide reserves of coal, oil and natural gas are called **non-renewable natural sources**. In one sense they are not truly non-renewable, but we could not hope to replenish them at the same rate as they are being used so they will eventually become exhausted.

Coal

Coal is formed from vast accumulations of plant litter, originally laid down in shallow tropical swamps in which the conditions were anaerobic. The transformation of plant litter into coal takes place in six or more steps, as follows:

plant → peat → lignites → brown → bituminous
litter   coal   coal
                                        (e.g. house
                hard coal ↙ coal)
                (e.g.
                anthracite)

The initial change, brought about by the action of anaerobic bacteria, results in the formation of peat, a low grade fossil fuel with relatively large amounts of water and relatively little carbon. Pressure from overlying deposits of sand or silt generally compresses layers of peat, squeezing out water and compacting the solid material. Lignites are brown granular deposits, which represent an early stage in coal formation. Brown coals and bituminous coals are more rock-like, representing intermediate stages in the formation of hard coals such as anthracite. Worldwide reserves of coal are vast. Mined at an annual rate of 4000 million tonnes, it is estimated that world

Large mechanical scraper mining lignite

reserves will last for another 200–250 years.

When coal is burned in air, it releases its potential energy as heat. The amount of heat generated however depends on the type of coal that is burned, or more specifically on its carbon content. Combustion of pure carbon can be represented by the following equation:

$$C + O_2 \rightarrow CO_2 \ (+ \ heat)$$

The complete combustion of one tonne of carbon requires 2.66 tonnes of oxygen (or 11.48 tonnes of air) and generates 3.66 tonnes of carbon dioxide. Therefore, burning bituminous coal (47–80% carbon) in houses and anthracite (85–95% carbon) in power stations releases substantial amounts of carbon dioxide into the atmosphere. In addition, whenever coal is burned, oxides of other elements are formed, as in equations (i), (ii) and (iii) below:

(i) $H_2 + O_2 \rightarrow \quad 2H_2O$

(ii) $S + O_2 \quad \rightarrow \quad SO_2$

(iii) $N + O_2 \rightarrow \quad NO_2$ (and other oxides of nitrogen)

Both sulphur dioxide, SO_2 and the oxides of nitrogen are atmospheric pollutants, contributing to the formation of acid rain.

Oil

Crude oil is probably formed from the remains of aquatic plants and animals that lived before, during and after the Carboniferous period. Again, as in the formation of coal, the initial stages of oil formation took place under anaerobic conditions, brought about by bacteria. This was followed by sedimentation with clays and silts, and compaction into rocks such as mudstones and shales. The transformation to hydrocarbons was probably completed by pressure and heating to around 180°C. Pockets of crude oil accumulated in porous rocks such as sandstones and limestones, capped by harder, impermeable layers of clays, shales and gypsum. Oil extraction is an expensive, skilled feat of engineering. It always involves drilling, often to considerable depths. The oil must then be brought to the surface, either unaided or with the help of a pump or high-pressure water injection. The crude oil that emerges varies in colour from green to brown to black. It contains nitrogen and sulphur, with traces of nickel and vanadium. After extraction, crude oil is split into fractions of different density at a refinery. These fractions are used to produce petrol, lubricating oils and a wide range of chemicals. Whenever any of these substances is burned, oxides of carbon, nitrogen, sulphur and hydrogen are produced. Consumed at its present rate of around 21 000 million barrels a year, world oil reserves will only last for another 50–90 years.

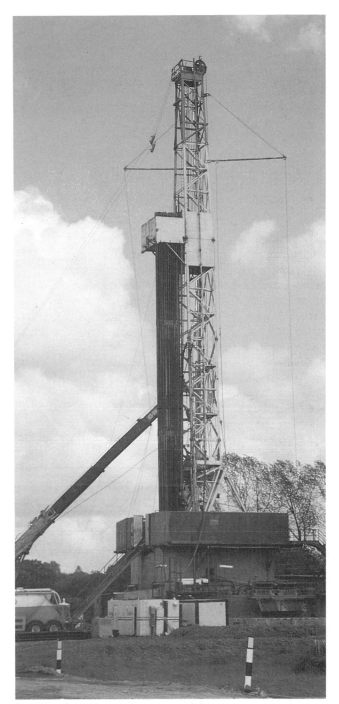

Drilling for oil

Natural gas

Pockets of natural gas often form above oil deposits, capped by dense non-porous rocks. Alternatively, they may form over water, without the presence of oil. The chief combustible components of natural gas are methane, ethane and propane. Other gases that may be present include hydrogen sulphide, carbon dioxide, nitrogen and occasionally helium.

QUESTIONS

1 The diagram below represents a part of the nitrogen cycle.

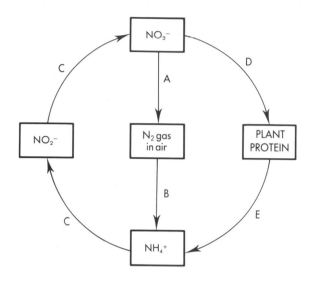

a) Name the processes represented by the letters A, B, C, D and E.
b) By what type of bacteria are processes A, B, C and E carried out?
c Which processes involve (i) oxidation and (ii) reduction of nitrogenous compounds?
d) Which compounds in the cycle can be absorbed by the roots of green plants?
e) Name three other nitrogenous compounds, not shown in the diagram, that feature in the nitrogen cycle.
f) What do you understand by the term 'nitrogen assimilation'?
g) Where does nitrogen assimilation occur in a green plant?
h) In what ways do humans contribute to the nitrogen cycle?

2 a) What is soil?
b) Name four natural processes that contribute to soil formation.
c) Distinguish between soil composition and soil structure.
d) Three soils from different habitats had the following composition.

COMPONENT	DRY MASS (%)		
	soil A	soil B	soil C
clay	25.1	9.3	1.2
sand	1.6	12.9	36.3
gravel	0.9	1.8	14.3
humus	5.8	25.1	0.8

e) State, with reasons, the soil that would be:
(i) coldest and wettest in winter;
(ii) driest in summer;
(iii) most likely to contain invertebrates and bacteria;
(iv) most acid;
(v) least fertile.
f) What additional compounds would each soil contain?
g) Suggest a habitat from which each soil could have been taken.
h) How would you treat soil A to produce a fertile loam, ideally suited for growing garden flowers or vegetables?
i) What soil factor, other than temperature, is most likely to determine the vertical distribution of earthworms? Explain your answer.

3 What do you understand by the 'ecosystem concept'?
Describe the (i) biotic and (ii) abiotic components of a named ecosystem.
Outline the principal exchanges that occur between the biotic and abiotic components of a named ecosystem.

4 How do each of the following abiotic factors affect the plants and animals that live in woodlands?
(i) temperature, (ii) humidity, (iii) light, (iv) soil.
(Refer in your answer to named species of plants and animals and the ways in which they are affected by these factors.)

5 Amplify and explain the statement that 'organisms in large ecosystems occupy different trophic levels, linked by food chains'.

6 Distinguish between:
a) producers and consumers,
b) food chains and food webs,
c) pyramids of numbers and of biomass,
d) micro-habitat and niche.

7 Using each of the following headings, describe the soil of one or more named natural habitats:
a) origin;
b) inorganic components;
c) organic components;
d) structure.
How would an agricultural soil, used to grow cereals or other crops, differ from the soil you have described?

8 Write an account of the carbon cycle, with particular reference to the formation of fossil fuels. Evaluate the ecological significance and consequences of using these fossil fuels as energy sources.

9 By reference to the nitrogen cycle, amplify and explain the differences between:
a) nitrogen fixation and assimilation,
b) nitrification and denitrification.
How do legumes obtain their nitrogen supply?

10 Give a full, illustrated account of two sedimentary biogeochemical cycles.

11 Explain how energy flows through ecosystems. Account for energy losses at each trophic level of an ecosystem. What is the relevance of the first and second laws of thermodynamics to this flow and loss of energy?

BIBLIOGRAPHY

Anderson, J W (1978) *Sulphur in Biology* (Studies in Biology No. 101) Edward Arnold

Boney, A D (1975) *Phytoplankton* (Studies in Biology No. 52) Edward Arnold

Brewer, R (1979) *Principles of Ecology* Saunders

Collins, M (1984) *Urban Ecology* Cambridge University Press

Dowdeswell, W H (1984) *Ecology, principles and practice* Heinemann

Etherington, J R (1978) *Plant Physiological Ecology* (Studies in Biology No. 98) Edward Arnold

Fitzpatrick, E A (1974) *An introduction to soil science* Oliver and Boyd

Hassel, M P (1976) *The dynamics of competition and predation* (Studies in Biology No. 72) Edward Arnold

Kormondy, E J (1969) *Concepts of Ecology* Prentice-Hall

Krebs, C J (1972) *Ecology* Harper and Row

Lewis, T and Taylor, L R (1967) *Introduction to experimental ecology* Academic Press

Mason, C F (1976) *Decomposition* (Studies in Biology No. 74) Edward Arnold

Odum, E P (1971) *Fundamentals of ecology* W B Saunders

Phillipson, J (1966) *Ecological energetics* (Studies in Biology No. 1) Edward Arnold

Postgate, J (1978) *Nitrogen fixation* (Studies in Biology No. 92) Edward Arnold

Putman, R J and Wratten, S D (1984) *Principles of Ecology* Crown Helm

Solomon, M E (1969) *Population dynamics* (Studies in Biology No. 18) Edward Arnold

Wood, M (1989) *Soil Biology* Blackie.

3 POPULATIONS

The ecosystems described in previous chapters support many different species of plants and animals. Each **species**, the lowest taxonomic group, contains many individuals which share recognisable physical similarities and a similar genetic make up. Furthermore, these individuals can normally interbreed freely and produce viable offspring which are themselves fertile. In the wild, species rarely, if ever, show uniform distribution throughout their habitats. More frequently they are organised into functional groups (populations) which interact with other populations of the same, or other, species.

3.1 SINGLE SPECIES POPULATIONS

A **population** is a group of interbreeding individuals of the same species occupying a particular place at a given time. e.g. the term could be applied to all the humans living in the UK on December 31 1991, or all the foxgloves in a named wood on June 21 1991. Precision in counting the numbers of plants and animals within defined geographical areas, finding out how numbers change, and explaining the reasons for such changes are among the primary aims of population studies.

Natural populations may be either open or closed. In an **open population** individuals are gained by immigration and lost by emigration, across the boundary defining the spatial limit of the population (Figure 1a). **Closed populations**, such as those of certain islands, are self-contained, without any gains from, or losses to, other populations. The actual size of a closed population at a given time is determined by its **birth rate (natality)**, **death rate (mortality)** and the **lifespan (longevity)** of its individual members. A closed population increases in size when the birth rate exceeds the death rate, decreases when the death rate exceeds the birth rate and remains constant when the two rates reach an equilibrium. Under conditions in which the birth rate remains constant, increased longevity will lead to a lower death rate and an increase in population. Conversely, a decrease in longevity will have the opposite effect, leading to a decrease in total population. Within large ecosystems such as woods, populations of organisms are often sub-divided into **demes**, or local populations, incompletely separated from other demes by physical boundaries, such as rivers or roads. Individuals can disperse from one deme to another, but such movements are the exception rather than the general rule (Figure 1b). Contemporary geneticists and evolutionists have broadened the population concept. They view

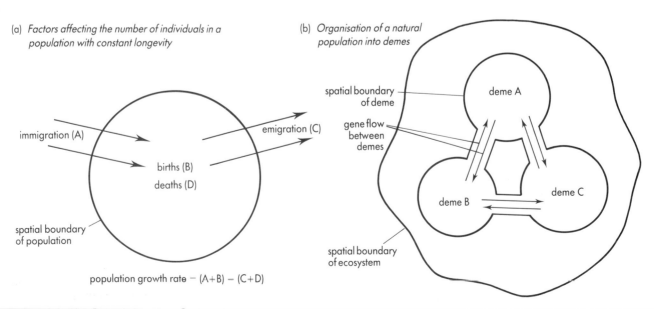

(a) *Factors affecting the number of individuals in a population with constant longevity*

immigration (A)

emigration (C)

births (B)
deaths (D)

spatial boundary of population

population growth rate − (A+B) − (C+D)

(b) *Organisation of a natural population into demes*

spatial boundary of deme

gene flow between demes

deme A

deme B

deme C

spatial boundary of ecosystem

Figure 1   Single-species population dynamics

each species as a collection of mixable genes, rather than a collection of individuals. All the mixable genes possessed by a species, together with their alleles, make up the **gene pool**. Clearly, the gene pool of each population shows less genetic diversity than that of the species as a whole. Similarly, within demes (which are essentially units of inbreeding individuals) one finds the smallest yet most active gene pools. **Gene flow** describes the limited transfer of genes beteen gene pools, as individuals disperse from one deme to another. Individuals are born and die, with a finite lifespan, but populations continue in time and their gene pool changes as time progresses. This change in the gene pool of populations is the raw material of **evolution**, on which the forces of **natural selection** act. If gene flow between neighbouring populations is high a species retains a fairly homogeneous gene pool and therefore undergoes very little evolutionary change. Conversely, if demes or populations become isolated, with little gene flow between them, active mixing produces novel gene combinations, leading to the formation of new species.

Population density

In any population the number of individuals per unit area, or **population density**, is principally determined by three factors:

(i) the carrying capacity of the environment,
(ii) the biotic potential of the population,
(iii) time.

The **carrying capacity of the environment (K)** is a measure of the maximum number of a species that could be accommodated in a defined space or habitat.

It is a factor determined by availability of water, food, space or other essential requirements. The **biotic potential** of a population is its maximum reproductive capacity, given unlimited natural resources such as food or space. Biotic potential represents an intrinsic rate of natural increase, or the inherent power of a population to grow. Biotic potentials are determined chiefly by the rate at which new individuals are produced. Among those traits that determine whether the biotic potential of a species is low or high are:

(i) the male: female ratio
(ii) the age at which reproduction begins,
(iii) duration of the reproductive period,
(iv) the number of offspring produced per reproductive episode,
(v) the time interval between successive reproductive episodes,
(vi) the survival rates of (a) offspring and (b) reproductive individuals.

In reality however, maximum reproductive potentials are never reached because environmental factors such as predators and parasites kill some individuals before their natural lifespan is completed. **Environmental resistance** is a measure of those factors, such as predation and parasitism, that tend to limit populations, preventing them from attaining their full biotic potential. The effects of these different factors on population density is illustrated in Figure 2. If the carrying capacity of the environment (K_1) is increased, perhaps because food increases or predation decreases, then the population generally increases to take advantage of the increased support provided by the environment.

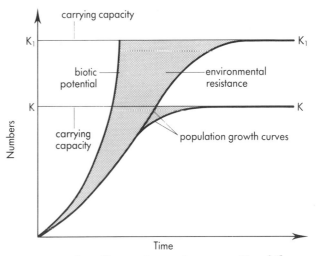

Figure 2 *The effects of carrying capacity of the environment, biotic potential and environmental resistance on the size of a population*

Time has the most marked effect on population density if the carrying capacity of the environment suddenly increases. For example, increased availability of food or space can often lead to an increase in population density. In many instances, species with a high biotic potential take advantage of this new opportunity sooner than those with a low biotic potential.

The description and analysis of plant cover at ground level often involves measurements of density, cover and frequency. All of these measurements may be made by using a wooden or metal frame called a **quadrat**. Conventionally a quadrat is a 1 m × 1 m square, subdivided into 10 cm × 10 cm squares, but both the size and shape can be varied for particular tasks. When measuring **density**, the quadrat is placed on the ground and the number of individual plants within the frame is counted.

Cover value is an estimate of the area covered by a given species, usually expressed as a percentage of the total area. Shoot cover may be estimated by counting the number of 10 cm² squares in which leaves of a given species occur. Alternatively, root cover may be estimated. This may give a very different result from an assessment of the number of plants present

(Figure 3). Results are commonly expressed numerically using the cover/abundance scales devised by Braun-Blanquet or Domin (Table 1). It should be noted however that estimates of cover value are sometimes incorrect because they are subjective, obtained by visual estimation and operator decision.

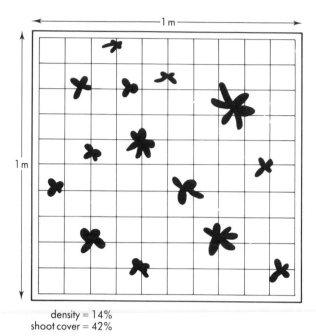

density = 14%
shoot cover = 42%

Figure 3   A quadrat

Table 1   Scales for estimating percentage plant cover

PERCENTAGE GROUND SURFACE COVER	SCALE	
	Braun-Blanquet	Domin
100		10
	5	
75–100		9
50–75		8
	4	
33–50		7
25–33	3	6
20–25		5
	2	
5–20		4
less than 5		3
	1	2
		1
single isolated plant	X	X

Frequency is a measure of the probability of finding a plant within any given area. Suppose a quadrat is thrown 48 times, and a given species found within 27 of the delimited areas after the quadrat had landed:

$$\text{frequency} = \frac{27}{48} \times 100 = 56.25\%$$

Frequency is dependent on quadrat size, plant size and the patterning of the vegetation. It is also affected by the number of times a quadrat is thrown. Clearly, the accuracy of estimates is increased by making a large number of throws.

Spatial distribution

The use of quadrats can be extended to include studies of spatial distribution by plotting the exact arrangement of individuals within a given area. Theoretically, three spatial arrangements of individuals are possible:

(i) **Uniform (regular) distribution** (Figure 4a). Such an arrangement is rare in nature, however.

(ii) **Aggregation**, where individuals are clustered into groups (Figure 4b). This arrangement is typical of many plants such as buttercups and daisies which grow in patches on lawns. Many animals also aggregate, especially around food sources, breeding grounds or in some optimal microclimate.

(iii) **Random distribution** occurs when individuals are neither arranged regularly, nor aggregated, but spaced in an irregular, unpredictable way that changes with time (Figure 4c). Theoretically, random distribution occurs when there is no interaction between individuals of a population. In practice however, there is always some interaction between individuals. This means that true random distribution is very rare in nature, although certain animal populations approach this condition.

Using the naked eye to decide if a population is aggregated or randomly distributed is clearly fraught with difficulties. Fortunately the problem can be resolved by using mathematics. To do this, ecologists need to know how to calculate arithmetic **means**, **standard deviations** and **variance**. The following example refers to Figure 4. In this diagram a population of 32 individuals is arranged (a) uniformly, (b) aggregated and (c) randomly distributed in a 16-square quadrat. The **arithmetic mean** is the best known and most useful form of average, usually referred to just as the 'mean' or 'average'. To calculate the mean number of individuals per square, proceed as follows.

Add together all the individuals shown in the quadrat.

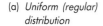

(a) *Uniform (regular) distribution*

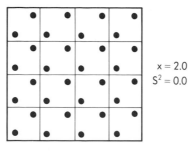

x = 2.0
S² = 0.0

(b) *Aggregated*

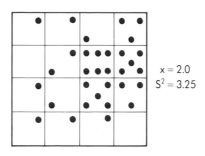

x = 2.0
S² = 3.25

(c) *Random distribution*

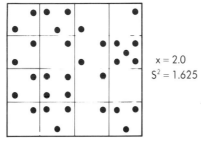

x = 2.0
S² = 1.625

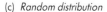

Figure 4   *The spatial distribution of individuals in a population*

Total number
 of individuals = 32
Total number
 of squares   = 16
The arithmetic
 mean (x)   = $\dfrac{\text{total number of individuals}}{\text{total number of squares}}$

So x = $\dfrac{32}{16}$

Note that in Figure 4 each small square in the quadrat has the same arithmetic mean of 2.0.

The **variance (S²)** is the best and most useful measure of population distribution. To calculate it you need to know the arithmetic mean (x) and the distance of deviation from the mean $(x - \bar{x})$. These figures are then squared, $(x - \bar{x})^2$, to produce squared deviations and remove the + and − signs. Next, the squared deviations are summed, $\Sigma(x - \bar{x})^2$, to produce the standard deviation. Finally, the standard deviation is divided by the number of observations (N) to give the variance (S²). Table 2 shows how variance is calculated from the data in Figure 4, counting from left to right and starting in the top row.

Table 2   *Data for calculating the variance (S²) of the population in quadrat b in Figure 4*

Arithmetic mean (x)	Distance of deviation from mean $(x - \bar{x})$	Squared deviation $(x - \bar{x})^2$	Standard deviation $\Sigma(x - \bar{x})^2$	Variance $\dfrac{\Sigma(x - \bar{x})^2}{N}$
2.0	− 1	1		
2.0	− 1	1		
2.0	− 1	1		
2.0	+ 1	1		
2.0	− 2	4		
2.0	0	0		
2.0	+ 4	16		
2.0	+ 3	9		
2.0	− 1	1		
2.0	− 1	1		
2.0	+ 3	9		
2.0	+ 1	1		
2.0	− 1	1		
2.0	− 1	1		
2.0	− 1	1	Sum	
2.0	− 2	4	= 52	$\dfrac{52}{16}$ = 3.25

From the three spatial distributions in Figure 4 we have:

a) Uniform (regular) distribution
   arithmetic mean (x) = 2.0
   variance (S²)   = 0.0
b) Aggregation
   arithmetic mean (x) = 2.0
   variance (S²)   = 3.25
c) Random distribution
   arithmetic mean (x) = 2.0
   variance   = 1.6

The figures obtained for the arithmetic mean (x) and variance (S²) provide valuable information about spatial distribution. A population is uniformly distributed if variance (S²) equals 0. If individuals are aggregated, the value of S² increases with increasing aggregation. For a perfectly randomly distributed population, the arithmetic mean (x) and the variance (S²) are equal. Such populations are rare in nature so the figures tell us that the population in quadrat (c) (1.62 − 2.0 = −0.38) is more randomly distributed than the population in quadrat (b) (3.25 − 2.0 = 1.25).

Estimating numbers

Populations of plants are easier to count than animals since they occupy fixed positions and their populations are not subject to immigration and emigration. When counting plants, quadrats can be used to make counts from a known proportion of the area they inhabit. Figures obtained from such counts are then multiplied by the appropriate figure to give an estimate of the population in the whole area. Populations of small, relatively immobile invertebrates such as slugs, snails and some soil-dwellers can also be estimated by using quadrats, but this method is unsuitable for fast-moving animals which run, jump or fly. For estimates of the numbers of individuals in the populations of these animals, ecologists use a **mark, release and recapture technique**. This technique relies on the principle that if marked animals are randomly mixed with other (unmarked) members of the population, and a random sample taken, the ratio of marked to unmarked individuals in the sample will be the same as in the whole population. The simplest mark, release and recapture technique for estimating population size is the **Lincoln Index**, expressed by the following equation:

$$\text{estimated total population (N)} = F_1 \times \frac{F_2}{F_3}$$

where:

F_1 = the number of marked individuals released into the population,
F_2 = the number of individuals captured in the second sample,
F_3 = The number of marked individuals in the second sample.

A sample of the population, ideally in excess of 20%, is captured in nets or traps. All of this first catch are then marked by painting, ringing or tagging, before being released into the general population. If paint spots are applied, they should not interfere with locomotion, nor make the animal more conspicuous to its predators. After allowing 24 hours for the marked individuals to become integrated into the general population, a second capture is made, and the number of marked individuals recorded. In work with froghoppers the following results were obtained:

$F_1 = 271$
$F_2 = 289$
$F_3 = 29$

$$\text{Population of froghoppers (N)} \simeq \frac{271 \times 289}{29}$$

$$N \simeq 2700$$

This method unfortunately takes no account of birth rate, death rate, immigration or emigration, but assumes a stable population with full integration of marked individuals. Furthermore, estimates of population size can be wildly inaccurate if only a very small percentage of the total population is marked and released.

A second method of obtaining a rough population estimate is called **removal sampling**. This technique is applicable to populations to froghoppers, grasshoppers and snails in grassland, or beetles and tadpoles in ponds. Selected sites are swept with a net, generally in a 'criss-cross'

manner, for 50, 100, 200 or 300 sweepings per sample. The number of animals in each sample is counted, and the animals retained in a container. This procedure is repeated between 5 and 20 times. Records are kept of the number of animals present in each sample. On returning to the laboratory, a table (similar to Table 3) is drawn, and a graph constructed (Figure 5). When the number of animals captures is plotted on the y-axis of a graph and the number previously removed is plotted on the x-axis, the points usually fall along a straight line, indicating that the probability of capture remains constant. If the line is projected to the zero mark (indicating theoretical 100% removal from the area) an estimate of population size is obtained. Figure 5, with a population of froghoppers, gives an estimate of around 600 individuals in the whole population.

Table 3   Tabulated results from removal sampling

SAMPLE NO.	NO. FROGHOPPERS CAPTURED	NO. PREVIOUSLY REMOVED
1	37	0
2	39	37
3	34	76
4	32	110
5	28	142
6	29	170
7	25	199

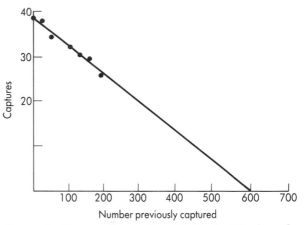

Figure 5   Removal sampling. Method of finding the approximate size of an animal population by extrapolation to the x-axis

Numerical fluctuations

The number of individuals in a population changes with time. Some populations show an orderly predictable pattern of growth and decline. Others show daily or seasonal fluctuations, typically with peaks and troughs of population density. Others are subject to cyclic fluctuations, the cycle being annual, or taking place over a longer period of time.

The classic model for population growth, where both space and food supply are limited, is provided by populations of bacteria or yeasts growing in a beaker of a nutrient solution. Such populations typically pass through a pattern of growth that is **'S'-shaped** or **sigmoid**. They then decline, as food runs out and toxic substances accumulate in their surroundings (Figure 6).

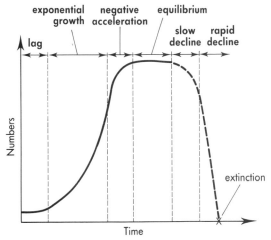

Figure 6 Phases in the growth of a population of yeast cells; the dotted line indicates phases that would occur only if the carrying capacity of the environment were to decline

Growth curves of this type may show all or only some of the following phases.

(i) A **lag phase** in which growth is slow, limited either by sparseness of breeding individuals or a shortage of some essential nutrient.

(ii) A phase of **logarithmic**, or **exponential growth**, in which the population increases by repeated doubling, in the sequence 1, 2, 4, 8, 16, 32 etc.

(iii) **Negative acceleration** in which the growth rate slows as a result of a shortage of food or the accumulation of waste products.

(iv) **Equilibrium**, in which the birth rate is balanced by the death rate.

(v) **Slow decline**, in which the death rate is slightly in excess of the birth rate.

(vi) **Rapid decline**, in which the death rate greatly exceeds the birth rate. When the last individual has died, the population is said to have reached a point of extinction.

Relatively few plants and animals from woods, ponds or rocky shores show sigmoid population growth curves. Those that do are most likely to be recent introductions into an established ecosystem (e.g. mink, coypu), or resident species which have spread into some newly created area of bare soil, perhaps the product of tree-felling, burning or digging. If woodland trees are felled, higher light intensities at ground level stimulate the germination of foxglove and other seeds. This leads to a marked increase in numbers, and often

an S-shaped growth curve, eventually limited by lack of space, light, water or nutrients.

Insect populations show marked variations in population density throughout the year. Adult froghoppers, for instance, are relatively short lived. Their populations build up to an annual peak in late summer, then decline (Figure 7). It is unusual to take any adult froghoppers in sweepings of vegetation within the period November to April. During this period of the year froghoppers are passing through diapause and eggs. Many other insect populations conform to this seasonal pattern of population fluctuation, as do populations of crustaceans, spiders, centipedes, molluscs and migratory birds. By contrast, populations of adult heather beetles, feeding on heather leaves, remain fairly constant throughout the year. Their populations may nevertheless show marked daily fluctuations, probably caused by variations in temperature, humidity and light intensity. Such population oscillations (Figure 8), both above and below the carrying capacity of the environment, probably show that this insect has reached a state of equilibrium.

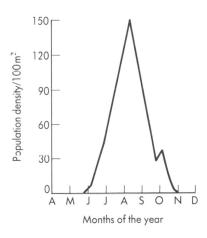

Figure 7 Fluctuations in the population density of froghoppers, Ashdown Forest 1987

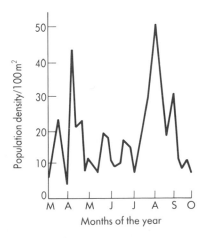

Figure 8 Fluctuations in the population density of heather beetles, Ashdown Forest 1987

Finally, some animals show cyclic oscillations in population density over several years. Foxes, mice and voles are examples of animals with well defined, regular and predictable changes in population density. In each of these animals, population density peaks every four years with one or more troughs between successive peaks.

In some animal species, there are physiological mechanisms for depressing the birth rate when population density rises above a particular threshold level. Resorption of embryos in the uterus occurs in foxes, rabbits and deer, as a direct result of overcrowding, shortage of food or stress. In mice, the smell of a 'strange' male mouse, i.e. one with which the female has not copulated, suppresses the secretion of prolactin in the female. As a result, her corpus luteum fails to develop and normal oestrus is restored. Among bees, only the queen is fertile. Although the workers possess ovaries, these are prevented from developing by the pheromone 9-ketodecanoic acid which is produced by the queen to act on the ovaries of the workers, preventing development of the eggs.

Age structure and survivorship

Populations rarely, if ever, consist entirely of individuals that are the same age. In most populations there are individuals of various ages, often described as **prereproductive**, **reproductive** and **postreproductive**. Age may be expressed in hours, days, weeks, months or years. If the population is divided into age groups, and the proportion of the population in each group displayed, an age pyramid is obtained (Figure 9). **Age pyramids** show the current age structure of a population. There are three basic types, from which future population trends may be predicted. In **expanding populations** (Figure 9a), with exponential growth, the pyramid is triangular and broadest at its base. **Stable populations** (Figure 9b) have somewhat bell-shaped, parallel-sided age pyramids. The age pyramids of **diminishing populations** (Figure 9c) may be diamond-shaped, broad in the middle and narrow at the base, as birth rates are reduced. By adding the percentage of males and females to each age group (the **sex ratio**) an **age-sex pyramid** is produced. This allows future population trends to be predicted with greater accuracy.

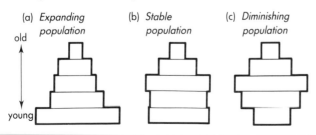

Figure 9   Age pyramids

The pattern of mortality in a population can be represented by a **survivorship curve**. These survivorship curves are of three types, as shown in Figure 10. Each curve shows the relationship between the number of individuals surviving and their age. In a **type I** curve, typical of the human population of the UK, most individuals survive to reach old age. After reaching old age though, there is a high mortality. A steady rate of mortality over the normal lifespan of the species is typical of **type II** organisms, including songbirds, lizards and small mammals. Survivorship curves approximating to **type III**, with the highest mortality rate occurring in juveniles, are common among insects, fishes, amphibians and reptiles.

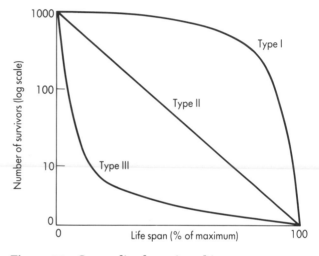

Figure 10   Generalised survivorship curves

3.2 POPULATION INTERACTIONS

Natural populations in ecosystems show individual-individual and species-species interactions. All such interactions affect population density. At one level, there is intraspecific competition as individuals of the same species compete with one another for natural resources such as food, water, light, breeding partners etc. The general relationship between species density and mortality is illustrated in Figure 11. Below a certain threshold level of density, individual members of a population have no need to compete for the resource because it is sufficiently abundant to meet the demands of all members of the population. As population increases however, there comes a point at which the resource becomes inadequate for all the individuals. At this point, individuals compete with one another for the resource. Further population increases lead to increased competition and a corresponding increase in mortality (Figure 11). This theoretically continues to a point where mortality reaches 100% because the resource has been exhausted.

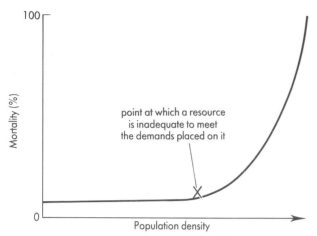

Figure 11   The general relationship between population density and mortality resulting from intraspecific competition

Interspecific competition

The interactions that occur between populations of different species can be categorised into different group, according to the ways in which each participating species benefits or is harmed by the interaction.

(i) **+ + interactions** are mutually beneficial to both participating populations, e.g. the mutualistic (symbiotic) associations that occur between *Rhizobium* bacteria and the roots of legumes, or between algae and fungi in lichens.

(ii) **+ o interactions** are of benefit to the population of one species, but do not affect the population of the other. Lichens growing on the trunks of trees are examples. Tree trunks provide the lichens with a suitable substratum, while the trees do not appear to suffer any adverse effects as a result of this colonisation by lichens.

(iii) **+ − interactions** are of benefit to one species but harmful to the other. Examples include interspecific competition for resources, predator-prey relationships, parasitism and herbivore grazing.

In the early 1930s a Russian ecologist, G F Gause, carried out a series of experiments in which laboratory-maintained populations of closely related species were studied (a) in isolation and (b) in competition with each other. Gause kept careful records of changes in population density, and some of his results are illustrated in Figure 12. Depending on the conditions that he provided, the inevitable result of this direct interspecific competition was the elimination of one population by the other. This

(a) *Population density when grown as separate cultures*

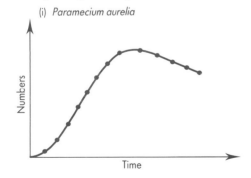

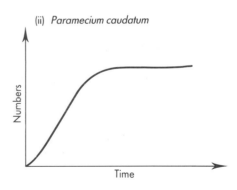

(b) *Population density when grown as a mixed culture*

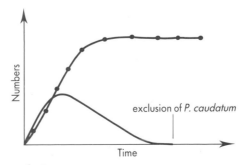

Figure 12   Interspecific competition between two species of Paramecium fed on bacteria

led Gause to formulate his **exclusion principle**, which states that competition between species results in the exclusion of one species by the other. Viewed another way, the exclusion principle implies that no two species have exactly the same requirements or, as modern ecologists would say, occupy exactly the same niche.

Later field studies of interspecific competition showed that, while some populations behaved as Gause had predicted, others did not. An alternative strategy of **coexistence** was commonly found among competing animal populations, each population utilising the resource in a different way. It also became clear that distantly related taxa, such as insects and cattle, could compete with one another for the same resource, the outcome resulting either in exclusion or coexistence. Furthermore, competition between animal species rarely involved a direct struggle between two, or even a few, individuals. It was more a case of the survival of the fittest, or best adapted, individuals with the elimination of those who were in some way handicapped and therefore unable to obtain the resources they required. Among plants, interspecific competition was more or less confined to the effect of individual plants on their neighbour's growth and reproduction. Such effects are now known to be widespread and are important in establishing the associations that occur between plants of different species.

Ecologists have known for many years that walnut trees inhibit undergrowth plants; their trunks tend to be surrounded by an almost barren patch, covering an area overhung by the branches. This inhibition is not caused by shading, soil drought, low nutrient status or root competition. Extensive research has shown that it is a chemical effect. Walnut leaves, fruits and twigs contain hydroxyjuglone, a non-toxic compound, oxidised by soil micro-organisms into juglone, a powerful plant growth inhibitor. Juglone, in common with other chemical compounds inhibiting germination, growth or the occurrence of other plants, is called an **allelopathic** substance. Chemical inhibition of one plant species by another, a '+ − interaction', is called **allelopathy**. This phenomenon is shown by many plant species which release compounds such as phenolic acids, coumarins, quinones, terpenes, essential oil, alkaloids or cyanides from their leaves, roots or decaying litter. For example, sunflower plants release allelopathics from all of these sources. The presence of these compounds in the soil does not affect the germination of sunflower seeds but strongly inhibits seed germination in some other species, therby giving the sunflower a competitive advantage. Oak trees release an allelopathic substance from their roots, which inhibits the germination of acorns. If a mature oak is felled,

causing the roots to die, this inhibition of acorn germination is removed, favouring regeneration of the site by oak seedlings. Heather plants, and the litter that forms beneath them, inhibit the growth of mycorrhizal fungi. This is one reason why trees, dependent on mycorrhizal associations for their nutrients, rarely grow on or invade heather moors. Another consequence of this is that if heather moorland is to be reforested, the heather plants must first be removed, otherwise tree saplings may fail to reach maturity.

Allelopathic substances probably exert a significant effect on the structure of plant communities, influencing both the succession and maintenance of the climax vegetation. Grasses tend to produce aromatic chemical substances, inhibitory to nitrogen-metabolising bacteria, and to the seedlings of other plants. Hence, grass-covered areas may change only slowly, or fail to show any succession. Where herbs are succeeded by shrubs, as in the regeneration of heathland after fire, alleleopathics from the shrubs become increasingly effective, until only a few herbs are left. In a similar way, allelopathics from mature woodland trees may inhibit those plants that occupied the same site at an earlier stage in the succession.

Predation, parasitism and herbivore feeding

Predation, parasitism and herbivore feeding all provide further examples of '+ − interactions' between different species. **True predators** (+) are carnivores, gaining their own sustenance by eating other animals, their **prey** (−). Predators are always larger and fewer in number than their prey. Predation inevitably results in the death of individuals from the prey population. **Parasites** (+) gain their sustenance by feeding on one or more parts of their **hosts** (−). Parasites are always smaller than their hosts, and generally more numerous. Parasitism always harms the host, and may even kill it. Following from parasitisation, host populations become diseased, showing impaired growth, reproduction or other adverse effects on their physiological processes. Herbivores (+) eat plants (−). Some appear to act like true predators, consuming individual plants for their own sustenance. Others, including aphids, behave more like parasites, weakening plants by feeding on the nutrients in their vascular tissue. In the past there has been a tendency to draw clear lines of demarcation between predators, parasites and herbivores. In many ways this is still justified but today's ecologists have found almost identical relationships between populations of the 'food source' (−) and 'feeder' (+) in each of these three groups. For this reason, they have simplified and generalised descriptions of these interactions in terms of a 'predator' (+) and 'prey' (−) relationship.

When changes in the population density of a predator and its prey are plotted on the same scale, two patterns may emerge. The first (Figure 13) shows the relationship between a population of ladybirds (predator) and a population of aphids (prey). Both the predator and its prey have seasonal populations which peak during the summer. Predator-prey interaction is possible only because both species live in close proximity of one another, occupying the same habitat. Populations of the prey appear before those of the predator. Throughout their range the prey is generally more numerous than the predator. At the end of the summer, members of the predator population persist after the last of the prey has died.

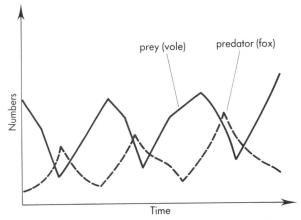

Figure 14   Cyclic oscillations of interdependent populations

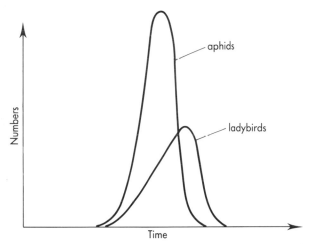

Figure 13   The relationships between populations of a predator (ladybird) and its prey (aphids)

A second predator-prey relationship occurs when long lived animals, such as mammals, interact. This interaction causes wave-like oscillations in the population density of both species which tend to be out of phase with one another. Foxes, for example, feed on voles, and both species have cyclic populations which peak every four years or so. In Figure 14, starting at a point where the fox population has peaked, increased feeding on voles reduces the vole population density. Next, the fox population declines, because there are fewer voles for foxes to eat. Finally, with less predation from foxes, the vole population recovers to a new peak, causing the cycle to be repeated.

As a conclusion to this section, it is worth noting that the populations of many animals, especially insects, are affected both by predation and by parasitism. e.g. populations of the large

cabbage white butterfly remain fairly constant from year to year. A single female may lay as many as 600 eggs per season, but of these only around 0.3–0.5% survive to become adults (Figure 15). Approximately 63% are parasitised by viral, bacterial and fungal agents of the larvae and pupae; 32% are parasitised by other insects, notably in ichneumon fly (*Apanteles glomerata*) and by the pupae of a fly (*Pteromalus puparum*). A further 4.7% or so are eaten by birds, chiefly great tits, blue tits and robins. From the 600 fertile eggs produced by the parents, only about two individuals survive to reproduce in the next season.

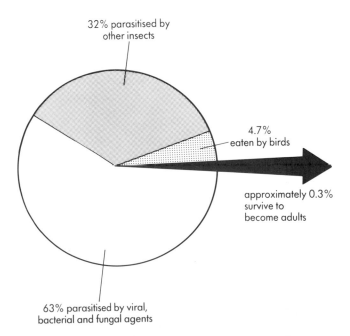

Figure 15   Agents causing mortality among larvae and pupae of the large cabbage white butterfly

QUESTIONS

1 The diagram below shows idealised cycles of predator and prey abundance.

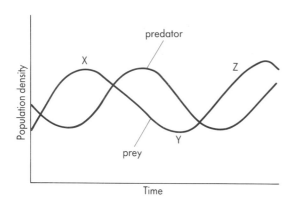

a) Name two organisms showing a relationship of this type.
b) Describe and explain the relationship between the two populations.
c) What is happening to the prey population at the points marked X, Y and Z?
d) If the diagram was not idealised, how might the population density of the prey differ from that shown in the diagram?

e) Populations of the snowshoe rabbit and lynx fluctuate on an eleven-year sunspot cycle. Can you suggest a reason for peaks in the rabbit population?
f) An ecologist made 10 sweeps of a small pond. Each sweep was made along a 10 m length of water. The number of pond snails captured after each sweep was recorded. The results were as follows:

SWEEP NO.	NO. SNAILS CAPTURED
1	59
2	44
3	38
4	33
5	29
6	24
7	17
8	14
9	11
10	7

From the data provided, estimate the size of the snail population.
g) What other methods could have been used to estimate the size of the snail population?

2 The diagrams below show two experimental procedures, (a) and (b), and their results, in an investigation involving grass plants and apple seedlings.

(a) *Each box watered from can*

(b) *Apple seedlings watered via grass box*

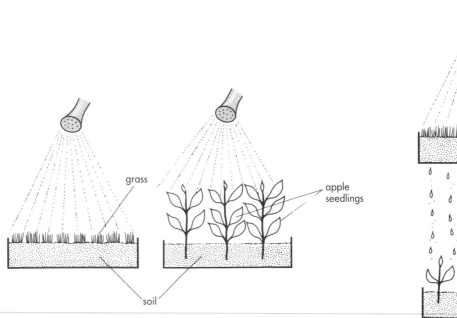

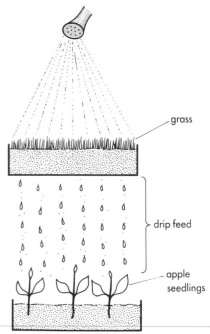

a) Make a drawing of the control you would use in this investigation.

b) What hypothesis is being tested?

c) If this hypothesis was supported by experimental evidence:
   (i) what type of compound is the grass producing,
   (ii) what advice would you offer to growers of apple seedlings?

d) Discuss the ecological significance of this and similar interactions between plant species.

3 a) What is a 'population'?

b) Distinguish between open and closed populations.

c) What factors affect the number of individuals in open populations?

d) Describe the organisation of populations in natural ecosystems such as woodlands.

e) What role do such populations play in the evolution of species?

4 Draw a diagram to illustrate changes in population density when a micro-organism, such as yeast or a bacterium, is grown in a unit volume of nutrient solution. Label stages in the growth curve, and explain each stage in terms of the processes that characterise it. What types of growth curve occur among populations of terrestrial insects?

5 The populations of different species affect one another in different ways, sometimes described as (i) ++, (ii) + o and (iii) +− interactions. Referring to one or more examples of each type, explain and illustrate this concept of species interaction.

6 Distinguish between:
a) a transect and quadrat;
b) cover value and frequency;
c) uniform, aggregated and random distribution;
d) biotic potential and carrying capacity of the environment.

7 Distinguish between intraspecific and interspecific competition.

For what resources do the individual members of a species compete?

In what ways do (a) the exclusion principle, and (b) the niche concept, help to explain the outcome of direct competition between closely related species?

Under what conditions can competing species coexist?

BIBLIOGRAPHY

Begon, M and Mortimer, M (1981) *Population Ecology* Blackwell

Kershaw, K A (1964) *Quantitative and dynamic ecology* Edward Arnold

MacArthur, R H and Connell, J H (1966) *The Biology of Populations* Wiley

Putman, R J and Wratten, S D (1984) *Principles of Ecology* Croom Helm

Sondheimer, E and Simeone, J B (1970) *Chemical Ecology* Academic Press

Van Emden, H F (1974) *Pest control and its ecology* (Studies in Biology No. 50) Edward Arnold

Wilson, E O and Bossert, W H (1971) *A primer of population biology* Sinaeur.

THE HUMAN POPULATION

Humans are relatively large social omnivores, occupying a terminal position in many food chains, both terrestrial and aquatic. If success can be measured in terms of dominance over other species, worldwide distribution and number of individuals, then humans are one of the most successful mammals that has ever lived. While some of these mammals owe their success to their size and physical dominance over other species, human success owes a great deal to behavioural characteristics, including the ability to solve problems and exert some control over the lives of other living organisms.

Present day Europeans, Africans and Chinese may look very different, yet are all closely related and can claim a common descent from a population, or populations, of *Homo erectus*, which existed probably no more than 500 000–2 million years ago. From the time when anatomically modern humans (*Homo sapiens sapiens*) first appeared, some 40 000 years ago, the human population has shown a continuous, if somewhat uneven, increase. At first the human species was sparsely distributed. Subsequent increases in population density followed increases in the carrying capacity of the environment, brought about as much by innovations in behaviour as by changes in soil or climate.

4.1 PHASES OF GROWTH

Three of the most significant phases of human evolution have been called the **tool-making** revolution, **agricultural** revolution and **scientific-industrial** revolution. Each of these phases was accompanied by a surge in population density (Figure 1). During the **tool-making revolution** that took place during the Stone Age, axes, choppers and knives were made by chipping flintstones. As a direct consequence, human populations of that period gained greater control over their environment. Before the **agricultural revolution**, some 10 000 years ago, humans lived as nomadic hunter-gatherers, consuming most of the available food in one area before they moved on to another. A different, more settled lifestyle was made possible by the domestication of animals and the monoculture of food crops. The steady supply of food provided by these innovations was sufficient

to sustain a steady increase in population. From Figures 1 and 2 you will see that the most spectacular increase in human population began about 500 years ago, two centuries or more before the start of the **scientific-industrial revolution**. After increasing arithmetically in the period to 1500 AD, world population then began to increase exponentially. Human numbers doubled in the period 1650–1850. They had doubled again by 1920, and yet again by 1970. Some of the factors responsible for this rapid increase in the UK were as follows.

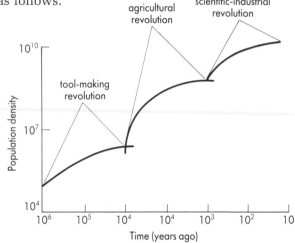

Figure 1   Three major phases in the growth of human population, expressed in the form of a logarithmic population curve (adapted from E S Deevy, 1960 The Human Population *Scientific American* 203, 195-204)

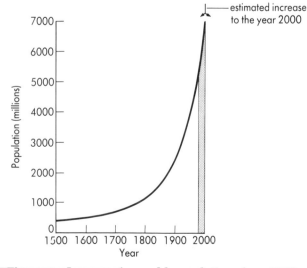

Figure 2   Increase in world population since 1500

(i) Food production was increased to a level at which starvation rarely acted as a limiting factor. Increases in food production resulted from improved methods of cultivation and the introduction of new food sources. i.e. a second agricultural revolution took place. Additional food was imported from foreign countries and methods of storage and transporation were improved.

(ii) As research revealed the life cycles of parasites, simple hygienic measures (such as keeping drinking water free from human excrement) helped to break the chain of parasite transmission from host to host. Advances in medicine, especially vaccination and the more recent introduction of antibiotics, reduced the effects of a number of infectious diseases. Other medical advances, including surgical operations and chemotherapy, prevented premature death so that more people reached reproductive maturity and went on to reach old age.

(iii) Improvements in housing and living conditions reduced the stress caused by coldness and dampness. In many instances, an increase in the general level of wealth meant that families could afford to have more children. Indeed, there were many distinct advantages in producing large families. Quite apart from increasing the labour force and family income, there were sons and daughters to care for the parents in their old age.

4.2 AGE STRUCTURE AND DISTRIBUTION

Human populations in different parts of the world are growing at different rates. The rate of population growth in any part of the world is influenced by the birth rate, death rate, immigration, emigration, and the longevity of individuals. If humans are assigned to three different age categories (prereproductive, reproductive and postreproductive) and analysed in terms of sex groupings, three distinct types of **age pyramids** may be obtained (Figure 15a, b, c):

(i) Broad-based triangular age pyramids are typical of developing countries such as those in South America and Africa. The typical family is large. Birth rate (the number of live births per 1000 of the population) and death rate (the number of deaths per 1000 of the population) are both high. There is also a high rate of infant mortality because standards of hygiene and nutrition are low. A poor diet, low in proteins, also delays the onset of sexual maturity until individuals reach an age of between 15 and 19 years. Finally, life expectancy, the average age at which people die, is low. Less than 50% of all individuals in the population survive beyond the age of 50. Only a very small number of postreproductive individuals reach extreme old age.

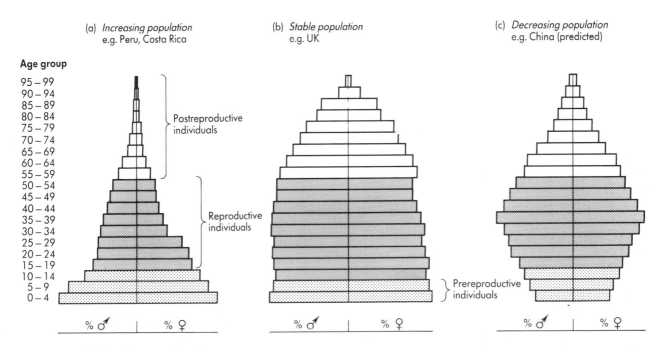

Figure 3   Idealised pyramids of age structure

(ii) Parallel-sided age pyramids are typical of populations in North America, Australia and parts of Europe. Typical families contain anything from 1–4 children, nourished on a balanced diet, maintained under hygienic conditions and well educated. The balanced diet, rich in proteins, advances the onset of sexual maturity into the 10–14 age range. There may also be an extension of reproductive activity beyond the age of 50. As birth rates and death rates are both low, most individuals reach postreproductive age. After that they die at a steady rate, killed by the diseases of old age.

(iii) Narrow-based, diamond-shaped age pyramids are typical of declining populations, where death rate exceeds birth rate. Such populations exist at the present time in Germany and the UK. Soon after the year 2000 however, China will provide the best example of this type, following rigorous birth control measures to restrict each married couple to one child.

Although all our early ancestors probably worked the land, there is now a marked division of labour between individuals, with many different types of work available. As a result, people have tended to aggregate in towns and villages, looking for work and depending increasingly on the specific skills of other individuals whenever they might need them. This movement of individuals into towns is called **urbanisation**, and it is an important aspect of present day population density and dispersion. At present, approximately 40% of the world's population lives in towns, and the figure may reach 50% before the end of the century. Some important environmental consequences of urbanisation are:

(i) Wildlife habitats and prime agricultural land may be used for developments such as housing or road construction.

(ii) If roads and railways cut across habitats, they may subdivide their natural populations into smaller, isolated units.

(iii) As human population increases, less land becomes available to meet increased demands for food.

(iv) Crowding increases the chances of epidemics, especially those caused by viruses and bacteria. In addition, new strains of virus commonly appear where populations are crowded, with humans living in close proximity to animals.

(v) Human effluent, notably sewage, may present an additional hazard to health unless measures are taken to effect its rapid and safe disposal.

4.3 INDUSTRIALISED SOCIETIES

One of the main reasons for the high standard of living in industrialised countries is that a substantial proportion of the adult population is skilled and organised into an effective **work force**. The adults in these countries, often after a long period of training, undertake jobs which serve the needs of other members of the population. Furthermore, the payment of a common currency in return for work ensures that wealth is distributed. Most members of the population can therefore afford essential goods and services. This economic and financial organisation, the basis of all industrialised societies, contrasts markedly with the situation generally found in developing countries. In those parts of the world where the adults are mostly unskilled, the work force is often inadequate to meet the needs of the people. As a result, goods are scarce, services poor, and many people depend on self-sufficiency for their survival.

Engineering, the application of scientific and mathematical principles to solve problems relating to matter and to energy sources has been largely responsible for creating wealth in industrialised societies. Engineers design, construct and use **machines**. Many of these machines have transformed the human environment while others have improved the quality of human life, e.g. by taking over menial tasks previously dependent on manual labour. Today there are 17 or more branches of engineering (Table 1), each making a contribution towards the improvement of goods and services. UK engineers are currently responsible for producing 11% of the nation's wealth as well as accounting for 40% of both imports and exports.

4.4 POPULATION CONTROL

In some parts of the world, human population has increased sixfold in a century. Clearly this rate of increase cannot be maintained indefinitely because the carryng capacity of the human environment is not infinite. We, like other species, are subject to population limitation, imposed by factors such as availability of food, water and land space. Unlike other species however, we can help ourselves by taking measures today designed to produce a stable, balanced population in the future, where the birth rate and death rate are closely matched. If we are to avoid some future catastrophic 'population explosion', there are

Table 1 The modern branches of engineering science, and some of their products

BRANCH OF ENGINEERING	PRODUCTION AND MAINTENANCE ACTIVITIES
Aeronautical	Civil and military aircraft, with their mechanical and electrical systems
Agricultural	Farm machinery, animal houses, glasshouses Land drainage and irrigation systems
Automobile	Cars, vans, lorries and buses
Biomedical	X-ray machines, body scanners, optical fibres, artificial joints, heart pacemakers, kidney dialysis machines, blood/urine analysers
Building services	Heating, water and ventilation systems, large scale refrigeration units, cranes, bulldozers, boilers, pumps
Chemical	Processed fossil fuels and mineral ores, food technology, drug production
Civil	Highways, railways, canals, reservoirs, bridges, dams, sewage disposal systems
Electrical	Electricity generators, lighting systems, refrigerators
Electronic	Telecommunications, computers, control systems
Engineering construction	Oil refineries, chemical plants, power stations
Materials	Chemically and physically processed metals, plastics, wood, concrete etc.
Marine	Machinery on ships, offshore platforms etc.
Mechanical	All types of land-based machinery, e.g. turbines, dentist's drills
Mining	Pumps and ventilation in mines; mechanical systems for extracting coal and mineral ores
Naval architecture	ships, yachts, oil rigs, oil tankers, submarines
Nuclear	Nuclear fuel plants
Production	Automated and controlled production processes

only two measures that could improve the situation; production of more food, and birth control.

The **production of more food** may however lead to further population increases in the long term. Furthermore, the capacity of the earth to yield more food is itself limited, implying that food production alone could never tackle the population problem at its roots.

Birth control offers the most direct solution to the problem of population regulation. Theoretically, world population would eventually stabilise if each woman produced two children. Allowing for infant mortality however, a figure of 2.1–2.5 children per generation would lead to population stability. In industrialised countries a

variety of methods of birth control are now available.

(i) **Behavioural control** involves avoiding sexual intercourse during the part of the menstrual cycles when the egg is most likely to be present, from day 11 to day 17 of each cycle. This is the **natural** or **rhythm method** of birth control, and its success depends on building up an accurate picture of a woman's pattern of ovulation over a period of several months. In order to do this, body temperature is measured daily, in the mouth or rectum, and recorded. Immediately before an egg is produced there is a slight fall in body temperature, followed by a rise, which is maintained until menstruation begins again on day 1 of the next cycle (Figure 4). Clearly some skill is required in interpreting this data because body temperature is influenced by many factors, emotional, physical and environmental. Equally, the applications of this method are likely to be limited in third world countries, where individuals may lack the resources required to interpret such small variations in body temperature. Even when the rhythm method is applied in accordance with scientific principles, it has no more than 80–85% success in preventing conception.

(ii) **Physical control** involves placing a barrier between the sperm and egg. **Condoms**, worn by men, are rubber sheaths which cover the penis. However, pausing to fit a condom can interfere with the behavioural sequence of love-making. Worn correctly, condoms are up to 98% effective in preventing conception. Furthermore, they give effective protection against sexually transmitted diseases, such as the virus that causes AIDS. **Diaphragms**, worn by women, cover the entrance to the uterus, thereby preventing sperm from entering. They are up to 98% reliable, but can be difficult to fit and may aggravate cystitis, a urinary infection. **Intra-uterine devices (IUDs)**, usually made of coiled plastic, have to be inserted into a woman's uterus by a doctor. Once fitted, they are about 99% effective and can be left in place for up to five years. Again, they may irritate surrounding tissues and cause bacterial infections.

(iii) **Chemical control** is directed either against the sperms or eggs. **Spermicides**, supplied as a foam and introduced into the vagina before intercourse, kill the sperms soon after ejaculation. **Contraceptive pills** are of two types, known as combined pills and mini-pills. **Combined pills** contain

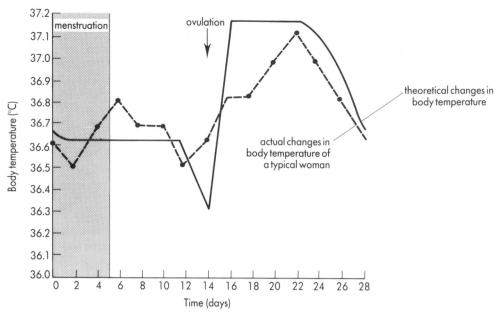

Figure 4 Body temperature during the menstrual cycle of a woman

substances similar to oestrogen and pregesterone, the natural female sex hormones. This type of pill works by stopping ovulation. Taken over many years the combined pill may slightly increase the risk of cardiovascular disease, especially in women who smoke or are obese. For most women though, it is not only risk-free, but helps to alleviate premenstrual tension, reduces the risk of fibroids, and gives some protection against cancer of the ovaries, cervix and breasts. The **mini-pill** contains only progesterone. It does not suppress ovulation, but maintains the uterus in a condition that prevents implantation of fertilised eggs. Mini-pills must be taken very regularly otherwise they fail to act as contraceptives. In most women they reduce periods but they may cause 'break-through' bleeding from the walls of the uterus. Women can now choose a progesterone **injection**, lasting for about two months. Administered by a doctor, it works like the mini-pill.

(iv) **Surgical control** is a 100% effective method of preventing births. By cutting and tying, either the Fallopian tubes of a woman or the sperm ducts of a man, the reproductive organs are isolated from their ducts. This prevents contact between the male and female gametes. Surgical intervention is called **tubal ligation** in a woman, and **vasectomy** in a man. Surgery may also be used on women who have already conceived. The surgical removal of a foetus is called an **induced abortion**. All forms of surgical control involve an element of risk,

and some are rather drastic because they cannot be reversed. Theoretically, men who have undergone vasectomy by having their sperm ducts tied can undergo a second operation for the reversal of this condition. It should be noted that in about 10% of these men the second operation is unsuccessful.

Trying to take a realistic, rational view of birth control is often difficult because so many complex issues are involved. Many people accept contraception as an effective means of preventing unwanted pregnancy. Others follow religious teachings that restrict interference with the natural processes of conception. Indeed, different solutions may have to be found in different parts of the world.

One of the most optimistic predictions about the future of human populations is that, after increasing to around 10 billion, they will stabilise. Advances in food technology might realistically be expected to provide enough food for a stable population of that size. Other alternative scenarios are more pessimistic, even gloomy. Like the populations of other animals studied by ecologists, the human population might exceed the carrying capacity of the environment. If this happened, it could precipitate a population 'crash'. Sudden, dramatic reductions in population might follow widespread famine, epidemics or incurable disease, earthquakes or global warfare. No-one really knows what will happen in the future; at best, these pessimistic predictions should encourage informed actions today, with a view to preventing some major catastrophe in the future. Unlike other organisms, humans can largely determine their own destiny.

QUESTIONS

1 The population of *Xenophobia* was 10 million on December 31 1990.
   a) List the factors that determine the numbers in this population.
   b) If the annual death rate in 1990 was 2.4%, how many people died in that year?
   c) Given an annual birth rate of 3.1% for 1990, how many babies were born in that year?
   d) What can you predict from these figures about future trends in:
      (i) population size,
      (ii) age structure?

2 Copy and complete the table below.

BIRTH CONTROL DEVICE	ADVANTAGES	DISADVANTAGES
a) Rhythm method	Doesn't interfere with metabolic processes	Only 80–85% Detailed records of menstrual cycle must be kept
b) Cap		
c) Condom		
d) Intra-uterine device (IUD)		
e) Spermicide		
f) Contraceptive pill		
g) Vasectomy		
h) Tubal ligation		

3 *'Humans are one of the most successful mammals that ever lived.'*
   Discuss this statement and suggest reasons for the biological success of the human species.

4 Describe increases in the human population since 1500 AD.
   What factors have increased the carrying capacity of the human environment?
   Outline some of the possible scenarios that might affect world human population in the future.

5 What do you understand by the terms '*age structure*', '*survivorship*' and '*urbanisation*'? How do human age structure and survivorship of human populations differ in different parts of the world?
   Describe some of the (a) causes, and (b) environmental consequences, of urbanisation.

6 Review different methods of birth control, referring to the advantages and disadvantages of each method. In addition to birth control, what other measures could be adopted to ensure that future generations do not exceed the carrying capacity of their environment?

7 Do you think that a policy of enforced birth control is acceptable?
   Try to find out about the birth control policies adopted by different countries and discuss their advantages and disadvantages.

BIBLIOGRAPHY

Beaujeau-Garnier, J (1966) *The Geography of Populations* Longman

Dasman, R F (1984) *Environmental Conservation* Wiley

Goudie, A (1990) *The Human Impact on the Natural Environment* Blackwell

Holmes, J H (1976) *Man and the Environment: Regional Perspectives* Longman

Lebon, J H G (1963) *An Introduction to Human Geography* Hutchinson

Leong, G C and Morgan, G C (1972) *Human and Economic Geography* Oxford University Press

James, P E (1966) *A Geography of Man* Ginn

Tivy, J and O'Hare, G (1989) *Human Impact on the Ecosystem* Oliver and Boyd.

AGRICULTURE

As human population increases, more food needs to be produced to satisfy demand. In industrialised countries, the availability of food has steadily increased over the last century. This is largely the result of advances in scientific knowledge, better farming techniques, and the selective breeding of crop plants and livestock. For high crop yields, farmers and growers must maintain their soil in a fertile condition, and control pests which would otherwise substantially reduce yields. In addition to the land, ponds, lakes, rivers and oceans can also be farmed to increase their natural output of fish, 'shellfish' (such as molluscs and crustaceans) or edible water plants.

5.1 SOIL CULTIVATION

Cultivated soils, the products of horticultural and agricultural practices, have been produced by human activity on soils that were originally covered by, for example, deciduous forests or grassland. The discovery that turning and mixing the soil improved crop yield was made thousands of years ago. Not only does digging or ploughing mix particles of different sizes, it also returns mineral nutrients to upper regions of the soil. Furthermore, enrichment of the soil by adding humus, mineral nutrients and lime helps to counteract the effects of leaching.

Soil constituents

A good cultivated soil, such as on a farm or in a garden, has seven essential constituents: mineral particles, mineral salts, humus, air, water, invertebrates and micro-organisms.

Mineral particles are formed from bedrock. Soils of siliceous origin may contain particles of different sizes, ranging from those that are less than 0.002 mm (clay) in diameter, to those that are greater than 2.0 mm (gravel). A sandy soil consists predominantly of coarse particles. It is light and easy to dig. Although well drained in winter, it tends to be hot and dry in summer, subject to erosion by wind. Rain, with dissolved CO_2, tends to leach out mineral salts from its upper layers, causing a fall in pH. By contrast, clay soils are heavy and difficult to work. They

retain both mineral salts and water. Waterlogging in winter (which retards plant growth) and cracking in summer are additional disadvantages of clay soils. Ideally, a good cultivated soil contains sand and clay particles, in a mixture known as **loam**. While retaining the desirable features of both sands and clays, a loam shows few, if any, of their disadvantages.

Mineral salts are released from the bedrock as it weathers, and from organic matter as it is decomposed by bacteria and fungi. For optimal growth, crop plants require relatively large amounts of seven **macro-nutrients**, together with much smaller quantities of seven **micro-nutrients**, or **trace elements**. These essential elements are listed in Table 1. Closely associated with the mineral ion content of a soil is the **hydrogen ion concentration**, or **pH**. Figure 1 shows how the pH influences the availability of cations to the roots of vascular plants. Maximum availability of most essential elements occurs at about pH 5.5, or in weakly acid soils. In soils that are more acid or alkaline, the availability of some ions is reduced. For most crop plants therefore, optimal yields are obtained when pH is maintained within the range 5.5–6.0.

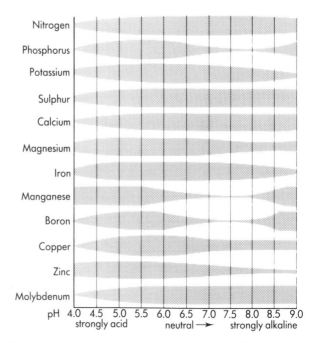

Figure 1 Influence of pH on the availability of plant nutrients in organic soils; widest parts of the shaded areas indicate maximum of availability

Table 1 Essential elements for most higher plants
(Note that some authors list iron as a micro-nutrient)

MACRO-NUTRIENTS	MICRO-NUTRIENTS
Nitrogen	Chlorine
Potassium	Boron
Calcium	Manganese
Magnesium	Zinc
Phosphorus	Copper
Sulphur	Molybdenum
Iron	Cobalt

Humus, an intermediate product in the breakdown of organic matter, binds with mineral particles to form a loose and crumbly structure, favourable for the growth of plant roots. Its presence in the soil binds soil particles, increases air content, and improves water-holding capacity. Agricultural practices frequently cause the fertility of the soil to decline. The process of harvesting fully grown crops and then removing them from the site on which they grew means that mineral salts are extracted from the soil and not replaced. In the absence of humus, the soil becomes harder and more compacted. Ploughing becomes more difficult, the soil loses its water-holding capacity, and roots become restricted in their growth. To remedy this, the farmer can apply farmyard manure or compost, which are broken down to produce humus.

(a) *Small, rounded particles*   (b) *Large, rounded particles*

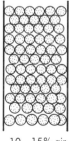
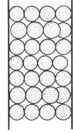

10 – 15% air   20 – 25% air

(c) *Irregularly shaped particles*   (d) *Aggregates of mineral particles and humus*

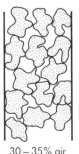

30 – 35% air   40 – 60% air

Figure 2 Effects of particle size, shape and arrangement on the air content of soil

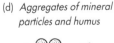

The **living organisms** that contribute to soil fertility are chiefly micro-organisms and invertebrates. Listing these organisms in functional groups, as decomposers, detritivores, herbivores, carnivores and omnivores, simplifies the description of a heterogenous group. Bacteria and fungi are the principal decomposers of plant litter and animal carcasses, recycling materials derived from them such as CO_2, water and mineral salts. Detritivores scavenge dead organic material, usually after it has been conditioned by micro-organisms. This activity by millipedes, woodlice and mites shreds dead leaves, softens them and

Earthworm, a detritivore

Snail, a herbivore

increases their nitrogen content relative to other contents. The common earthworm, (*Lumbricus terrestris*), lives in burrows. It pulls leaves and other plant material into the mouth of its burrow before feeding on it. During feeding, it also ingests insoluble mineral particles. These two components of a soil are mixed in the earthworm's alimentary canal, then transported through the soil, often to be deposited at the surface in the form of 'worm casts'. The leaf litter is shredded, softened and partly digested as it passes through the alimentary canal. As a result, fungi and bacteria can more readily decompose organic material subjected to this treatment. The calciferous glands of earthworms secrete calcium carbonate which helps to neutralise the acidity of humus. Burrows made by earthworms improve soil drainage, bringing oxygen to plant roots. Soil herbivores include slugs, snails and the larvae of several flies, beetles and moths. Centipedes, spiders and carabid beetles are the principal carnivores. Finally, a number of mites and insects are omnivores, feeding on plants and other soft-bodied soil invertebrates.

Maintaining soil fertility

The fertility of agricultural soils must be maintained because the soils rapidly deteriorate if neglected. **Digging** by hand was the first innovation to result in better yields because turning the soil and burying weeds created a loose, well aerated top layer into which seeds could be sown. As the seeds grew into seedlings, buried organic matter decomposed to form humus from which mineral salts were slowly released. Autumn digging, assisted by winter frosts, broke up solid clods of earth into a more crumbly and manageable soil for spring sowing. As agricultural techniques improved, digging gave way to **ploughing**, a more rapid method of turning soil, initially dependent on the labour of horses or oxen. It was relatively late in the scientific-industrial revolution when ploughing eventually became mechanised. Petrol-driven trators pulled high speed ploughs, thereby reducing both the time required for soil cultivation and the manpower. At about the same time, tractor-drawn harrows, rakes and hoes were used to increase the area of soil under cultivation, again speeding up the process of soil preparation.

Liming, applying a mixture of calcium carbonate and calcium hydroxide to soil, is an ancient practice which can improve soil fertility in any of the following ways.
   (i) It neutralises soil acidity and supplies Ca^{2+} ions to plants.
   (ii) It encourages colonisation of the soil by earthworms, and by nitrifying bacteria responsible for the formation of nitrates

from other nitrogen-containing compounds.
(iii) It binds small wet clay particles into aggregates, promoting the formation of an aerated crumb structure.
(iv) It binds sand particles, chiefly as they dry out, acting like cement to hold the particles together. This effect is of greatest importance in exposed regions, where soil particles may be removed by wind erosion.

Both ancient and modern agricultural practice is characterised by **plant monoculture**, the simultaneous growth of large numbers of crop plants of similar age and type within a defined area. It was soon discovered however that, if the same crop was grown on the same plot year after year, yields progressively declined. We now know that this decline results, in part, from mineral salt depletion. In addition, conditions for the crop plant's pests and parasites become ideal, especially for those that overwinter in the soil. The Romans found a simple practical solution to this problem by rotating their crops so that no crop was grown on the same strip of land for two years in succession. A three-year **crop rotation** was practised by Roman farmers (Figure 3a) in which legumes, which fix nitrogen, were grown as a key crop. Each field was left bare, or **fallowed**, after it had grown legumes, then manured before a cereal crop was sown in the following spring. The Roman system persisted essentially unchanged throughout medieval times, but it was gradually replaced during the eighteenth century by other systems. One of these, the Norfolk rotation, was a four-year crop rotation which eliminated fallowing. The crop of legumes grown in year 4, together with manuring, supplied sufficient nutrients for crops of wheat, barley, roots or potatoes (Figure 3b).

(a) *Roman system*

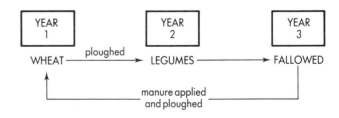

(b) *Norfolk system*

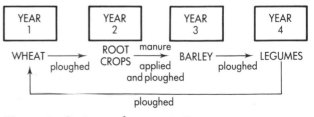

Figure 3 Systems of crop rotation

5.2 FERTILISERS

In most large ecosystems, such as woodlands, the fertility of the soil does not decline. The mineral nutrients extracted by growing plants are returned to the soil when the plants die and decompose to be absorbed again by plants of the next generation. This is in marked contrast to what happens in an agro-ecosystem where crop plants are grown for maximum productivity: at harvest, the plants are removed from the site on which they grew, together with the mineral salts they contain. If nothing is done to replace these losses, succeeding crops suffer mineral deficiencies and become more prone to diseases. Therefore, only by replenishing the soil with a fresh supply of mineral salts applied as a **fertiliser** after harvest, can productivity of the land be maintained.

Research has shown that the best crop yields are obtained when farmers and growers use a combination of organic and inorganic fertilisers. **Organic fertilisers** (decomposing plant or animal remains) change the physical characteristics of soils; they promote the formation of a porous, crumbly upper layer which is readily penetrated by plant roots. **Inorganic fertilisers** (a mixture of mineral salts) change the chemical properties of soils, chiefly by providing essential elements in the form of cations and anions.

Manures

Some of the most widely used organic fertilisers include farmyard manure, deep litter poultry manure, spent mushroom compost and

composted vegetation. These 'manures' add bulk to the soil, increase the amount of air present, and contribute soluble mineral salts. As they break down, all manures form humus, a vital component that increases soil fertility in many ways (Figure 4). Applying manure to soil has the following beneficial effects.

(i) Manures are generally complete fertilisers, containing all of the mineral ions necessary to prevent deficiency diseases.

(ii) The contain nitrogen in a variety of forms, some quick-acting and others remaining in the soil for longer periods of time. Manures are usually long-lasting in their effects. They steadily and continuously release nutrients into the soil following the breakdown of organic material by soil organisms.

(iii) They provide food for earthworms. The presence of earthworms has a desirable effect on soil structure and fertility; earthworms improve aeration, mix together organic and inorganic particles, and reduce the size of particles passing through their alimentary canals.

(iv) The growth of saprophytic bacteria and fungi, the soil's principal decomposers, is encouraged.

(v) The mechanical, physical and chemical properties of a soil are improved, following the development of a desirable crumb structure and increased water-holding capacity.

(vi) Crops grown with organic manures appear to be less prone to disease.

In contrast, organic manures have some disadvantages. Most are in short supply, bulky, difficult to handle and expensive. Furthermore, they are often too slow-acting to achieve any significant improvements in yield during a single growing season.

Organic (farmyard) manure

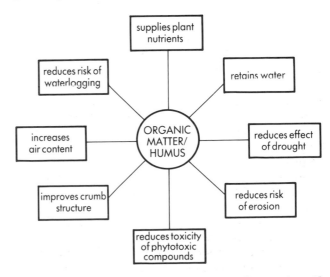

Figure 4   The effects of organic matter/humus in soil

Alternative approaches to organic manuring depend on the use of plants to produce so-called **biofertilisers**, e.g. growing legumes to enrich the soil with ammonium (NH_4^+) ions from bacterial activity in their root nodules. In a similar way, many cyanobacteria (blue-green algae) and the water fern (*Azolla*) can be used to fix nitrogen in aquatic agro-ecosystems. The practice of 'green manuring', used mainly by market gardeners and farmers, is roughly comparable in its effects on soil nitrogen status. A quick-growing crop, such as rape or turnips, is grown in the autumn, then ploughed into the soil before the winter. These young seedlings are rich in proteins and decompose before the following spring, enriching the soil with NH_4^+ and NO_3^- ions.

Chemical fertilisers

Inorganic fertilisers are mostly mixtures of mineral nutrients. They are formulated to provide essential elements in a water soluble form. As annual crops remove chiefly nitrogen, phosphorus and potassium from the soil, a common practice is to apply a **N-P-K fertiliser**, containing a mixture of salts of these elements. Inorganic fertilisers are relatively easy to apply, are required in fairly small amounts (e.g. 4–12 kg/hectare) and are generally quick-acting. Applied to most soils, they will stimulate plant growth immediately and lead to increased yields. Indeed, the rapid stimulatory effects of these fertilisers cannot be overemphasised for they have already been a major factor in doubling or trebling crop yields. The excessive or indiscriminate use of inorganic fertilisers however can have a number of disadvantages.

(i) They do not improve the physical character of soils. In addition, they have no power to promote the formation of a crumb structure, or to increase water-holding capacity.

(ii) They are rapidly removed from the soil. In addition to the fraction taken up by plant roots (15–20%), another fraction is lost as gas to the atmosphere (10–20%) following chemical reactions. In regions of high rainfall, a third fraction (25–35%) may be leached from the top soil and carried downward to levels that are out of range of plant roots.

(iii) The indiscriminate use of nitrogen-containing fertilisers may pollute water supplies and pose a threat to human health. If heavy rain washes fertiliser into rivers, ponds and lakes, the first effect may be an 'algal bloom' as algae increase in numbers stimulated by abundant nutrients. At this stage the water may become green, viscous and slow flowing. The short lived algae soon begin to die, turning yellow-brown as they are decomposed by saprophytic bacteria and fungi. These large populations of saprophytes deplete the water of oxygen so that fish and other oxygen-requiring species may die of suffocation.

This increase of nitrates and other nutrients in natural waters is called **eutrophication**. In the final stage of this process, anaerobic bacteria in the water may reduce nitrate (NO_3^-) to nitrite (NO_2^-); both nitrates and nitrites are toxic compounds. In view of their toxicity, the EEC has set a limit of 11.3 ppm total nitrogen in drinking water, a figure that has been exceeded in parts of the UK, notably East Anglia. Above this level, nitrites especially pose a threat to human health. In reactions taking place mainly in the stomach, they may be converted into highly carcinogenic substances called nitrosoamines. A second risk is to infants up to three months old: nitrites oxidise ferrous iron in haemoglobin into ferric iron, thereby reducing the oxygen-carrying capacity of the blood's red pigment. The result is methaemoglobinaemia, a condition in which babies turn blue because there is insufficient haemoglobin available for oxygen transport.

A bag of artificial (inorganic) fertiliser

5.3 WEEDS AND PESTS

Efficient crop plant monoculture on cultivated soils may be thwarted by two groups of unwanted organisms, namely weeds and pests. Both have been encouraged by human activities, and both can seriously reduce crop yields, even on soils that have been cultivated to perfection.

Weeds

Weeds are native plants found growing in the wild that colonise cultivated soils. Among their more important characteristics are short life cycles, high seed production, tolerance of extreme environmental conditions, and rapid vegetative reproduction. Many are well adapted to open, exposed, nutrient-deficient and physically stressed conditions. Biologists recognise several different types of weed, grouped according to their particular adaptations:

(i) **Fast-growing weeds** of cultivated soil (e.g dandelion, dock, chickweed). These weeds compete with crops for mineral salts, water and light. Some may eventually grow to a greater height than the crop, shading it from sunlight. A number of these weeds harbour pests, such as aphids, which may attack the crop; others restrict crop growth by releasing growth retardants from their roots or leaves. Attempts to remove these weeds by digging often fail because many can regenerate complete daughter plants from leaf, stem or root fragments.

(ii) **Tall weeds** of cereal crops (e.g. poppy) of which the seeds contaminate the grain harvest.

(iii) **Inedible weeds** of fields and meadows (e.g. stinging nettle, thistle). These may be toxic to sheep and cattle or less nutritious than grass.

(iv) **Low-growing weeds** of lawns (e.g. daisy, clover) that spoil the appearance of a lawn and make it less hard-wearing.

(v) **Spreading weeds** of lakes and waterways (e.g. Canadian pondweed, pondweed) that cause silting up, with loss of fish or other forms of animal life, or blockage of water channels.

Hoeing, to remove weed seedlings before they get a hold, is the traditional method of weed control. It works quite well in gardens but is laborious, slow and expensive if applied to field crops covering large areas. **Flame gunning** is an alternative. The operator walks between rows of crop plants, burning weed seedlings with a broad fanned flame that emerges from the nozzle of a paraffin-burning flame gun.

A significant advance in weed control was made during the 1940s. It was found that synthetic auxin-like substances (phenoxy compounds) could be used to kill broad leaved weeds. The two main phenoxy herbicides are 2,4–D and 2,4,5–T, the former used against herbs and the latter against shrubs. Both are **selective herbicides**, lethal to dicotyledons, but not to monocotyledons such as grasses or cereals. For this reason, they are sprayed over meadows and cereal crops to eradicate broad leaved weeds. The stems of treated dicotyledons elongate, coil and fail to open their terminal buds or leaflets. Secondary roots grow in abundance; mature leaves curl and blacken. At the cellular level, permanent tissues become meristematic, forming new growth which interferes with the translocation of materials in both the xylem and the phloem.

Other herbicides, known as **contact herbicides**, destroy only the plant tissues they actually touch. Sulphuric acid and sodium chlorate are examples. Dissolved in water to form a solution, sodium chlorate is effective in clearing ground of weeds, but it has two major disadvantages:

(i) dry vegetation killed by this compound

Poppies are weeds of cornfields

Spraying herbicide on a crop

becomes highly inflammable, exploding in flames if ignited;

(ii) soils treated with sodium chlorate cannot be resown with crops for several years because the compound inhibits seed germination and plant growth.

These problems can be solved by using paraquat, a contact weedkiller that is rapidly broken down and rendered ineffective by soil bacteria. For example, if used to remove weeds from future garden site, the ground can be dug and planted with crops only 3–4 weeks after treatment. The usefulness of this compound however, is partly offset by its extreme toxicity to humans and to other vertebrates. For humans, one teaspoon is a lethal dose and there is no known antidote. Furthermore, absorption through the skin, following splashes onto clothing, has resulted in some fatalities, with victims suffering progressive shrinkage of their lungs over a period of 2–3 weeks.

One significant outcome of the large scale use of selective herbicides has been an increase in **herbicide-resistant weeds**. These plants, which either always existed in the population or arose through mutation, synthesise enzymes which break down the herbicide and render it ineffective. A current aim of genetic engineers is to transfer genes for herbicide resistance from weeds into dicotyledonous crop plants. This, in theory at least, would make many crops resistant to herbicides, and would allow farmers to apply herbicides to these crops for effective weed control. Another possible scenario however is that the increased selective pressures resulting from increased herbicide application could generate 'super-resistant' weeds, thereby defeating the plans of the genetic engineers.

Pests

Pests are the fungal and animal counterparts of weeds. **Parasitic fungi** such as the late blight of potatoes are adapted to obtain their nutrients from crops by interfering with their metabolic processes. As a result, photosynthetic activity is impaired and yields are reduced. **Animal pests** are a more diverse group. **Standing crops** are attacked by many animal pests, especially insects, molluscs, pigeons, rabbits and deer. All parts of the plant are vulnerable to attack at some stage of their development. Freshly sown seeds such as peas may be dug up and eaten by magpies and mice. Wood pigeons pluck newly planted seedlings from the ground. The foliage of mature plants may be perforated by caterpillars or slugs, or stripped by larger animals such as rabbits. Small birds, including sparrows and chaffinches, eat flower buds and peck into the seed pods of legumes. Larger birds, such thrushes and blackbirds, eat raspberries, strawberries, cherries and other soft fruits. Pests of standing timber eat buds and leaves, uproot saplings, gnaw bark or bore into wood, destroying its commercial value. Even seasoned timber has its pests; old wooden furnishings in and around houses may be attacked by furniture beetles whose larvae feed on dry wood.

Stored crops may also be attacked and ruined by animal pests. Grain weevils and flour beetles attack stored cereal grains, eating most of them and contaminating others with their droppings. Potatoes, turnips and other 'root crops' may be gnawed by rats and mice, or pitted by burrowing slugs, millipedes and woodlice.

A fourth group of animal pests that bite, sting or crawl over food are vectors of disease, either by puncturing the skin and injecting disease-causing micro-organisms into the blood stream, or by spreading pathogenic bacteria onto food. These animals therefore constitute a hazard to health. Throughout the UK, the health risk from these pests is greatest during the summer months when wasps, mosquitoes and houseflies are on the wing.

Every year, about one quarter of total world crop production is destroyed by pests. Two general approaches to the problem of pest control have been adopted:

(i) **chemical control**, using toxic manufactured agents known as pesticides;

(ii) **biological control**, by promoting the natural predators and parasites of the pest.

Pesticides

Pesticides are an important group of agricultural chemicals (agrochemicals) that have been very effective in controlling many pests. In addition to herbicides, the term 'pesticide' covers insecticides, fungicides, ascaricides (used to kill spiders and mites), nematocides (used to kill nematode worms), molluscicides and rodenticides. Every year in the UK more than 4500 million litres of liquid pesticides are sprayed over crops. The general practice is to mix the pesticide with a surfactant to wet the leaf surfaces, a 'sticker' to make it adhere to leaf surfaces, and a synergist to enhance the effectiveness of the bioactive ingredient. An ideal pesticide is effective at low dosage against its specific target; it is also inexpensive to manufacture, non-polluting, plentiful and easy to apply. Any breakdown products should be harmless to non-target organisms in the air, soil and water. Although the use of chemical pesticides has generally brought enormous benefits in terms of increased food production, few, if any, have proved entirely beneficial in their effects. Indeed, pesticide manufacture and use has been dogged by three problems: environmental pollution, pest tolerance and harmful residues. According to Oxfam, 375 000 people in the Third World are poisoned every year by pesticides, 10 000 fatally.

Insecticides, fungicides and molluscicides are among the most widely used pesticides (Table 2).

Insecticides are used to control harmful insects. Early insecticides were mainly of three kinds: stomach poisons, tar oils and plant extracts. Stomach poisons were salts of heavy metals, effective after hydrolysis in an insect's alimentary canal. Tar oils were sprayed onto trees during the winter, chiefly to kill overwintering insects but also to prevent insects from climbing trees from the soil. Plant extracts containing pyrethrum (from the disc florets of an African daisy) and nicotine (from tobacco plants) were widely used in the 1950s and 1960s. The active chemicals in these compounds were enzyme inhibitors, paralysing an insect's nervous system or blocking its respiratory chain.

Since the 1940s, there have been three main trends in insecticide manufacture. The manufacturers have shifted from chlorinated hydrocarbon compounds to organophosphate compounds and then, most recently, to carbamates.

(i) **Chlorinated hydrocarbon compounds (organochlorines)** (e.g. DDT, dieldrin, aldrin) were applied as emulsions or dusted onto plants in the form of a powder. They were extremely effective against insects but very persistent, remaining in the soil for many years after application. Research into the ecological effects of DDT showed that it tended to accumulate in the fat deposits of animals where it acted as an inhibitor of cytochrome oxidase. Furthermore, DDT was concentrated along food chains because animals could not excrete the compound (Figure 5). Birds seemed particularly vulnerable, with birds of prey showing the most severe symptoms of poisoning. Many died, while others produced thin-shelled eggs which failed to hatch. When it became clear that DDT posed a threat to useful animals, and to humans themselves, further use of this insecticide was prohibited.

Table 2   Chemical pesticides

GROUP	EXAMPLES	
Insecticides	PLANT EXTRACTS	Nicotine
		Pyrethrum
	ORGANOCHLORINES	DDT
		Dieldrin
	ORGANOPHOSPHATES	Malathion
		Diazinon
	CARBAMATES	Carbaryl
		Propoxur
Fungicides	Captan	
	Benomyl	
Molluscicides	Metaldehyde	
	Methiocarb	
Rodenticide	Coumatetralyl	

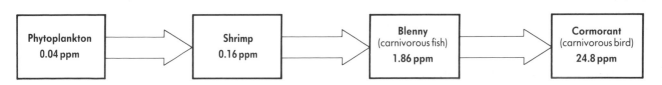

Figure 5   The concentration of DDT through a food chain (concentrations are ppm dry mass)

(ii) **Organophosphate compounds** (e.g. malathion, diazinon) inhibit the enzyme acetycholinesterase in the nervous system. Extremely toxic to insects and to humans, this group of compounds found favour because they were less persistent than the organochlorines, and less likely to accumulate along food chains.

(iii) **Carbamates** (e.g. carbaryl, propoxur, aldicarb) are organic nitrogen compounds that also inhibit acetylcholinesterase. These compounds do not leave long lasting residues in the environment. Carbaryl is only moderately toxic to humans but can be lethal to non-target organisms, especially bees.

During the last 50 years, some of the disadvantages of using insecticides have become clear:

(i) A number of insect pests have become genetically resistant to the three main groups of insecticides as a result of enormous selection pressures exerted on pest populations by their extensive use. This has necessitated a constant search for new insecticides, as potent as those already in use yet chemically unrelated.

(ii) Useful insects may be killed by insecticides. Bees are particularly vulnerable. Whenever bee populations are reduced by insecticides, there may be a related failure in cross-pollination, resulting in reduced yields of soft fruits, beans, peas and tomatoes.

(iii) The natural enemies of the pest (its parasites and predators) may be killed by the insecticide, so that the pest population may no longer be subject to biological control. This may result in the emergence of 'secondary pests' – organisms that were never sufficiently abundant to be pests before the insecticide was used. e.g. the emergence of a spider mite as a pest of apple orchards followed the use of malathion to control aphid and other pests. The insecticide also destroyed natural predators to the mite, allowing it to increase its numbers. Enormous numbers of these mites fed on mesophyll cells of leaves and reduced them to leaf skeletons.

(iv) The accumulation of insecticides along food chains poses a threat to human health. Humans are at the end of many food chains, both terrestrial and aquatic.

Fungicides, sprayed over the leaves of crops or onto soil, kill parasitic fungi. Bordeaux mixture, formulated from copper (II) sulphate and lime, is still widely used to treat late blight of potatoes and to spray fruit trees. Modern fungicides used in the field often contain compounds of heavy metals, highly effective in killing fungi but toxic to animals and humans within 1–3 weeks of application. Systemic fungicides, such as benomyl, are safer. These compounds, absorbed by plant roots and circulated within the vascular system of the plant, are often effective in preventing the spread of fungal infection. This helps the plant's own defence system.

Molluscicides are used to control slugs and snails. Metaldehyde, which causes dehydration following secretion of copious amounts of mucus, is the active ingredient in most slug pellets. It is mixed with bran or bean meal so that molluscs will ingest it with these foods.

Biological control

Biological control involves the use of one organism, or its products, to regulate the numbers of another. It is advantageous in that the control achieved is often species-specific; other related organisms present in the locality are not affected. In certain circumstances, unwanted plants and animals can be controlled by those animals that normally feed on them, or by their natural parasites. Herbivores, especially insects, may be used to control unwanted plants. For example, the introduction of prickly pear cactus into Australia was followed by the rapid spread of the plant which, in 1925, covered thousands of square miles. Effective control was achieved by introducing larvae of the *Cactoblastis* moth. By boring holes in the stem of the plant, this insect provided a point of entry for parasitic fungi to attack and kill the cacti.

Carnivores may be used to control herbivores. This type of control in the UK is largely restricted to insect pests in glasshouses. A good example is the regulation of aphids on tomatoes and lettuces by ladybirds. Less well known is regulation of the greenhouse whitefly *Trialeurodes vaporariorum* by a parasitic wasp, *Encarsia formosa*. The red spider mite *Tetranychus urticae* is controlled by a larger predatory mite *Phytoseiulus persimilis*, originally imported from Chile. Biological control of this type is never fully effective but it generally helps to keep the number of pests in check, making the use of toxic pesticides unnecessary. Parasitic micro-organisms provide an alternative means of biological control. The bacterium *Bacilllus thuringensis* attacks the caterpillars of butterflies and moths, causing fatal disease. This organism has been mass cultured and marketed in dried, powdered form. Mixed with water, and applied to cabbages, it provides a specific treatment against cabbage white caterpillars.

A second approach to biological control involves disrupting the breeding of pest species, notably insects. One way of doing this is by modifying the action of growth hormones. Three hormones, brain hormone, ecdysone and juvenile hormone, regulate the growth of insects. Juvenile hormone keeps an insect in its larval or nymphal state, preventing metamorphosis to the adult form. Ecdysone regulates moulting. By feeding a chemical analogue of insect juvenile hormone to cattle, fly and mosquito larvae that normally feed on cattle droppings have been kept in their larval state. This has reduced the numbers of flies and mosquitoes in and around cattle sheds. Another technique for disrupting the life cycles of insect pests can be applied only to insects that mate once in their lives. Males are bred in the laboratory, irradiated or treated with chemicals to kill their sperm, then released into the wild. Any females that mate with these males will produce infertile eggs. The technique has been applied with good effect to the screw worm fly, a parasite of cattle, in the southern United States. Mosquitoes, boll weevils, sheep blowflies and tsetse flies are other pests that could be controlled this way.

A third approach to biological control is through the use of behaviour-controlling compounds, acting primarily on sense receptors of smell or taste. These compounds include **pheromones**, compounds that affect interactions between members of the same species. Pheromones are produced by many different insects. For example, a female moth or butterfly emits a sex pheromone, attracting males to her for mating. Males may be attracted from 1–3 kilometres downwind of the female. An ingenious method of pest control has been based on this response: male pea moths, attracted to a synthetic sex attractant ((E)–10–dodecanyl acetate) in a trap, are caught on a sticky material on the floor of the trap (Figure 6). A similar method has been used to catch gipsy moths, a pest of coniferous forests.

5.4 CROP AND LIVESTOCK IMPROVEMENT

Previous sections have described how the input of fertilisers and pesticides has improved crop yields. These inputs can be thought of as supplementing the input of solar energy because their manufacture involves consumption of energy in the form of fuel to drive machinery. An alternative approach involves the selection and breeding of high yielding plants and animals. These organisms are efficient converters of energy, with the ability to utilise a high proportion of the sunlight, or food, that the environment provides, and convert it into their own biomass.

Crops

Selective breeding has been used for many years to produce new varieties of crop plants from existing ones. Higher yields, larger size, improved appearance, enhanced flavour and a longer shelf life have been among the primary objectives of selective breeding programmes. However, some plants, such as strawberries and potatoes, have been bred for their resistance to disease. Others, including sweetcorn and grapes, have been bred for more rapid growth and shorter annual cycles so that crops may be successfully harvested in more northerly latitudes. Frost-resistant tomatoes are a relatively recent introduction, as are thornless blackberries, and cucumbers from which the bitter-tasting component has been eliminated. Pea growers can take advantage of a

'Leafless' pea supported by intertwined tendrils

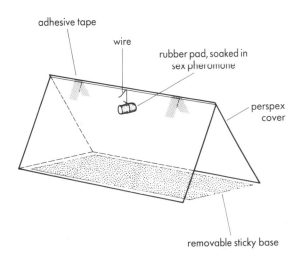

adhesive tape

wire

rubber pad, soaked in sex pheromone

perspex cover

removable sticky base

Figure 6   A pea moth trap

leafless pea, with a large number of robust tendrils; when planted in fields this pea clings to other plants, forming a self-supporting crop, without the need for additional support from pea sticks. With mechanised harvesting, farmers have favoured short-stemmed wheats, and peas which produce pods at the same time along the entire length of their stems.

Genetic engineering offers a means by which genes may be transferred from one plant to another. When existing techniques are perfected, it should be possible to transfer desirable genetic traits, such as the ability to fix atmospheric nitrogen, disease resistance, drought resistance, better fertiliser utilisation, herbicide resistance etc. into crop plants. **Micro-propagation**, in which large numbers of daughter plants are grown from sterilised meristems on nutrient agar, is another promising new technique. The heat treatment of meristem cultures has been used to eliminate viral infections from strains of strawberries, potatoes and other crops. More importantly, very large numbers of genetically identical daughter plants have been produced from a single parent. This technique, called **cloning**, has greatly reduced the time required for large numbers of a desirable new variety to become generally available to farmers and growers.

Livestock

Animal breeders have concentrated on meat production, with particular reference to **protein conversion rates**:

$$\text{Protein conversion efficiency} = \frac{\text{Mass of protein produced}}{\text{Mass of protein consumed}}$$

Although cattle and sheep have relatively low protein conversion efficiencies, they can be maintained on diets composed of plant materials high in cellulose which cannot be digested by humans. Pigs and poultry, with higher protein efficiencies, nevertheless have to be fed diets containing more protein.

In the future, the quality of farm animals may be improved by novel breeding methods. **Embryo manipulation** has made it possible for farmers to obtain more offspring from their livestock. Female sheep and cattle produce, on average, one offspring per pregnancy; twins are rare. The relatively simple technique of bisecting the fertilised egg at the two-celled stage and transplanting each half into different regions of the uterus has almost doubled the reproductive rate. Among treated animals, twin births become the rule and not the exception. The technique of **embryo surgery** used to produce twin births is currently being extended to help conserve rare breeds. After fertilising their eggs in the laboratory, the young embryos of rare animals are dissected into anything from 2–8 cells. Each cell, successfully transplanted into a **surrogate mother** of a common breed, grows to produce a new individual of the rare type. Another variation of the technique allows surrogate mothers to carry embryos of a different species.

Bovine somatotrophin (BST), also called growth hormone, is a natural protein hormone produced by a cow's pituitary gland. The hormone has three different physiological effects:

  (i) it stimulates growth,

 (ii) it affects the balance between fat and carbohydrate metabolism,

(iii) it increases milk production, partly by boosting food intake, but also by diverting a larger proportion of the cow's food into milk production.

During the 1970s, genetic engineers inserted the gene for BST into bacteria. As a result, large amounts of BST became available. Injected into cows, it was found to increase milk production by anything from 25–40%. The meat was also leaner, making it more attractive to the consumer.

The growth rates of cattle, sheep, pigs and poultry may also be considerably improved by **factory farming**. Productivity in these animals is increased by genetic selection, intensive feeding and the restriction of movement. Furthermore, chemical compounds may be added to food to promote growth and prevent disease. These compounds include antibiotics, hormones and colouring agents used to improve the appearance of meat or egg yolk. Common hormones used in factory farming are **anabolic agents (steroids)**. These are either synthetic androgens (male sex

Factory farming: chicken in battery cages

hormones) or oestrogens (female sex hormones). In sheep and cattle for example, a subcutaneous implant may be made 3–4 months before slaughter. The best results have been obtained by treating female animals with androgens, males with oestrogens and castrated animals with a mixture of the two compounds. Anabolic agents increase nitrogen retention and protein deposition. Androgens act directly on muscle cells, increasing protein synthesis and decreasing the rate of protein turnover. Oestrogens exert a less direct effect, acting chiefly through the secondary hormones GH and insulin. The greatest potential hazard of using anabolic agents is that chemical residues may be found in meat sold for human consumption. While levels of residues in treated meat do not normally exceed that in meat from untreated animals, there is still a possibility that continuous consumption of synthetic anabolic agents could exert a long term carcinogenic effect on the human population.

Whatever the ethics of factory farming practices, the results have been quite impressive. Egg production in poultry has been improved up to 80%; milk yields in cows have risen by about one third; and the time taken to produce animals for slaughter has been markedly reduced, sometimes by as much as one half.

5.5 FISH FARMING

Considerable attention has recently been focused on fish as a source of high quality protein. Fisheries supply around 25% of the world's protein and a livelihood for millions of people. Most of the fish eaten in the UK and in Europe are from 'free range' stocks, taken from the seas by traditional methods of fishing. As these natural stocks diminish, scientists are looking for novel methods of replenishing them. **Fish farming** is the deliberate cultivation of fresh water species, marine species and shellfish (crustaceans and molluscs). It has been practised in China for centuries. Satisfying European tastes has proved rather more difficult; Europeans are reluctant to eat fresh water fish, preferring natural stocks of marine species.

The protein conversion efficiencies of fish are high, partly because they do not maintain high body temperatures and partly because they live in a supporting aqueous medium. Two other biologically significant features of fishes are their relatively slow growth rates and enormous reproductive potential. The latter is rarely realised because large numbers die before reaching maturity. The bulk of the world's fish harvest is caught by highly mechanised **commercial fishing fleets**, using technology designed to maximise catches. In many cases, a large 'mother' factory

Traditional fishing, using a net

ship processes and packs the accumulated catches of a dozen or so auxiliary vessels. Consequently, in the face of such efficient catches, some seas have been fished to the point of depletion. In the North Atlantic, the herring has been fished to the verge of extinction and stocks of cod and haddock have been severely depleted. Furthermore, some natural populations of fish, such as plaice in the North Sea, have been greatly reduced by disease. It seems probable that this demise is at least partly related to increased pollution of the North Sea, used as a dumping ground for various industrial wastes.

During the 1980s shortages of herring, cod and haddock, combined with steep price rises, stimulated research into **intensive methods of fish farming**. One useful practice consists of collecting fish eggs, hatching them under laboratory conditions, and releasing the young fish when they are old enough to fend for themselves. For example, keeping plaice in the laboratory until they are about 10 cm long, greatly increased the numbers that survived to maturity. Another example is rearing salmon and lobsters in large fish tanks, feeding them on a protein-rich diet until they are large enough to be eaten. In fact, the intensive rearing of salmon by this method has been particularly successful, increasing the supplies and reducing the cost to the consumer.

Mussels are farmed in shallow river estuaries. One method is to use submerged ropes, threaded through plastic rings and supported by wooden stakes or frames. Plastic floats buoy up the ropes and mark their position. The mussels attach to the

A salmon fish farm

In the future it seems probable that salmon, cod, halibut and other types of fish will be farmed in ocean cages. An **ocean cage** is essentially a massive, mobile fish net, slung beneath a 4–5 sided floating aluminium support. The fish, retained by the mesh, are fed pelleted food from a central cabin, and allowed to grow for several years before they are harvested. If it is more convenient, the cage can be towed behind a ship to a position in the ocean where plankton is abundant, and this is allowed to enter the cage via the mesh. Fish cages large enough to hold 30,000–40,000 individuals are in operation, but when large numbers of fish are kept under these conditions they become particularly liable to parasitisation by sea lice. These parasites perforate the skin, cause loss of body fluids, and prevent the farmed fish from being sold in the open market. One treatment lies in the use of a toxic pesticide called 'Nuvan', while another depends on biological control by small fish called wrass. These wrass feed on sea lice, keeping the farmed species relatively untroubled by the parasite.

rope and remain attached to it as they grow. After 2–3 years, the mature mussels are harvested by cutting the ropes, removing the mussels, washing them, grading and despatching to the fish markets.

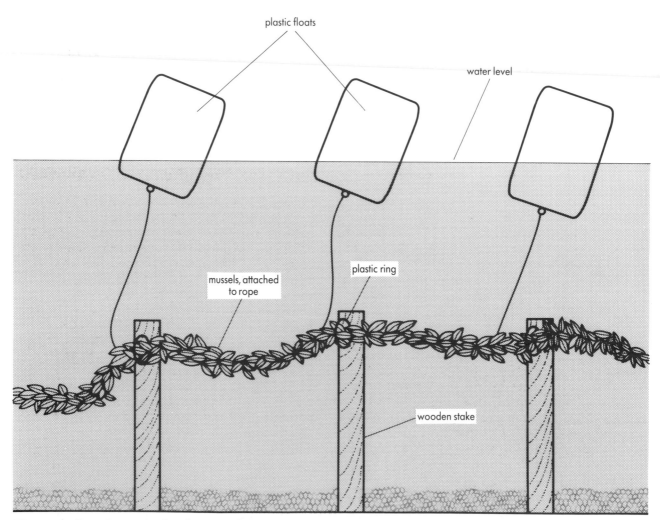

Figure 7 Farming mussels; the mussels grow attached to ropes, supported by wooden stakes and plastic floats

5.6 AGRICULTURAL ENGINEERING

The increasing yields and larger harvests that have characterised agriculture in parts of Europe, North America and Australia for much of the twentieth century have been obtained, in part, by **mechanisation**. Labour intensive processes such as harvesting crops, feeding animals, milking cows and preparing meat for the table were once carried out by hand but are now done by machines. A wide range of these machines has allowed the various jobs on a farm to be done more quickly, with lower production costs and generally less waste. For instance, combined harvesters cut, thresh and sack grain crops in a single operation. The mechanisation of crop protection measures means that yields can be increased by treating crops with fertilisers or insecticides, in immediate response to the first signs of possible crop failure.

Agricultural engineers, who design and manufacture farm machinery, work principally in the three main areas outlined below.

(i) **Vehicle manufacture**, including tractors, harvesters and four-wheel-drive vehicles for trekking over uneven, muddy surfaces.

(ii) **Farm organisation**, the design and layout of milking parlours, greenhouses, crop dryers, cow stalls, and pig and poultry houses. Most of these buildings now include computer control systems to regulate temperature, humidity and the rate at which food and water are suppiled to animals.

A modern milking parlour

(iii) **Field engineering**, including soil improvement mainly by drainage or irrigation. This work may also involve ploughing, transferring top soil to greenhouses, adding organic material or removing large stones.

Needless to say, the skills of agricultural engineers are particularly in demand in developing countries where food shortages and crop failures are most frequent.

QUESTIONS

1 a) Define each of the following terms in a way that clarifies the differences between them:
   (i) predator, (ii) prey, (ii) parasite, (iv) pest.
   b) What numerical relationship would normally exist between ladybirds (predator) and aphids (prey)?
   c) Copy and complete the table below.

GROUP	EXAMPLES	
	PESTS	PARASITES
Insects	(i) (ii)	(i) (ii) (iii)
Molluscs	(i) (ii)	
Fungi	(i) (ii) (iii)	(i) (ii) (iii)
Flowering plants	(i) (ii) (iii)	(i) (ii)

A combine harvester

d) Copy and complete the table below.

AGROCHEMICALS	EXAMPLES
Insecticide	(i)
	(ii)
	(iii)
	(iv)
Herbicide	(i)
	(ii)
	(iii)
	(iv)
Molluscicide	(i)

2 a) What is humus?
   b) Describe how you would determine the percentage of humus in a sample of soil.
   c) How may the humus content of agricultural soils be increased?
   d) Name three groups of micro-organisms which decompose humus.
   e) List five end products from the breakdown of humus.
   f) State four different ways in which the nitrogen (N) content of a soil may be increased. For each process, state one reason why it is effective.

3 List the constituents of a good agricultural (or garden) soil.
   Briefly explain the functions of each constituent in determining soil fertility.
   How may fertility be maintained in soils that are used to produce annual crops?

4 Describe the chemical composition of artificial fertilisers, and explain how they are applied to land used for agriculture or horticulture.
   What are the advantages and disadvantages of using artifical fertilisers?

5 Distinguish between:
   a) sand and clay,
   b) artificial fertilisers and manures,
   c) insecticides and herbicides,
   d) pests and parasites.

6 What are weeds?
   How do the weeds of cereal crops differ from those of lawns?
   Survey the range of herbicides (weedkillers) currently available to farmers and growers, referring to any environmental hazards that might result if they are misused.
   If all chemical weedkillers were banned, what alternatives could be used for weed control?

7 Explain the importance of insect herbivores to farmers and growers.

Review the use of chemical insecticides to control these insect pests.
What problems have arisen as a result of using chemical insecticides on crop plants?

8 What is meant by the 'biological control' of pests?
   Referring to specific examples, describe the advantages and disadvantages of this approach to pest control.
   What other methods can be used by growers of 'organic' fruit and vegetables to protect their crops?

9 List those factors that limit the productivity of wild fish stocks in the seas. How may fish farmers increase stocks of:
   a) fresh water fish,
   b) marine fish,
   c) marine molluscs or crustaceans?

BIBLIOGRAPHY

Addison, H (1961) *Land, Water and Food* Chapman and Hall

Bayliss-Smith, T P (1982) *The Ecology of Agricultural Systems* Cambridge University Press

Corbett, J R (1974) *Biochemical Mode of Action of Pesticides* Academic Press

Courtenay, P P (1965) *Plantation Agriculture* Neill and Co

Davidson, J and Wibberley, G (1977) *Planning and the Rural Environment* Pergamon

Green, M B, Hartley, G S and West, T E (1977) *Chemicals for Crop Protection and Pest Control* Pergamon

Gunn, D L and Stevens, J G R (1976) *Pesticides and Human Welfare* Oxford University Press

Horsfall, D (1983) *Agriculture* Blackwell

Huggett, R and Meyer, I (1980) *Agriculture* Harper and Row

Morgan, W B and Munton, R J C (1974) *Agricultural Geography* Methuen

Perring, F H and Mellanby, K (1977) *Ecological Effects of Pesticides* Academic Press

Russell, E W (1973) *Soil Conditions and Plant Growth* Longman

Schnitzer, M and Kahn, S U (1978) *Soil Organic Matter* Elsevier

Waites, B Wheeler, K S and Giggs, J A (1971) *Patterns and Problems in World Agriculture* Blond Educational.

6 ECOSYSTEM DISRUPTION AND CONSERVATION

Increases in the human population have resulted in land development at sites previously occupied entirely by wildlife. Ideally, humans need a place to live, a place to work and places for their recreation. This has led to debates about land use. Frequently wildlife suffers when land is used for farming, housing, industrial and recreational purposes. The conservation movement has grown from an awareness of the harm humans can do to their environment and to other species. It has both an ethical and aesthetic basis. Polluting the environment to the detriment of ourselves and other species is unethical, as is the indiscriminate extermination of wildlife by habitat destruction, collecting, hunting, trapping and other means. Conversely, the countryside and its wildlife offer a source of aesthetic pleasure, in an age when people have increasing amounts of time for leisure activites. Each ecosystem supports a community of plant and animals, interconnected by food webs. Destruction of any part of a habitat, or changes in the numbers of any species, poses a threat to wildlife and may cause the existing balance between organisms to change.

Deciduous and coniferous forests

Throughout the UK, deciduous and coniferous forests have been felled to provide land for agriculture, and the production of timber and wood pulp. Conifers are the principal source of wood pulp, which is used as a raw material in the manufacture of paper. Vast amounts of newspaper, and tissue paper of different types, are used every day. As very little of this paper is recycled by industry, forests are felled to keep pace with demand. Trees, the largest individual plants in terrestrial ecosystems, perform three major roles in the biological recycling of materials.

(i) **Carbon dioxide**, a raw material for photosynthesis, is removed from the atmosphere.

(ii) **Oxygen**, a byproduct of photosynthesis, is released into the atmosphere.

(iii) **Water**, as vapour, is returned to the atmosphere from the soil. Individual large deciduous trees, such as oaks, may transpire as much as 1000 dm^3 water per day during the summer.

Tree-felling on a large scale therefore increases the CO_2 content of the atmosphere, reduces its

6.1 ECOSYSTEM DISRUPTION

All human activities result in increases and decreases of other species which, as we have seen, are likely to alter the functioning of ecosystems. Those human activities that are currently having a major disruptive effect include deforestation, hedgerow clearance, drainage and burning. In this section we review some of the effects of these practices in the UK and consider the ecological consequences of ecosystem disruption in tropical rain forests.

Deforestation

Much of the earth's land surface was originally covered by forests. By felling trees and burning standing timber, humans have removed about 30–40% of this vegetation, replacing it with agricultural land, grassland and scrub.

Waste paper

oxygen content, and creates a drier atmosphere. Soil conditions may become wetter, as evaporation is generally slower than transpiration in returning water vapour to the atmosphere.

The leaf litter in coniferous and deciduous forests contains anything from 10–50% of the total organic material in the eosystem. If these forests are cut down, a substantial proportion of the nutrients remains in the soil. This means that soils cleared of deciduous trees are normally very fertile and suitable for immediate planting with crops. The soils of coniferous forests on the other hand are unsuitable for agricultural purposes, because pine needles contain toxic compounds which act as growth inhibitors.

Large scale deforestation in temperate zones has adverse effects on several animal populations. In parts of Europe for example, it has led to the virtual extinction of some large birds, wolves, bears and wild pigs. In Scotland, the osprey has become a rare bird after the felling of pine forests.

Tropical rain forests

Tropical rain forests cover approximately 10% of the Earth's surface. Large areas, covering millions of hectares, occur in South America, central Africa, South East Asia and Australia. Taken together, all of the world's rain forests carry out a significant fraction of global photosynthesis, mopping up carbon dioxide and releasing oxygen. The horizontal layering of vegetation in a rain forest bears a superficial resemblance to that seen in European deciduous woodlands. Large trees are understoreyed by smaller trees and shrubs. Here, however, the resemblance ends. Most of the large trees in the rain forest are old and sturdy, sometimes braced by buttress flanges. Yet they have shallow roots, covering an area below ground no wider than the tree's crown. Space above ground is crowded by the closeness of the large trees, whose densely packed branches shade the soil beneath. Further dense crowding of the smaller trees and shrubs virtually excludes light from the soil surface, which, in the absence of herbs, is covered at all times by a deep layer of leaf litter. This litter layer however, contains no more than around 10% of the total organic matter in the ecosystem. Total biomass per hectare may weigh from 400 to 600 tonnes, compared with about 200 tonnes in broad leaved deciduous woodlands. Throughout the rain forest, there is great species diversity. More than 100 different species of plant grow in a typical hectare. Animals too are abundant and taxonomically diverse. Most are herbivores (e.g. leaf-eating primates, elephants etc.) and litter feeders (e.g. millipedes, worms). The carnivores are mainly small birds and reptiles.

Progressive destruction of the world's tropical

Tropical rain forest

rain forests, by logging and burning, is a cause for international concern. In the period 1880-1980 some 40% of all tropical rain forests had gone. The current rate of destruction is estimated at about 6–10 million hectares per year. Destroying mature trees, to satisfy a runaway demand for timber, chip, paper and other wood products, has been widely practised in some third world countries as a means of paying off national debts. Among the first trees to suffer have been mahogany, teak and other hardwoods. Cropped areas may take from 30–50 years to regenerate. All available evidence suggests that the regenerated forest supports fewer plants and animals per hectare. Clearly, amounts of timber felled should never exceed the reproductive capacity of a species in a given area, or damage the ecological stability of the forest.

Slashing and burning to clear rain forest land for farming is currently the major cause of rain forest destruction. Economically important crops, including coffee, cocoa, tea, sugar, bananas, citrus fruits, pineapples, maize and peanuts can be grown in forest clearings, but only if the terrain is fairly flat and the soil is cultivated to maintain its fertility from year to year. When trees are burned, all of their mineral salts are released in a single pulse, and generally deposited as a pile of ash on the soil surface. Unless it is immediately dug into the soil, this ash is dispersed by heavy tropical rains, washed down hillsides and leached into rivers. Cleared areas may sustain a few generations of agricultural crops, but they soon become mineral-deficient, with crop failure as the inevitable result. Once the trees have been felled, they can no longer return water to the atmosphere by transpiration. Consequently, the soil becomes wetter, less compacted and more easily eroded. Digging or ploughing further loosens the topsoil, assisting the process of soil erosion by heavy rain. When crops fail through lack of nutrients, the cultivators move on, leaving barren patches of land physically unlike the rain forest ecosystem.

Beyond the local effects of rain forest destruction are its global effects, which affect everyone. Among the many trees and shrubs of the rain forest are some with medicinal properties. The Madagascan periwinkle, for example, yields an effective treatment for leukaemia. Other rain forest plants contain anticoagulants, heart stimulants, hormones, tranquillisers and antibiotics. The extinction of any plant species before their chemical properties have been investigated could amount to an incalculable loss. Large scale forest clearance may also affect

climatic conditions. If all the rain forests of the world were burned before the end of the century, atmospheric CO_2 would rise by some 15–20%, contributing significantly to the 'greenhouse effect' (see section 7.4). Furthermore, removing vegetation from parts of the world where the heat received on each hectare is greater than in any other part of the globe, would result in additional heat absorption by bare soil and raise the temperature of the lower atmosphere. This could result in more frequent and intense winds, an additional factor capable of destroying vegetation and accelerating erosion.

Hedgerow clearance

Anyone who has looked from an aeroplane must have noticed the neat system of hedgerows that cover much of the UK. These hedges are more than physical boundaries, separating grass from other crops or confining farm stock within certain areas. In many cases, hedges act as wind breaks, restricting soil erosion from ploughed fields and reducing wind damage to tall crops such as maize. In addition, hedges provide a habitat for wildlife. Approximately one third of our native flora grows in hedges. The variety of hedgerow plants increases with the age of the hedge. None of these plants however is particularly rare, so that a

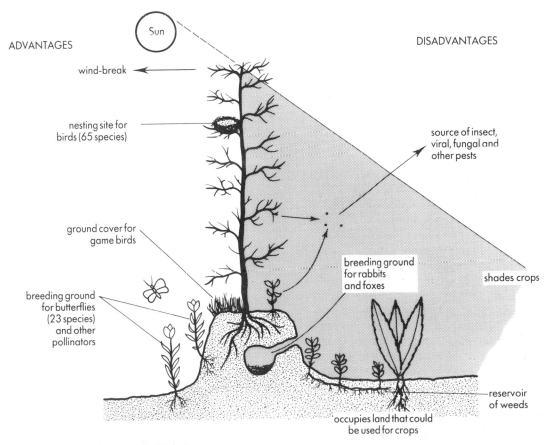

Figure 1   Some advantages and disadvantages of hedgerows

complete loss of hedgerows is unlikely to threaten any plant species with extinction. The position of animals would be more serious if hedges were to vanish. From 28 species of British lowland mammals, 21, including rabbits, foxes and badgers, breed beneath hedges. These hedges also provide the breeding grounds for 65 species of British birds and 23 different butterflies. These are mainly woodland species, using hedgerows as an alternative to the margins and scrub areas of woodland.

Throughout the twentieth century, farmers have carried out hedgerow destruction at the rate of around 8000 km or more per year. Hedgerows are difficult and expensive to maintain; hedge cutting, even with a flail cutter, is time-consuming. The hedge occupies land that could otherwise be used for growing crops. Furthermore, it casts a shade that reduces crop yield. More importantly, a hedge may contain a reservoir of pests and parasites, spreading outwards during the growing season to compete with, or attack, crops. Hedges harbour weeds. In certain parts of the UK, herbicide-resistant species such as cleavers (*Galium aparine*), cow parsley (*Anthriscus sylvestris*) and sterile brome grass (*Bromus sterilis*) are particularly troublesome. Broad bean aphids spread from spindle trees to attack bean crops in April to July. Crown rust spreads from buckthorn and fireblight, which attacks apples and pears, spreads from hawthorn.

You will see that there are powerful arguments for and against the retention of hedges. On balance, it seems most farmers will probably retain existing hedges, mainly for their landscape value and as game cover for pheasants and partridges. Where footpaths exist across farmland, hedges may serve the additional purpose of preventing walkers from trespassing across fields.

Draining wetlands

The soils of marshes, bogs and fens are mainly organic, formed from plant material in various stages of decomposition. Effective drainage of these habitats produces a fertile soil, suitable for growing cereals and vegetables. Beginning in Saxon times there has been widespread wetland destruction by conversion into farmland. The drainage of these wetlands has also been encouraged to destroy the breeding grounds of water-bourne parasites. These included the anopheline mosquito, responsible for transmitting human malaria in lowland regions of the UK until the early nineteenth century; and snails which acted as intermediary hosts in the transmission of 'liver rot' to sheep, caused by a fluke. During the industrial revolution, extension of the canal system, conversion of estuarine sites into ports, and the banking of rivers to prevent flooding,

Cutting peat in a blanket bog

contributed to wetland destruction. In Ireland, Russia and Canada, large areas of upland bogs have been destroyed by removal of peat for fuel, and for horticultural use as a soil conditioner. Needless to say, wetland destruction has led to a loss of many wetland species. Beavers, storks, cranes and spoonbills have vanished from the UK. At the present time, otter populations are under threat, declining rapidly in lowland areas, especially where water is polluted by human sewage. Swallow tail butterflies, once common throughout the fens, are now rare. Plants that have suffered a similar demise include the marsh gentian, a species found on wet heaths, and the lesser reedmace, found at the edges of lakes, ponds and slow-flowing rivers.

Fire

Fires, started by lightning or by human activities, are of two main types.

(i) **Surface fires** of grasslands and heathlands sweep rapidly over the ground, destroying the shoots of herbs and shrubs, together with surface deposits of litter.

(ii) **Crown fires** of coniferous and deciduous woodlands spread rapidly through the tree canopy. These fires are most likely to occur during prolonged summer droughts, when leaves are dry and covered by resins and sugary deposits.

Many heather-dominated heathlands throughout the UK are regularly burned in the spring or summer, some deliberately, others accidentally. **Controlled burning** is used to encourage the growth of young heather plants, an evergreen fodder for sheep and cattle, and the staple diet of the red grouse in the Scottish highlands. The principal effects of frequent burning are detrimental, and may be summarised as follows:

(i) loss of nutrients from the system,
(ii) initiation of soil erosion,
(iii) destruction of the surface organic soil layers,
(iv) reduction in the variability of the heather community,
(v) drastic modification of the micro-climate immediately above the soil surface,
(vi) an increase in bracken at the expense of heather, and the creation of conditions particularly suitable for birch seedlings.

Heather, gorse and bracken are **fire-resistant species (pyrophytes)**, capable of rapid regeneration after fires. Some part of each plant, usually below ground, sends out new shoots some weeks after the fire has passed. Heather has fire-resistant seeds, stimulated into germination by the heat of a fire (100–200°C).

A fifth major disruptive influence in ecosystems is **pollution**, the subject of chapter 7.

A heathland fire

6.2 ECOSYSTEM MODIFICATION

There are a number of human activities that often interfere with the functioning of ecosystems but rarely act as major disruptive influences. Activities of this type include road building, reservoir construction, quarrying and the introduction of foreign species.

New **roads and railways** cut across existing ecosystems, dividing them up into smaller areas. Some of these areas may not be large enough to support large carnivores. Furthermore, mammalian carnivores must cross busy roads to cover their territory, a factor that inevitably leads to some fatalities. Any marked reduction in the carnivore population may lead to an increase in the number of herbivores. There is evidence that populations of kestrels have increased along motorway verges, which are relatively undisturbed by humans. Throughout England and Wales, roadside verges cover an estimated 420 000 hectares. These man made ecosystems support more than 700 species of flowering plant and have become an important sanctuary for wildlife. Railway banks that border tracks also provide open wildlife habitats, relatively free from human disturbance. Typically, south-facing banks provide warm habitats for small mammals while north-facing banks provide cooler, moister conditions, ideal for mosses and ferns.

Reservoirs, built in response to the increasing demand for water, are often created by submerging terrestrial ecosystems. These large open areas of still water are particularly important for birdlife, notably as resting places for migrants. Fluctuations in the water level expose mud around the margins of most rservoirs. These areas provide an ideal habitat for mud ephemerals such as red goosefoot (*Chenopodium rubrum*) and common mudwort (*Limnosella aquatica*).

Land scarification describes unsightly earthworks such as quarries, sand pits and mine tips. **Open cast mining** probably causes most ecological damage because it completely removes the top layer of soil. Mine tips around copper, tin and lead mines generally contain toxic materials. Large heaps of subsoil may take from 20–25 years before they are covered by vegetation. Soil dumps, with soil transported from distant sites, may introduce new plant species into an area which then spread into the surrounding ecosystem and interfere with its function. The flora and fauna of these tips is generally sparse, with little species diversity.

Rubbish tips may have both short term and long term effects on the fauna of an ecosystem. Household rubbish, for example, attracts houseflies and their predators. Populations of rats and mice are also likely to increase because the rubbish provides suitable nesting sites as well as food.

Overgrazing in meadows by cattle and horses leads to an increase in weed species, notably coarse leaved thistles and ragwort (*Senecio jacobea*), which the animals will not eat. Goats are probably the most destructive of all grazers. Kept in a confined space, they will strip meadows of almost all their vegetation, including shrubs and young tree saplings.

The **importation of foreign species** usually has adverse effects on one or more members of the native flora or fauna. For example, house sparrows were first introduced into the USA from Europe in 1853; they displaced native songbirds, damaged crops and acted as vectors of some diseases. Similarly, the American grey squirrel (*Sciurus carolinensis*), introduced into a number of sites in the UK in the nineteenth century, displaced the native red squirrel (*S. vulgaris*) in deciduous woodlands and became the more abundant species. Mink (*Mustela lutreola*) escaped from fur farms in the 1940s–60s, and became naturalised along river banks. These carnivorous animals, feeding on fish and birds, occupy a niche that is very similar to that of the native otter. Direct competition between these two species had resulted in the demise of the otter in some parts of the country, a species that is also highly sensitive to water pollution. Plants, too, can have similar effects if they become naturalised. A well known example is the mauve-pink flowered rhododendron (*Rhododendron ponticum*), originally a garden plant brought from the Himalayas. Throughout large areas of the west country, this plant is now a major understorey species in deciduous woodlands. Its dense foliage and toxic litter forces out other species so that it often becomes the sole occupant of the shrub layer. This reduces plant variety, with a corresponding decrease in the number of grazing woodland animals.

6.3 ENDANGERED SPECIES

No one knows exactly how many species of living organism the Earth currently supports. Estimates range from 3–10 million. Whatever the true number, it represents only around 1–2% of all the species that have lived on Earth since the evolutionary process began. The vast majority of the Earth's earlier occupants, including the large, and once dominant, dinosaurs and tree ferns, have become extinct chiefly as a result of climatic, geological and biotic changes. Today, human activity has taken over as the primary cause of species extinction, possibly accounting for losses of anything from 5–25,000 species per year world wide. Although extinction is a natural part of the evolutionary process, many biologists have become alarmed by the recent dramatic increase in its rate. Since 1900 for example, 13 species of native plant have become extinct in the UK, compared with only 7 in the period 1600–1900. A similar fate threatens many animals, including some large mammals. Regrettably, there are currently fewer than 30 white rhinos, 400 mountain gorillas, 1000 giant pandas, 4000 tigers and 15 000 polar bears. These demises have three primary causes which, if unrestrained, will lead to extinction:

(i) loss of habitat, often as a result of human activities

(ii) overhunting by humans,

(iii) unsuccessful competition with an introduced (foreign) species.

Beyond that, species may become endangered through a failure to reproduce successfully; or a new, virulent parasite may evolve and kill most of its victims. For many years it has been recognised that the thoughtless elimination of species is unpleasant, unnecessary and, in the case of animals, often selfish and cruel. More recently, it has been recognised that each species may represent an important human asset, a potential source of food, useful chemicals, or disease-resistant genes. There is therefore a need for **species conservation**, the planned preservation of wildlife.

The task of identifying endangered species, and preventing their extinction, was initiated by the International Union for the Conservation of Nature and Natural Resources, based in Switzerland. Information, compiled by researchers in many parts of the world, was presented in **Red Data Books**. Volumes include *(1) Mammals, (2) Birds, (3) Amphibians and Reptiles, (4) Fish* and *(5) Angiosperms*. The Red Data Books assign each species threatened with extinction to one of five categories, defined as follows.

(i) **Endangered** – species and subspecies (taxa) in immediate danger of extinction (e.g. white rhino, giant panda).

(ii) **Vulnerable** – taxa with recently reduced, often small populations, following from overexploitation, habitat destruction etc. (e.g. ocelot).

(iii) **Rare** – taxa localised within particular habitats, usually thinly scattered over an extensive range (e.g. Dorset heath (*Erica ciliaris*) on heaths in southern England)

(iv) **Indeterminate** – taxa about which insufficient information exists to determine if they are endangered, vulnerable or rare.

(v) **Out of danger** – formerly endangered,

African elephant, a threatened species

vulnerable or rare taxa, whose numbers have recovered following from appropriate conservation measures (e.g. *Sphenodon punctatus*, a New Zealand lizard-like reptile).

The first **British Red Data Book** (vascular plants) was published in 1977 by the Society for the Promotion of Nature Conservation. This book lists the present and recent distribution of species, and gives numerical assessments of their attractiveness (to collectors), remoteness and accessibility.

Table 1 lists the UK's endangered species. World wide there is probably most concern with the fate of the large and familiar animals, such as elephants and polar bears, that are faced with extinction. Table 2 lists some of these animals and comments on the size of their current populations and reasons for their losses in numbers. Whales, not listed in Table 2, are also in danger of extinction, as the following account will show.

Table 1 Endangered species in the UK

GROUP	SPECIES
Mammals	Pine marten Red squirrel Scottish wildcat
Birds	Black-throated diver Golden eagle Golden plover Greenshank Osprey
Angiosperms	Alpine fleabane Alpine gentian Bog orchid

Table 2 Endangered animals

ANIMAL	COUNTRY OF ORIGIN	COMMENTS
African elephant	Central Africa	100 000 killed per year in late 1980s for ivory trade Approximately 750 000 remain in wild
Black bear	North America	Killed for its gall bladder, a highly prized item in the pharmocopoeia of the Far East
'Flying Fox' (a fruit bat)	Pacific Islands	Eaten as a delicacy; its habitat destroyed by burning rain forests
Giant panda	China	Feeds exclusively on bamboo shoots Approximately 1 000 in wild and 50 in zoos
Grevy's zebra	Ethiopia, Somalia, North Kenya	Fences, erected by farmers, have interrupted its migration routes
Jaguar	South America	Threatened by trappers and the disappearance of tropical rain forests
Mountain gorilla	Central Africa	Approximately 400 in wild
Polar bear	Canada, Russia, Norway	Protection measures (1973) doubled numbers, now estimated at 10 000–20 000
Snow leopard	Asia	Trapped for its fur
Tiger	Bengal, Sumatra, Siberia, China	Trapped for its fur Approximately 5000–10 000 in wild
White rhinoceros	Central Africa	Killed for horn Only 25–30 remain in wild
Caiman (reptile)	South America	Skins used for making handbags, shoes etc.

Whales

Whales, the world's largest marine mammals, have been hunted for centuries. Grouped according to their feeding habits, zoologists recognise **toothed** and **baleen** types. Toothed whales feed on vertebrates and squid. The sperm whale, for example, feeds on fish, while the killer whale attacks and eats seals and sea lions. Baleen whales feed by sieving small invertebrates from mouthfuls of water, using the tough, fibrous strands of baleen at the sides of their mouths as

Japanese whaling vessel with a harpoon ready for firing

filters. For example, grey whales feed on worms and molluscs, scooping them from the sea floor, while blue whales feed on krill, shrimp-like crustaceans found mostly in open water.

European whaling probably began in the sixteenth century. After exhausting European stocks, the whalers moved to the seas off Greenland, then Newfoundland, and finally, at the beginning of the twentieth century, into the Atlantic. At first, the whales were hunted for their oil which was used as a fuel in oil lamps. Some whale meat was also eaten, but was never very popular with Europeans. For the early whalers themselves, whaling from open boats was a risky but profitable occupation. By the late 1870s however, hand harpoons had been replaced by explosive harpoons, a Norwegian invention, and open boats were replaced by steam boats. Equipped with this new technology, many whalers persued whales relentlessly, greatly increasing the numbers that were killed. Hump back whales, a large slow-moving and white-finned species, fish in groups and proved easy to kill. Grey whales, undertaking an annual migration between Mexico and the Arctic, were slaughtered at both ends of their migration route. Sperm whales were exploited for their oil, used in the twentieth century as a lubricant, candle ingredient and in margarine manufacture. Soon, to satisfy increasing demand, whaling was extended to include the fin whale and blue whale, the largest animal that has ever lived with a length of up to 30m and a mass in excess of 200 tonnes. Both of these species sink when dead; whalers with open boats and hand harpoons had great

difficulty in handling these animals and so tended to ignore them. The introduction of steam boats, fitted with lifting gear, overcame this problem, making these species as vulnerable as the others. By the 1960s the Japanese had built up a massive whaling fleet with 100 or more factory ships, each with 6–10 attendant catcher boats, equipped with exploive harpoons. In Japan there was a considerable demand for whale meat, processed and deep frozen at sea before sale to consumers. Needless to say, whaling on this scale led to 'boom and bang', an economic bonanza at the expense of the whale, followed by a decline in the numbers of many species to a point of near extinction. As a result of a catastrophic decline, blue whales were given total protection in 1965, and the International Whaling Commission was set up to safeguard the world's whales. Although largely successful in saving threatened species, the IWC has not been able to prevent heavy exploitation of the smaller species. This is particularly true in Japan and the Far East, where the demand for whale meat remains high and the exploitation of whale populations continues.

6.4 CONSERVATION

Humans are heavily dependent on environmental resources. There are of two types.
   (i) **Renewable resources**, which include plants and animals (capable of reproducing their own species), wind, solar energy and tides.
   (ii) **Non-renewable resources**, which include coal, fuel and limestones, formed from organisms which have mostly become extinct.

The term **conservation** applies to all human resources, both renewable and non-renewable. For renewable resources, the aim is to preserve today's species and the places where they live for future generations. The conservation of non-renewable resources consists of regulating rates of consumption so that reserves are used economically, without unnecessary wastage.

Renewable resources

Conservationists aim to preserve ecosystems and the communities they support, especially those threatened by extinction. No species lives in isolation. Each threatened plant species has its own biotic, climatic and soil (edaphic) requirements. Similarly, each threatened animal species needs food, water, shelter and conditions favourable for reproduction. Ecosystems provide these needs. Establishing and maintaining suitable ecosystems for threatened species is therefore a prerequisite of species conservation. The responsibility fo preserving areas of exceptional national interest against disorderly development and spoilage, together with safeguarding their flora and fauna is now partly a function of Government. in the UK, *The National Parks and Access to the Countryside Act* (1949) established National Parks, National Nature Reserves and Sites of Special Scientific Interest (SSSI). Today, there are 11 National Parks (Figure 2), more than 100 National Nature Reserves and nearly 5000 SSSIs in the UK.

The National Parks, such as Dartmoor and the Lake District, are large areas of countryside, with wild and lonely places unchanged by human habitation. Although much of the land in the National Parks is privately owned, overall responsibility for maintenance rests with local authorities who encourage and control public access. Nature reserves include the habitats of rare plants and animals. In addition to the National Nature Reserves, others have been established on land purchased by the National Trust (NT) and the Royal Society for the Protection of Birds (RSPB). Brownsea Island in Poole Harbour, owned by the NT, is one of the last haunts of the red squirrel in southern England. Sites of Special Scientific Interest, selected by the Nature Conservancy Council are mostly on private land. They include uncommon habitats, such as ancient hedgerows and rare species of ecological interest. Public access to these sites may be restricted.

Badger, a threatened species

The **Nature Conservancy Council (NCC)** is the government body that promotes nature conservation in the UK. It gives advice on nature conservation to government and to all those whose activities affect wildlife and wild places. its range of publications include a series of leaflets on the conservation of major habitats, such as broad leaved woodlands, lowland heathland, and lakes. In proposing schemes of **management** for each of the major ecosystem types, it seeks to conserve species diversity. To maintain lowland heathland in southern England for example, the NCC, in effect, makes the following recommendations.

(i) Encourage heather. Maintain uneven-aged vegetation structure in heather stands, with as many large patches of heather as possible, preferably within close proximity of one another so that insects and birds can move between them.

(ii) Retain patches of bare ground, boggy areas and overgrown, undisturbed heathland, blanketed by bushes such as gorse.

(iii) Discourage tree saplings, by pulling them up or felling, and bracken, by grazing in spring and cutting in late summer.

(iv) Carry out controlled burning to encourage the growth of young heather shoots.

(v) Take precautions to prevent uncontrolled heathland fires. Cut or rotavate strips across the heathland, broad enough to prevent fire from crossing the strip.

(vi) Prevent uncontrolled human activity such as motorcycle scrambling, horse-riding, picnicking, car parking etc.

Conservation in the UK however is not confined to the activities of the Nature Conservancy

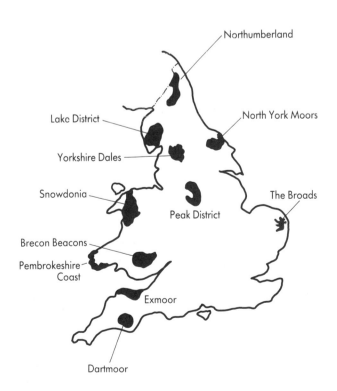

Figure 2   National Parks in England and Wales

- Northumberland
- Lake District
- North York Moors
- Yorkshire Dales
- Snowdonia
- The Broads
- Peak District
- Brecon Beacons
- Pembrokeshire Coast
- Exmoor
- Dartmoor

Jacob sheep ram, a rare animal

Council. Public education, such as publicising the advantages of retaining hedges, and generally making land owners aware of the benefits of conservation, have done a lot to change the climate of public opinion. In the UK and many other countries, endangered species are protected by law. **Legislation** has been introduced to prevent overgrazing, overfishing, the hunting of game, collection of bird's eggs, picking of wild flowers and collection of plants. Badgers and otters have been the subjects of Acts of Parliament, designed to halt the decline in their numbers. Nature reserves managed by wardens, have been established as sanctuaries for threatened species, where plants and animals can live protected from human interference. The effective management of wildlife sometimes entails **culling** individuals, particularly when sick animals are present or when populations have exceeded optimal levels. Long term conservation strategies involve establishing **gene banks**. These may contain unfashionable varieties of vegetables, flowering plants or farm animals, which may one day provide the genes for new improved varieties.

Non-renewable resources

Enormous reserves of non-renewable carbon-containing resources (coal, oil, limestone) lie beneath the land masses and seas (see section 2.5). Even so, amounts of each of these resources is finite. Once removed, there is no way in which stocks can be replaced. Again, in order to conserve these resources, legislation may regulate their rate of removal or define the uses to which they may

be put. As an alternative strategy, these resources may be sufficiently highly priced that consumers are forced to use them economically, thereby preserving some of the resource for future generations.

Another important non-renewable resource is nuclear fuel, used in the nuclear power industry. **Nuclear fuels** are of three types, each used in a different type of reactor:

(i) Uranium-235 (scarce), used in fission reactors,

(ii) Uranium-238 (reasonably abundant), used in fast breeder reactors,

(iii) Deuterium or 'heavy water' (plentiful in sea water), which would be used in fusion reactors if they come into operation.

Bearing in mind that non-renewable energy resources may eventually be depleted, increasing attention is likely to be focused on alternative sourcs of energy, notably the renewable energy technologies (see section 7.5).

6.5 TRANSFORMING WASTE LAND

Throughout the UK there are more than 45 000 hectares of waste land, formerly occupied by buildings, mine workings, railway lines etc. These sites are described as **derelict waste lands** if they cannot be reclaimed without treatment to detoxify waste, stabilise soil or clear away old buildings. Spoil heaps from mining operations, disused factories, docks and gasworks are examples. A second category consists of **neglected waste lands**, mostly around urban fringes, where illicit rubbish dumping has created an untidy, disorganised wilderness. Land reclamation is usually an expensive, time-consuming process because it almost always involves clearing and levelling. In addition, certain sites may require detoxification and filling. After the initial stages of preparation, land-based sites may need to be covered with topsoil then left for a time to stabilise. Figure 3 shows some of the ways in which reclaimed waste lands can be developed. The list of possibilities is almost endless. Some developments though are more cost effective than others; costs incurred by local councils can often be recovered if the land is subsequently used for development, agriculture, sport or leisure.

Disused railway cuttings may be used as **land fill sites**. Such sites may initially be lined with impermeable materials such as clay or plastic, especially if they are to be used for domestic or hazardous chemical wastes. Tipping, to fill up the hole, must be carried out with appropriate treatments to ensure that the tipped material is spread evenly and compacted. After filling the

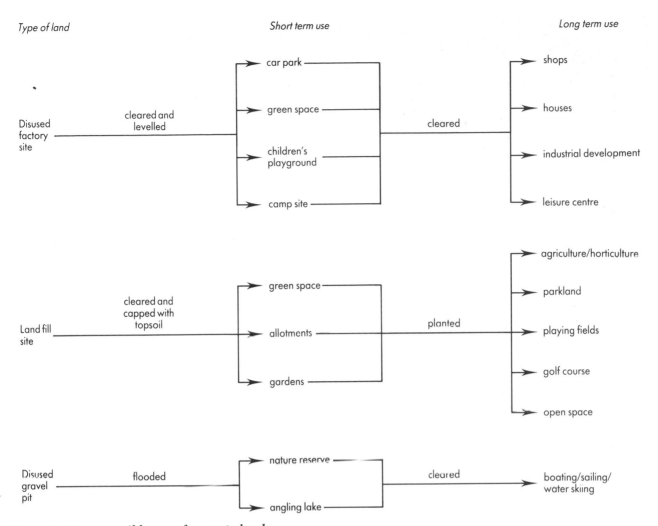

Figure 3   Some possible uses for waste lands

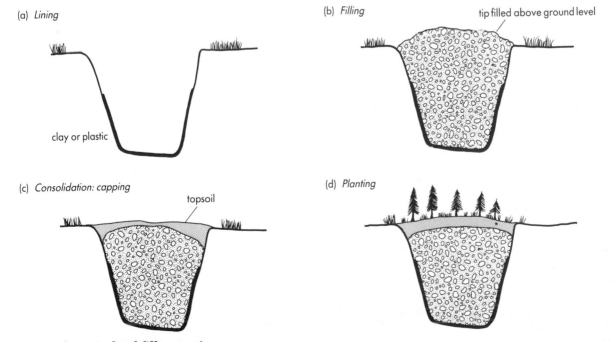

Figure 4   Stages in land fill operations

Land fill site used as a rubbish dump

Flooded gravel pit used for sailing

hole above the surrounding ground level, the tipped material is left for a year or two to undergo partial decomposition and to settle. In the final phase, the site is capped with top soil and may be planted with grass or trees, depending on the intentions of the planners. Attempts to use land fill sites for building however have been dogged by a number of problems.

(i) Toxins from sites may be leached into the local drinking water supply.

(ii) Explosive gases, notably methane, from decomposing rubbish may enter buildings. This can happen many years after a site has been capped with top soil.

(iii) Land subsidence may cause structural damage to buildings.

Extensive mining for sand or gravel frequently leaves the countryside scarred by deep, unsightly hollows known as **gravel pits**. Some of these fill naturally with water, while others are filled artificially to create reservoirs or boating lakes. The scenic value of a water-filled gravel pit is usually greater than that of a dry one. Mature flooded gravel pits may contain a wide variety of habitats, including extensive willow scrub, alder carr and reedmarsh. These man made wetlands support a rich diversity of bird life, visited by more than 100 migrating species. They also provide overwintering for wildfowl, thrushes, finches and buntings. In many cases however, the pleasures of the ornithologist conflict with the economic interests of the land developer. Excellent profits have been made by flooding gravel pits, clearing away vegetation, stocking the water with fish, and providing facilities for boating, water-skiing etc. Clearing away

vegetation destroys the habitats of wildlife. The noise made by people and boats frightens away migratory birds. Oil from boats kills the birds' food supply and pollutes their nesting sites. Only the largest flooded gravel pits can therefore satisfy the requirements of ornithologists, anglers, boaters and water-skiers. In most cases however, a flooded gravel pit can provide an amenity for only one of these groups.

QUESTIONS

1 a) Define the term '*conservation*'.
   b) Otters are '*protected*' species in the UK.
      (i) Suggest two reasons for their recent demise.
      (ii) Suggest two protective measures that should allow their numbers to recover.
   c) A primary aim of conservationists is to preserve a wide range of habitats. Suggest reasons for this.
   d) In what ways do each of the following activities contribute to conservation?
      (i) lawn mowing,
      (ii) culling,
      (iii) fox hunting,
      (iv) tree felling,
      (v) making compost,
      (vi) preserving the seeds of 'old fashioned' fruits and vegetables.

2 Female Nile crocodiles actively protect their eggs and defend their young against predators, especially monitor lizards and olive baboons. The table below shows the extent of predation at sites visited by tourists in open boats, and at sites not visited by tourists.

Table 3 Based on J M Edington and M A Edington (1977), Ecology and Environmental Planning, Chapman and Hall, London

BREEDING GROUNDS	NUMBER OF NESTS	NESTS DESTROYED BY PREDATORS
Tourist sites		
1	13	13
2	10	10
3	13	7
Sites not visited by tourists		
1	36	17
2	7	2
3	22	4
4	7	0

Describe and discuss the effect of tourism on this crocodile population.

3 What is 'deforestation'?
Argue the case for and against tree felling in the UK.
Why has there been progressive destruction of the world's tropical rain forests? Describe the (a) local, and (b) global, effects of rain forest destruction.

4 By reference to any three of the following, describe how human activities may pose a threat to wildlife:
a) burning tropical rainforests,
b) hedgerow clearance,
c) draining wetlands,
d) fire,
e) importing foreign species.

5 What are 'endangered species'?
For what reasons have some species become endangered?
How may these species be conserved for future generations?

6 Write an essay on 'Whales and whaling'.

7 In the UK what has (a) central government, and (b) local government, done to conserve natural habitats and wildlife?
Briefly state the aims, interests and achievements of two of the following groups:
The Worldwide Fund for Nature;
The Nature Conservancy Council;
The National Trust;
The Friends of the Earth;
The Sports Council;
The Forestry Commission.

8 Describe how waste land originates, and how it can be developed to produce amenity sites and leisure facilities.

BIBLIOGRAPHY

Allaby, M (Ed.) (1989) *Thinking Green* Barrie and Jenkins

Curry-Lindahl, K (1974) *Conservation for survival* Gollanz

Green, B (1985) *Countryside Conservation* George Allen and Unwin

HMSO (1986) *Transforming our waste land: the way forward*

Huxley, A (1984) *Green Inheritance* Gaia Books.

POLLUTION

Pollution is the fouling of air, water or soil by materials that are harmful to living organisms, especially to humans and those plants and animals on which we depend. In most cases, organisms have no previous evolutionary experience of contact with chemical pollutants. Large scale pollution is a relatively new phenomenon, and possibly the most threatening one associated with increases in human population density. Urbanisation and combustion of fossil fuels, together with advances in agriculture and manufacturing industries, have been contributory factors. When pollution occurs the air, water or soil becomes contaminated with potentially harmful substances. Unless some measures are taken either to control pollution at its source, or to neutralise its effects, each pollutant may pose a hazard to human health, or threaten the efficiency of agricultural production.

7.1 THE ATMOSPHERE

Above the earth's surface are two gaseous regions or spheres, the lower one called the **troposphere** and the upper one the **stratosphere**. In the **troposphere**, extending upwards to about 15 km, gases circulate. Pure air in the trophosphere is a mixture of gases, in the following proportions:

Nitrogen	79%
Oxygen	20%
Carbon dioxide	0.03%
Inert gases	trace

As one ascends through the troposphere, the atmospheric gases retain their relative proportions but decrease in density; i.e. their molecules become fewer in number and more widely spaced. Above the troposphere is the stratosphere, a layer

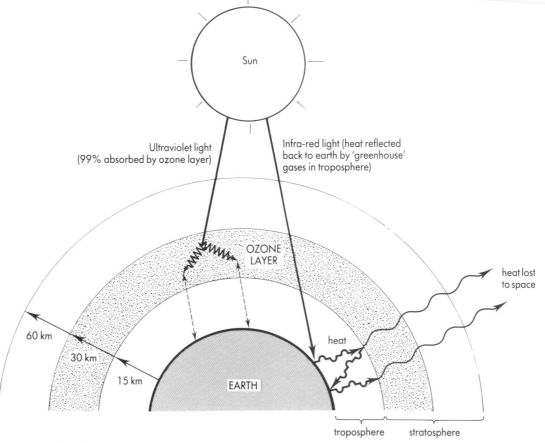

Figure 1   Structure of the atmosphere, and absorption of ultraviolet and infra-red light

of sparse, non-circulating gases, extending upwards to about 60 km (Figure 1).

In the lower layers of the stratosphere, some 15–30 km above the Earth's surface, is an **ozone layer**. The ozone molecules in this layer are quite rare, accounting for only a few out of every million gas molecules at this height. Ozone (O_3) forms in the stratosphere from oxygen (O_2) in a photochemical reaction catalysed by the ultraviolet (UV) rays of sunlight. The process has two stages. In the first stage, (i), atoms of oxygen are formed which then combine with molecules of oxygen to produce ozone, (ii). As ozone is unstable, it slowly reverts back to diatomic oxygen, (iii):

(i) $\quad O_2 \xrightarrow{\text{UV light}} 2O$

(ii) $\quad 2O_2 \;+\; 2O \xrightarrow{\text{UV light}} 2O_3$

$\qquad\qquad\qquad\qquad\;\; \downarrow \text{UV light}$

(iii) $\qquad\qquad\qquad\qquad 3O_2$

The biological importance of ozone molecules in this region of the stratosphere, together with processes leading to their formation, lies in UV light absorption. The so-called 'ozone layer' has the ability to absorb some of the sun's ultraviolet light. It therefore acts as a global 'sunscreen', filtering out harmful, mutagenic UV light, the cause of some human cancers and premature ageing. As it absorbs UV light, the earth's ozone layer is warmed. This affects convection currents in the troposphere below, the force that drives the world's weather. If there were no warming layer, convection systems would rise higher in the atmosphere, and clouds would form at greater heights. In the early 1980s scientists, using a device called a Dobson Spectrophotometer, discovered an **ozone hole** over Antarctica. Careful monitoring of the size of this hole has provided a useful method for monitoring the state of the ozone layer itself. Intriguingly, scientists discovered that the depletion of ozone was stronger in odd-numbered years (1983, 1985, 1987) than in even-numbered years, but have not yet provided a satisfactory explanation of this phenomenon.

A second component of sunlight is its heat-producing infra-red (IR) light. This fraction is retained by water vapour and certain gases, including carbon dioxide in the troposphere. These are the 'greenhouse' gases (see section 7.2).

7.2 AIR POLLUTION

Air becomes polluted when harmful materials in the form of solids (particulates), liquids or gases are added to it.

Particulate pollutants

The major particulate pollutants are smoke particles, from the combustion of coal and oil, and radioactive dust from atomic explosions and nuclear-powered power stations.

Smoke particles blacken the surfaces of plants, reducing the amount of light that reaches photosynthesising cells. Acids in the soot damage the epidermis and mesopyll, causing leaves to become yellow as chlorophyll is broken down. These same acids are also harmful to humans. Inhalation of smoke particles irritates the lungs, partly because the smoke is acid, and partly because the particles are irregular in shape, often with needle-like projections at their surface. A number of respiratory diseases, notably bronchitis, emphysema and asthma, are aggravated by a smoke-polluted atmosphere. Buildings also suffer from the effects of smoke. A covering of soot blackens a building, making it unsightly; it also attacks some types of stone, chiefly sandstone and limestone, causing the surface to flake. In time, structural weaknesses develop as the stone crumbles.

Large towns, with concentrations of manufacturing industries, are often situated on estuaries in valleys. If such towns, or any low-

(a) *Normal pattern of particle dispersion*

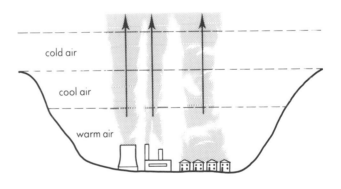

(b) *Smog formation*

Figure 2   Thermal inversion

lying town, are surrounded by higher ground, **thermal inversions** may occur during the winter, trapping a layer of cold air beneath a warmer layer. The effect of thermal inversion is to prevent the escape of smoke and other products of combustion. The smoke remains close to the ground, and may combine with droplets of water to form a **smog**. Visibility is reduced by a smog. More importantly, some of the chemicals in the smoke dissolve in water droplets to form acids, which irritate and damage the respiratory system and eyes. Smogs are particularly likely to occur in regions where there are a large number of consumers of coal and oil. Smoke from coal and oil fires contains oxides of sulphur and nitrogen. During rain, these gases are carried back to Earth as dilute solutions of nitric and sulphuric acids. Acidification of the soil may accelerate leaching, so that mineral nutrients are removed from topsoil. We shall return to a fuller discussion of the problem later in this section.

Radioactive dust, from atomic bomb tests, or routine or accidental release from nuclear power stations, emits subatomic particles. Natural background radiation from rocks, and cosmic radiation from space, are additional sources of some of these subatomic particles. Among the fission products of uranium–235 are a number of biologically active isotopes, notably strontium–90, caesium–137 and iodine–131. Apart from entering human tissues directly via the lungs, these isotopes are also concentrated along food chains, and so pose a threat even to those not directly in contact with atomic radiation. Strontium–90 is concentrated in human bones, while iodine–131 is concentrated in the thyroid gland. As radioactive isotopes are unstable, their nuclei disintegrate to release subatomic particles of three types.

(i) **Alpha radiation**, which has little penetrating power and only damages cells if it is emitted from a radiation source within human tissues and organs.

(ii) **Beta radiation** is capable of penetrating a couple of centimetres and damages cells via contact with the skin, lungs or alimentary canal.

(iii) **Gamma radiation**, similar to X-rays, has great penetrating power and high velocity. Gamma particles can damage human cells at distances of several metres from the radiation source.

Alpha, beta and gamma particles are known collectively as **ionising radiation**, because they damage cells by ionising materials in them i.e. by adding or removing electrons. Exposure to high radiation doses causes vomiting, bleeding, loss of hair and often death. Those who survive may later develop leukaemia, or some other form of cancer, and cataracts. Many become sterile, while others

produce children with genetic defects or increased susceptibility to certain diseases, especially cancers. Repeated exposure to low radiation doses can eventually produce the same illnesses because ionising radiation is accumulative in its effects.

Car exhaust fumes

Almost every household in the UK has at least one car or motorbike. The internal combustion engine, driven by petrol, produces many different substances in its exhaust. Some of these substances are serious air pollutants. The list of **primary pollutants**, emitted at source from the engine, is as follows.

(i) Carbon monoxide (CO), an odourless and highly toxic gas which combines irreversibly with haemoglobin in the blood, preventing it from carrying oxygen.

(ii) Carbon dioxide (CO_2), a 'greenhouse' gas.

(iii) Unburned hydrocarbons, the compounds responsible for the unpleasant smell of car engines. They are probably carcinogenic.

(iv) Nitrogen oxides, especially nitric oxide (NO) and nitrogen dioxide (NO_2). Amounts of these gases increase when engine temperatures are high. Nitrogen dioxide is a toxic eye and lung irritant.

(v) Sulphur dioxide (SO_2), another toxic eye and lung irritant.

(vi) Lead (from leaded petrol only), a toxic heavy metal.

Ozone is a **secondary pollutant**, produced in the troposphere about heavy traffic in hot, sunny cities such as Los Angeles, Athens and Sydney. Nitrogen dioxide undergoes photolysis to produce nitrogen oxide and atomic oxygen (O):

$$NO_2 \xrightarrow{\text{UV light}} NO + O$$

This atomic oxygen then rapidly combines with molecular oxygen to produce ozone (O_3):

$$O + O_2 \rightarrow O_3$$

Ozone is the main ingredient of photochemical smogs and, like NO_2, is a toxic compound causing eye and lung irritation, headaches, reduced physical performance and reduced resistance to infections and respiratory diseases. Unfortunately, ozone formed at this level in the troposphere cannot replace ozone depleted from the stratosphere.

Fine particles of **lead** are emitted from the exhausts of cars which burn petrol containing tetraethyl lead, an additive that prevents engine knocking. Since 1985 the lead limit for petrol in the UK has been 0.15 g per litre. Lead is a toxic heavy metal. The symptoms of lead poisoning in adults begins with fatigue, irritability, headaches, sleeplessness, anaemia and loss in weight. Severe lead poisoning leads to muscle weakness, confusion, coma and eventual death. Very low concentrations of lead, such as those found in busy streets and around motorways, are believed to adversely affect development of the brain and nervous system of children, with a significant effect on their mental functioning. For this reason, 'lead-free' petrol is now available, backed by government tax concessions and extensive advertising to encourage its wider use.

Removing the toxic gases from car exhaust fumes can be achieved by fitting a **catalytic converter** (Figure 3). These 'bolt-on' devices are attached to the exhaust pipe of a car, generally between the engine and the silencer. They reduce noxious gas output but do increase the volume of carbon dioxide emitted into the atmosphere. A catalytic converter contains a honeycombed metallic catalyst or metallic oxides embedded in a porous supporting medium such as pelleted clay. The catalysts (which may be platinum, stainless steel, or the oxides of iron, copper or chromium) affect the removal of nitric oxide through its reduction by carbon monoxide.

$$2NO + CO \rightarrow N_2 + CO_2$$

The further removal of carbon monoxide, together with hydrocarbons, is achieved by oxidation, using any of the catalysts listed above:

$$2CO + O_2 \rightarrow 2CO_2$$

$$C_nH_m + (n + \frac{M}{4})\, O_2 \rightarrow nCO_2 + \frac{M}{2}\, H_2O$$

The removal of NO is a reduction and therefore poisoned by the presence of oxygen; and the removal of CO and hydrocarbons are both oxidations, dependent on the presence of NO. This clearly presents problems for manufacturers. **Dual converters**, capable of catalysing both the reducing and oxidising reactions, are available but are currently expensive. This reflects the complex processes involved in their manufacture.

Gases from solid fuel combustion

Coal, the principal solid fuel used for industrial and domestic heating, consists mainly of carbon but also contains compounds of sulphur and nitrogen. Complete combustion of coal results in the formation of several polluting gases: (i) **carbon dioxide**, (ii) **sulphur dioxide** and (iii) oxides of nitrogen, principally **nitrogen dioxide**:

$$\text{(i)} \quad C + O_2 \quad \rightarrow \quad CO_2$$
$$\text{(ii)} \quad S + O_2 \quad \rightarrow \quad SO_2$$
$$\text{(iii)} \quad N + O_2 \quad \rightarrow \quad NO_2$$

In 1980 the total emission of SO_2 from all sources in the UK was 4 680 000 tonnes, with an estimated 61% from coal burning. World wide in that year sulphur dioxide emissions amounted to more than 100 million tonnes. Emissions of NO_2 from coal burning were about 10% lower by mass than emissions of SO_2 both in the UK and world wide. Even so, more NO_2 entered the atmosphere in that year because *additional* amounts came from car exhausts and the breakdown of nitrogenous fertilisers in fields. When carbon

(a) *Radial flow type*

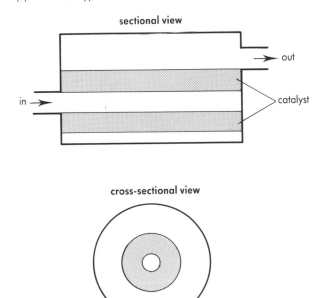

(b) *Flat bed type*

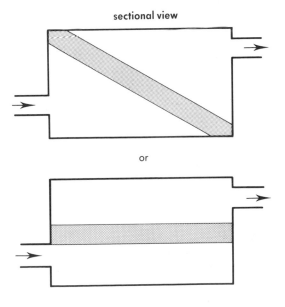

Figure 3 *Arrangement of the catalyst in a catalytic converter*

dioxide, sulphur dioxide and nitrogen dioxide dissolve in water they produce carbonic, sulphuric and nitric acids respectively. These fall to the earth as acid rain.

Antipollution measures have concentrated mainly on preventing SO_2, the major pollutant from coal burning, from entering the atmosphere. Two general approaches have been used.

(i) In **flue gas desulphurisation**, waste gases are 'scrubbed' with alkaline solutions before they are released into the atmosphere (Figure 4).

A typical reaction is as follows:

$$CaCO_3 + SO_2 \rightarrow CaSO_3 + CO_2$$

calcium   calcium
carbonate   sulphite

The calcium sulphite is dumped. It is a waste product.

(ii) In **fuel desulphurisation**, sulphur is removed from coal before it is burned. One technique uses micro-organisms for this purpose.

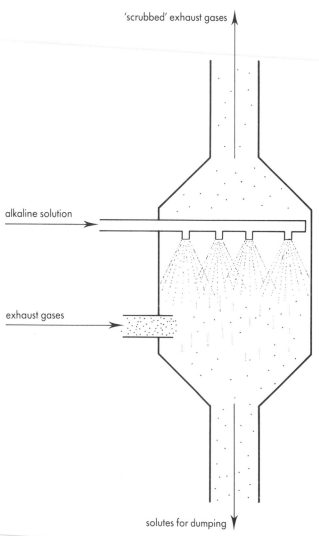

Figure 4   *Flue gas desulphurisation by 'scrubbing'*

Acid rain

If smoke from industrial processes is blown by wind, irradiated by sunlight and combined with water droplets, the product eventually returns to earth as **acid rain**, often hundreds of miles from the place where it originated. Pure water is neutral, with a pH of 7.0. Acid rain is formed chiefly from sulphur dioxide (SO_2) and oxides of nitrogen (NO and NO_2) released into the atmosphere by industrial processes, vehicles and power stations. Acid rain can have a pH as low as 3.0–4.5. While in the air, these gases are oxidised to form a mixture of sulphuric and nitric acids, possibly with ozone, magnesium and sunlight acting as catalysts. Further reactions between ammonia, from chemical fertilisers, and sulphur dioxide result in the formation of ammonium sulphate, a secondary pollutant. Wind may blow the pollutants many hundreds of miles from their source. Acid rain originating in Europe's industrial areas may fall over woodlands in Scandinavia; that from the USA may fall over Canada. Adverse effects have been demonstrated in mature forests and lakes. Humans may also be affected.

Mature fir trees affected by acid rain begin to lose their needles and become discoloured. The youngest branches of yews and beech die off. The acid rain causes magnesium and calcium ions to be leached from leaves, leading to symptoms of deficiency. Furthermore, normal sugar-starch metabolism is affected so that high levels of sugar accumulate in leaves. This attracts insect pests and encourages the growth of fungi and acid-tolerant lichens. Soils beneath affected trees contain toxic amounts of aluminium, liberated by accumulations of acidic ammonium sulphate. The ammonium sulphate damages roots and kills fungal mycorrhizae, decreasing the ability of trees to absorb water and mineral salts from the soil. Heavy rain leaches both calcium and magnesium from the soil.

The initial effect of acid rain on lakes is to lower the pH. This is accompanied by a change in the algal flora, notably diatoms, together with the death of some flowering plants and animals. In addition, organisms in lakes slowly die, poisoned by toxic accumulations of aluminium, a much more potent killer when calcium and magnesium ions are absent. Under these conditions, aluminium crosses cell walls and membranes, binds with proteins and disrupts biological processes. In time, all organisms in the lake are killed as the water becomes more acid and toxic. Aluminium is soluble only in water that has become strongly acidic. It may pass from a lake into tap water used for human consumption. A different source of aluminium poisoning was responsible for an event at Camelford in Dorset, when a lorry load of aluminium sulphate was accidentally tipped into the tank from which domestic water supplies were drawn. Certain forms of senile dementia, including Parkinson's disease and Alzheimer's disease, have been attributed to aluminium poisoning; patients who have these conditions were found to have high concentration of aluminium in their brains.

Lichens, that grow on tree trunks and walls, are especially sensitive to concentrations of sulphur dioxide in the air. Hence they have been used as **indicators of pollution**. Counts can be made either of the total number of lichen species in a locality, or of the distribution of a single species within a given area. Two widely distributed species of particular interest are *Xanthoria*, an orange-brown lichen that grows on chalk, limestone or cement walls, and *Usnea*, a grey-green leaf-like lichen that covers the trunks of trees. Even school laboratories, which emit very small amounts of sulphur dioxide, may be surrounded by a zonation of lichen species, increasing in numbers of individual plants and species with increasing distance from the building.

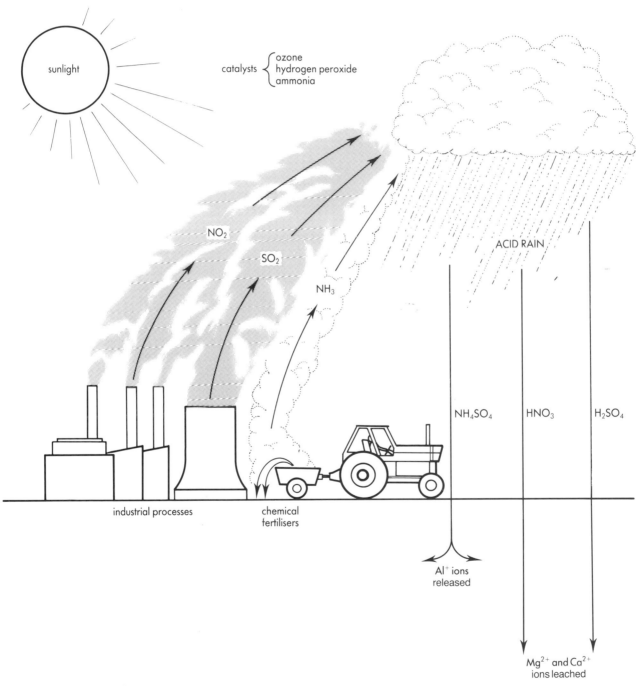

Figure 5 **The formation, components and effects of acid rain**

Bhopal: victim with eye injuries

Chernobyl: the damaged nuclear reactor

Factory accidents

Occasionally, lethal or extremely toxic substances may be released into the atmosphere following factory accidents. There are many examples, but some of the worst have occurred at Seveso, Bhopal and Chernobyl.

Seveso

A chemical disaster took place at **Seveso**, an industrial suburb of Milan, Italy on July 11 1976. Workers in a chemical plant producing trichlorophenol (TCP), from which some weedkillers are manufactured, had left for the weekend. At noon on that Saturday the chemicals heated up and blew the safety valves. A gas cloud containing white flakes escaped from the factory and covered the surrounding area. Not for some 8–13 days after the accident however was it realised that the flakes contained the extremely toxic compound dioxan, which scientists believe can cause cancer in humans. By this time, plants and animals were dying and people were attending local hospitals suffering from vomiting and chloracne, a severe blistering of the skin. The long term effects of this disaster were probably more serious than its immediate aftermath. Rates of stillbirths, natural abortions and birth defects increased. Animals and plants within the affected area had to be destroyed. Top soil was removed and buried, while fresh top soil was brought in from other areas.

Bhopal

On December 2 1984, a cloud of toxic gas escaped from a pesticide factory in **Bhopal**, India. The identity of the gas is still something of a mystery but it may have been hydrogen cyanide, phosgene, methyl isocyanate or a mixture of these gases. Following its release, the gas cloud hugged the ground and spread to cover an area of about 40 square kilometres, affecting nearly 200 000 of the city's population. Those who were exposed to the gas suffered blistering of the skin, blindnesss and acute respiratory distress. A majority of those afflicted by blindness later recovered their sight, but continued to suffer from irritating inflammation of their eyes. As at Seveso, rates of stillbirths, natural abortions and birth defects increased. Nursing mothers produced insufficient breast milk to feed their babies. The children of these victims were generally underweight. In years to come, the disaster will probably claim many more lives, as the damage caused to tissues and organs leads to chronic disease.

Chernobyl

On April 25 1986, there was an explosion in a reactor at the nuclear-powered electricity generating station at **Chernobyl** in the Soviet Union. The blast blew a hole in the reactor, allowing some 15–20 megacuries of iodine–131 and 1–2 megacuries of caesium–137 to escape into the atmosphere. A south-easterly wind blew the radioactive materials over Poland and by April 28 they were detected over Sweden. Later that month, following a change in the direction of the wind, there was radioactive fallout over parts of the UK and most of western Europe as radioactive particles were deposited over vegetation by rain. Soon after the disaster, a number of precautionary measures were taken. Around 130 000 people living close to the reactor were evacuated. The parents of Polish children were advised against giving them fresh milk. Vegetables harvested from much of the Soviet Union and parts of eastern Europe were thrown away. A ban was placed on the sale of Welsh lamb, as the animals had accumulated toxic amounts of radioactive materials after feeding on contaminated hillsides. The number of human cancers that could be caused by the fallout form Chernobyl has been estimated at something in excess of 100 000. Direct inhalation of iodine–131, and its consumption in milk, is expected to cause cancers of the thyroid gland, only a small percentage of which are expected to prove fatal. By contrast, consumption of caesium–137 will cause a wider variety of cancers, such as leukaemia, of which about one half may be fatal.

Greenhouse gases

Certain gases in the atmosphere, known as 'greenhouse' gases, are able to absorb and emit heat. When sunlight strikes the earth's surface it warms up, and emits heat which radiates upwards into space. This heat warms up the 'greenhouse' gases so that they also emit heat, some into space and some back down to the surface (Figure 7). It is this fraction that radiates back to earth which provides additional **global warming**. Without any greenhouse gases in the atmosphere, the average surface temperature of the earth would be a very cold, inhospitable −18°C. Today's 'greenhouse' gases radiate sufficient heat back to earth to give an average global temperature of +15°C. In the future, if concentrations of greenhouse gases increase, there will be additional global surface warming, the so-called '**greenhouse effect**'. It is therefore essential that we try to keep the greenhouse gases near to their present concentration to avoid the occurrence of dramatic climatic changes.

Table 1 lists the gases that are known to have a 'greenhouse' effect and shows their major sources. The origin and effect of some of those gases is now considered in greater detail.

Table 1   Greenhouse gases

GAS	SOURCE OR ORIGIN
Water vapour (H_2O)	Evaporation and transpiration
Carbon dioxide (CO_2)	Combustion of fossil fuels, wood etc.
Chlorofluorocarbons (CFCs)	Refrigerators, aerosol sprays
Methane (CH_4)	Cattle, rice fields, bogs, rubbish tips
Nitrous oxide (N_2O)	Denitrification
Ozone (O_3)	Secondary pollutant from car exhausts

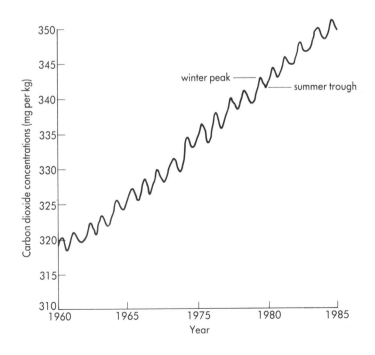

Figure 6   Carbon dioxide concentrations in the northern hemisphere

Water vapour is an efficient 'greenhouse' gas, present in the troposphere in variable amounts, depending on climatic conditions. A complete cloud cover can have a cooling effect because the clouds reflect sunlight, preventing it from reaching the earth's surface. If there is no cloud cover at all, heat can radiate more directly into space resulting in a rapid cooling after the sun has set. A partial cloud cover, however, can increase surface temperatures. Surfaces are warmed when the sun shines on them, and some of this heat is radiated back to earth by the clouds.

Carbon dioxide concentrations of the troposphere have been rising steadily since the Industrial Revolution. From a preindustrial level of 250–290 ppm, concentrations have risen to 345 ppm (1984). If this rate of increase continues, levels will reach approximately 660 ppm by the middle of the next century. Over the northern hemisphere there is a seasonal flux in CO_2 concentrations, reflecting seasonal photosynthetic activity in plants (Figure 6). Levels of atmospheric CO_2 are always higher in winter than in summer because less is removed by photosynthesis.

The primary cause of the current rise in CO_2 concentration is the combustion of fossil fuels, especially coal, oil and natural gas. A secondary cause is the burning of virgin forests. Between 5 and 10^9 tonnes of fossil carbon are released into the atmosphere every year. Not all of this CO_2 however remains in the atmosphere because there are two major **CO_2 sinks**, capable of removing it; these are plants and large expanses of water. CO_2 fixation in photosynthesis, with its subsequent conversion of nutrients, is one of these sinks. Tropical rain forests, the most efficient CO_2 sink on land, can fix annually between 1–2 kg of carbon per m². Burning tropical rain forests

therefore adds more CO_2 to the atmosphere, while at the same time reducing the amount of forest available to act as a CO_2 sink.

The figure for temperate deciduous forests is less, estimated at between 0.2–0.4 kg per m² each year. Phytoplankton in the oceans fixes roughly the same amount of CO_2 per unit area. As the surface area of the oceans exceeds that of the land masses, total amounts of CO_2 fixed by marine plants is probably greater than that fixed by terrestrial vegetation.

Water in the oceans is the second major CO_2 sink. A litre of distilled water will dissolve 1019 cm³ CO_2 at 15°C. Sea water can take roughly eight times more carbon dioxide than distilled water because sea water contains carbonate ions (CO_3^{2-}) which react with dissolved carbon dioxide to form hydrogen carbonate (bicarbonate, HCO_3^-). Reactions between carbonates and calcium ions in sea water form molecules of **calcium carbonate** which slowly sink to the bottom of the oceans. Here they aggregate and undergo compression in the first stage of chalk and limestone formation. That fraction of CO_2 molecules which take part in this reaction are effectively removed from circulation, possibly remaining bound for millions of years before they are again recycled.

Chlorofluorocarbons (CFCs) are complex volatile compounds containing atoms of carbon, fluorine and chlorine. Two of the most widely used CFCs, known as CFC 11 and CFC 12, are manufactured by combining carbon tetrachloride with hydrogen fluoride:

carbon tetrachloride + hydrogen fluoride

↓

$$CClF \quad + \quad CClF_2$$
(CCF 11)　(CCF 12)

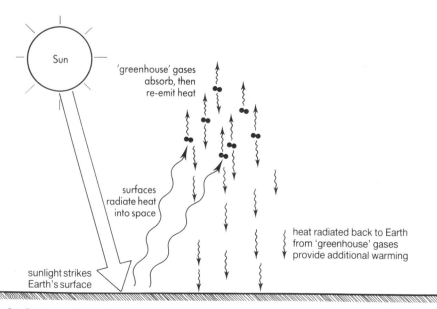

Figure 7　The way in which 'greenhouse' gases may warm the Earth's surface

CFCs are used as coolants in refrigerators, propellants in aerosols, and as foaming agents polystyrene manufacture. It is believed that CFCs are primarily responsible for the ozone hole over the Antarctic and the depletion of ozone in the stratosphere. The CFCs undergo chemical decomposition in the stratosphere to form chlorine atoms, the agents of ozone decomposition. For example:

$$CCl_2F_2 \xrightarrow{\text{UV light}} Cl \xrightarrow{O_3} O_2 + ClO$$

(activated chlorine atoms)   (chlorine oxide)

$$O_2 + Cl$$

(activated chlorine atoms which can react again)

Researchers have estimated that in the stratosphere 10 atoms of chlorine destroy a million or more molecules of ozone. The **ozone depletion potential (ODP)** of a CFC depends on its percentage by weight of chlorine and its lifetime in the atmosphere. As a reference point, CFC 11 has been given an ODP of 1.0. One of the most 'ozone friendly' CFCs is CFC 22, with an ODP of 0.05, and a low boiling point. This compound is already widely used in refrigerators.

Methane (CH_4) comes primarily from the anaerobic breakdown of cellulose. Annual emissions into the atmosphere exceed 100 million tonnes. Most of this comes from cattle. An adult cow, for instance, produces 200 g methane per day, releasing the gas from both ends of its alimentary canal. Other major sources are bogs, marshes and rice fields. Land fill sites also emit methane, generally as part of a toxic and explosive mixture of gases, including CO_2, ethyl butanoate and methanethiol.

Nitrous oxide (N_2O) comes chiefly from the denitrification of nitrates. in the stratosphere, nitrous oxide undergoes photochemical decomposition to form nitric oxide (NO), atomic nitrogen (N), molecular nitrogen (N_2) and atomic oxygen (O):

$$N_2O \xrightarrow{\text{UV light}} NO + N$$

and $$N_2O \xrightarrow{\text{UV light}} N_2 + O$$

Some of the nitric oxide reacts with atomic oxygen or ozone to form nitrogen dioxide (NO_2). This compound combines with water to form nitric acid:

$$NO \xrightarrow{\text{O or } O_3} NO_2 \xrightarrow{+H_2O} HNO_3$$

The first stage in this reaction can damage the ozone layer, because it can break down ozone in the stratosphere.

7.3 THE 'GREENHOUSE' EFFECT

Global warming as a result of heat emissions from 'greenhouse' gases is known as the **greenhouse effect**. The term is misleading for at least two reasons.

(i) As we have seen, greenhouse gases radiate heat back to earth. Glass in greenhouses doesn't do that. Rather, greenhouses stay warm principally because the glass shelters the plants from the wind.

(ii) Glasshouses on the whole provide a very hospitable, pleasant climate, where plants grow better. Yet if the greenhouse effect were not controlled, the world would be an inhospitable stressful place in which plants would grow less well and all our social, economic and agricultural systems would suffer.

Most scientists are now convinced that the greenhouse effect is a reality, and that it could have major long term effects on the Earth's climate and vegetation.

Climatic effects

If 'greenhouse' gases continue to increase at their present rate, it is predicted that the Earth's average surface temperature will rise by 1–5°C between the beginning and end of the twenty-first century. This global warming though will not be evenly distributed. Polar regions will warm most rapidly, possibly by as much as 6–12°C. The increase in temperate zones will be somewhat less marked, while equatorial regions will warm by no more than 1–2°C. General global warming will have two major effects on climate.

(i) The polar ice caps will begin to melt. Sea levels throughout the world will rise, increasing by an estimated 20–200 cm before the end of the twenty-first century. This, in turn, will flood many low-lying coastal regons, for example in parts of East Anglia, Holland, Bangladesh and Australia. Rivers will flood their banks. Rocky shores, shingle beaches and mudflats will be eroded. Salt water will intrude into coastal land, making it unfit for agriculture. As the polar ice caps melt, less sunlight will be reflected from the earth by snow. More sunlight will be absorbed to compound the greenhouse effect.

(ii) In a warmer world, more water will be returned to the atmosphere via evaporation and transpiration. Clouds will rise to a greater height, carried by stronger convection currents. Total cloud cover may increase, although this effect will not be evenly distributed. There will also be an increase in total rainfall, especially in equatorial regions. Temperate zones may also experience heavier rainfalls, accompanied by stronger winds. The Earth's main climatic zones will extend further from the equator, so that southern England may experience a more mediterranean climate, with less snow in winter, and hotter, drier, sunnier summers. Parts of Spain, now covered by sparse vegetation, may turn to desert.

Biotic effects

Changes in the Earth's main climatic zones may eventually lead to the extinction of some plants and animals, together with the redistribution of others. It is predicted that the vast treeless tundra, covered by lichens such as 'reindeer moss', will move north and diminish in total area. Moose, reindeer and other tundra-dwelling animals may experience severe selection pressures, possibly sufficient to cause a significant demise of their populations. In a similar way, areas of coniferous forests will move north and be squeezed around their margins.

Botanists have shown that elevated concentrations of CO_2 affect C_3 plants (plants that fix CO_2 in combination with ribulose bisphosphate to form two molecules of phosphoglyceric acid) and C_4 plants (plants that fix CO_2 in combination with phosphoenolpyruvate to form oxaloacetate) in different ways. Given more CO_2, it seems that C_3 plants which abound in temperate zones respond with increased yields. By contrast, C_4 plants, including maize, sorgum, sugar cane and many other plants from hot, sunny climates, barely change their growth rates. This bodes well for future C_3 crop yields, but also suggests that certain C_3 weeds may become more serious pests. Almost all C_3 plants grown at elevated CO_2 levels have been found to develop extremely vigorous root systems. This results in an increased uptake of both water and mineral salts. As a result, cultivated soils become drier and mineral-deficient. These effects, however, are partly offset by the effect of increased CO_2 levels on stomata which close for longer periods, thereby reducing water losses. Among the other effects produced in response to elevated levels of CO_2 were increased branching, reduced flowering period, flower bud abortion, a decline in seed production and reduced seed quality, notably a decline in stored nutrients.

7.4 WATER POLLUTION

Water may be polluted by liquids, solutes or solid particles. **Oil** is a liquid pollutant of coastal waters, lakes, inland canals and larger rivers. Even small amounts of oil spread over the surface of inland waters by pleasure boats may prevent oxygen from reaching aquatic plants and animals. One consequence of this may be putrefaction of the vegetation, resulting in the release of hydrogen sulphide, a foul toxic gas which smells like rotten eggs. More importantly, coastal waters may be polluted by oil from grounded, damaged tankers. Crude oil is a tar-like, sticky, gelatinous compound which is toxic to plants and animals on rocky shores. It clogs the feathers of sea birds, preventing them from swimming and flying. Furthermore, oil-covered feathers lose their capacity for retaining heat so that the birds suffer from hypothermia and die as a result of their heat loss.

Toxic solutes pollute mainly rivers and lakes. These solutes originate either from factories, or from farmland. Ions of heavy metals, ammonia, cyanide, acids and alkalis have all been discharged into rivers as components of industrial effluent. Salts of mercury, copper, zinc and cadmium may pollute rivers that pass through industrial areas. Discharge of mercury into **Minimata Bay** in Japan had tragic consequences for the local population of fishermen. Micro-organisms in the water converted inorganic mercury compounds to organic forms, such as methyl mercury chloride. This compound was concentrated through food chains. Although concentrations were insufficient to kill molluscs and fish that lived in the Bay, humans who consumed them in large numbers developed mercury poisoning and suffered severe neurological disorders.

Drainage of nitrates and phosphates from farmland into rivers presents a different problem. Excessive enrichment of the water with nutrients leads to a condition known as **eutrophication**. The first phase in this process is an 'algal bloom', caused by the effects of fertilisers on the growth of microscopic green algae. The algae grow so rapidly that they shade other vegetation, causing the death of higher plants. Flow rates in the river may slow down as the slimy green growths of algae spread. When some of the older algae begin to decompose, and bacterial populations increase, the water becomes yellow-brown and deoxygenated. At this stage fish are killed and the entire food web of the river is disrupted. Fish may also die if **detergents**, another source of phosphates, should seep into rivers. This is particularly true of synthetic 'hard' detergents which lower the oxygen absorption capacity of the water. The presence of these detergents in sewage at one time presented a formidable problem. Foam built up on the surface of sewage tanks and on polluted rivers, forming so-called 'foam swans' which presented a health hazard. A

An algal bloom, the first stage in eutrophication

Dead fish in deoxygenated water, the final stage in eutrophication

solution to the problem was provided by the introduction of 'soft' detergents which had relatively simple molecules, readily broken down by bacteria. Today almost all household detergents are of this type. Even water itself may sometimes act as a pollutant, especially if it is at a higher temperature than the bulk of water in a river or lake.

Thermal pollution may affect rivers or stretches of coastal waters close to power stations. Large volumes of water are used to cool reactors in electricity generating stations. When this water is returned to its source, it is often too hot and with insufficient oxygen to support life. It therefore acts as a pollutant, killing those organisms with which it comes into contact. Further from the outfall, the warm water may attract many different species, stimulating some individuals to grow to a large size.

Particulate pollutants include fine mud and sewage. Mud may be washed from ploughed fields during heavy rain, or come from building sites, clay pits, or water-pumping stations. If the mud should remain in a river for more than 3–4 days, it may shade plants from sunlight or block the gills of fishes. A much more serious participate pollutant is **sewage** which contains nutrients and oxygen-consuming bacteria, including pathogenic species. Seepage of sewage into rivers therefore constitutes a hazard to human health. It also affects the flora and fauna of the water, covering plants and suffocating animals. As bacteria in the sewage complete the process of decomposition, the polluted water begins to emit an obnoxious odour, resulting from the release of ammonia,

hydrogen sulphide and sulphur dioxide to the atmosphere. Few, if any, of the river's original inhabitants survive this change.

Just as the presence of certain lichens indicate the extent to which air may be polluted, so certain species of plants and animals can be used as indicators of pollution in fresh water. In a classic study of the effects of discharging untreated sewage into a river, Hynes recorded levels of solutes and animal numbers at different distances

Water starwort, an indicator of relatively unpolluted water

the outfall. His results are ... 8 and 9. He found that clean, ... and heavily polluted water each ... characteristic fauna. By removing and identifying the animals in any stretch of water, it was possible to gain a rough indication of the extent to which the water was polluted (Figure 10).

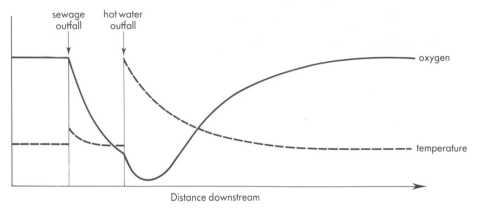

Figure 8   The effect of a heated effluent on an organically polluted river. (Based on Hynes, 1960)

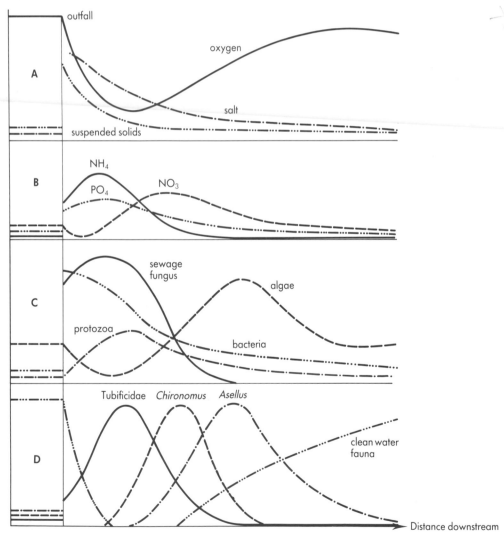

Figure 9   The effects of an organic effluent on a river, at different distance downstream from the outfall. A and B = physical and chemical changes; C = changes in micro-organisms; D = changes in larger animals. (Based on Hynes, 1960)

108

(a) *Clean, almost neutral water (pH 6.5)*

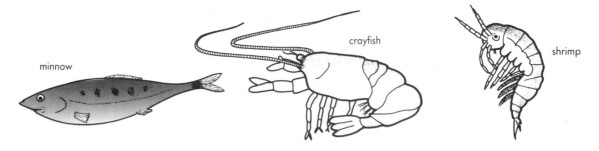

(b) *Clean, slightly acid water (pH 6.0)*

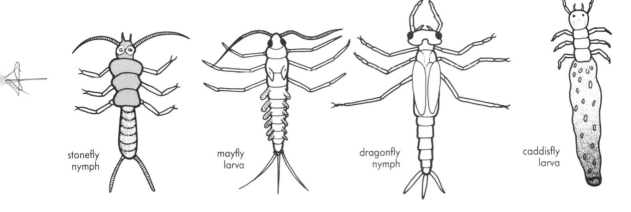

(c) *Water with some organic pollutants*

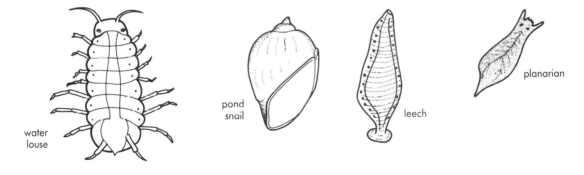

(d) *Water with heavy organic or chemical pollution*

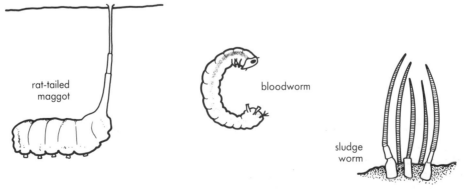

Figure 10   Fresh water animals used as pollution indicators (not drawn to scale)

Rain water is naturally slightly acidic, reacting with carbon dioxide in the air to produce weak carbonic acid with a pH of around 5.6. Minnows, crayfish and shrimps live only in water that is more alkaline than this (pH 6.0–6.5), partly neutralised by basic ions from the soil. At pH 5.6, the exoskeletons of crayfish soften, they become infected with parasites, and their eggs are overrun by fungi. The larvae of caddisflies, and the nymphs of stoneflies and dragonflies (Figure 10b) have a high oxygen requirement and tend to occur only in relatively unpolluted, oxygen-rich water, with little bacterial activity. Less demanding are the water louse (hoglouse), pond snails, leeches and planarians (Figure 10c). The water louse is of particular interest because it can live only in water where concentrations of Ca^{2+} ions exceed 10 mg/dm^3. Typically, the water louse and other animals in this group live in water where there is abundant plant material and decomposing vegetation. Least demanding of all fresh water invertebrates are the rat tailed maggot (the larva of a hoverfly), the bloodworm (the larva of a midge) and the sludge worm. These animals can live in heavily polluted water where there is a low oxygen concentration. In fact, both the bloodworms and sludge worms have haemoglobin in their blood, which binds oxygen.

House with domestic solar water heater

7.5 RENEWABLE ENERGY

A large number of the pollutants that are emitted into the atmosphere, or get into water, are products that originate from fossil fuels. Finding alternative cleaner sources of energy is therefore a priority, both to reduce pollution and because supplies of fossil fuels are finite. Some of these alternative energy technologies, such as windmills, water wheels and tidal mills, go back a long way in history. Today, the main renewable energy resources are solar power, water power and wind power.

(i) **Solar power** is used mainly at present to drive small scale energy conversion units in sunny regions of the world. Used principally to provide hot water, **solar collectors** are fitted to roofs; they consist of blackened absorber plates in a glass-fronted box. Water is pumped through tubes embedded in the plate and carried away to a storage tank from where it can be tapped off. **Solar cells**, based on advanced semi-conductor technology, convert sunlight directly into electricity. Storage of this electricity enables the user to have a continuous supply of electricity throughout the year, regardless of day to day conditions. Large scale **solar thermal electric systems**, used in parts of California and the Middle East, use mirrors to focus sunlight and generate very high temperatures.

(ii) **Water power** drives **hydro-electric power stations**, already providing more than 25% of the world's grid-supplied electricity. Jets of water, directed against the blades of turbines, result in a spinning action that generates electricity. The basic requirement is a downward flow of water, with power generating capacity directly related to the volume of water involved, and the height through with it falls. **Dams** and extensive waterways are built in some cases to create man made waterfalls for electricity generation, e.g. the Aswan Dam in Egypt. **Tidal power stations** generate electricity from the rise and fall in water levels as the tide ebbs and flows. Small prototypes operate near Bergen in Norway.

(iii) **Wind power** drives **wind turbines**. These propeller-like machines, designed by engineers from the aerospace industry, may have blades some 50 metres or more across. Clusters of 20–30 wind turbines on exposed hilltops generate electricity efficiently and cheaply. e.g. a wind turbine in Orkney generates 2–4 megawatts (MW).

Renewable energy technologies, popular with conservationatists, may create one or more of the following problems.

Wind turbines

(i) Solar collectors in the UK, especially small models on houses, are inefficient on cloudy days and for most of the winter.

(ii) Solar and wind power are both extremely variable energy sources, affected by changes in weather patterns.

(iii) Tidal schemes can be unsightly and generally have adverse effects on plant and animal life around the shoreline.

(iv) Vast areas of arable land have been flooded by dam projects. People have been uprooted from their homes. Those living in dry valleys, below dams, may run a risk of being flooded. In tropical countries, the water in dams has provided a breeding ground for mosquitoes and other human parasites.

(v) Most large solar, water or wind-powered generators do not produce more than a few MW of electricity. This means that large numbers of generators must be set up to produce enough electricity for feeding into the National Grid.

(vi) Some of the best wind generator sites, on the tops of hills, are often in areas of outstanding natural beauty.

QUESTIONS

1 Copy and complete the following table.

AIR POLLUTANT	SOURCES	EFFECTS
a) Carbon dioxide (CO$_2$)		
b) Sulphur dioxide (SO$_2$)		
c) Nitrogen dioxide (NO$_2$)		
d) Nitric oxide (NO)		
e) Nitrous oxide (N$_2$O)		
f) Ozone (O$_3$)		
g) Methane (CH$_4$)		
h) Chloroflurocarbons (CFCs)		

2 A list of stages leading to the pollution of river are given below:

algae bloom; fish and plants die; fertiliser applied; toxic gases emitted; river water becomes viscous; heavy rainfall; oxygen levels fall; nitrogen-enrichment of river; bacteria and fungi increase; leaching and drainage; river stagnates.

a) Rearrange these stages into their proper sequence.
b) What name is given to the whole process?
c) Describe a different sequence of events leading to the same end result.
d) If the river had become stagnated, in what form would you find:
   (i) nitrogen-containing compounds
   (ii) sulphur-containing compounds?
e) Explain why the stagnant water would be unfit for human consumption.

3 Distinguish between the troposphere and stratosphere.
How do the (a) troposphere, and (b) the ozone layer of the stratosphere, affect life on Earth? In what ways do air pollutants interfere with the structure and functions of these layers in the atmosphere?

4 Write an essay on air pollution, under the following paragraph headings:
a) particulate pollutants,
b) car exhaust fumes,
c) gases from solid fuel combustion,
d) 'greenhouse' gases.

5 Describe the origins and biological effects of acid rain.
What measures can be taken to reduce the emissions of acid-producing gases into the atmosphere?

6 Explain and criticise the term '*greenhouse effect*'.
What are the causes of the 'greenhouse effect'? Suggest how the 'greenhouse effect' might affect (a) climate, (b) plants, and (c) animals by the middle of next century.

7 Write a general account of water pollution in the UK.
How may the fauna of ponds and rivers be used to indicate their degree of pollution?

8 What industrial disasters happened at
(a) Chernobyl, (b) Seveso, (c) Bhopal,
(d) Minimata Bay?
How can the authorities in the UK best provide
safeguards against similar accidents?

BIBLIOGRAPHY

Goldsmith, E and Hildyard, N (1988) *The Earth
Report* Mitchell Beazley

Henderson-Sellers, A and Blong, R (1989) *The
Greenhouse Effect* New South Wales University
Press

Holdgate, M W (1979) *A Perspective of
Environmental Pollution* Cambridge University
Press

Hynes, H B N (1971) *The Ecology of Running
Water* University of Liverpool Press

Leadley Brown, A (1987) *Fresh Water Ecology*
Heinemann

Macan, T T (1973) *Ponds and Lakes* Allen and
Unwin

McCormick, J (1985) *Acid Earth* Earthscan

Mills, D H (1972) *An Introduction to Fresh Water
Ecology* Oliver and Boyd.

GLOSSARY

Abiotic factors: non-biological, physical or chemical conditions, such as temperature, humidity and pH, that form part of an organism's environment

Adaptation: any change in an organism that improves its ability to survive and reproduce in its habitat(s)

Allelopathy: chemical inhibition of one species by another

Autecology: the ecology of a named plant or animal species, its food sources, predators etc.

Biological control: pest control by promoting the pest's natural predators and parasites

Biomass: the dry mass (weight) of all the living organisms in a given population, or given unit of space such as m^2 or hectare

Biosphere: that portion of the Earth's surface occupied by living organisms

Biotic factors: biological conditions, such as food sources and interspecific competition, that form part of an organism's environment

Carrying capacity: the maximum number of a species that can be supported indefinitely by a given habitat or environment

Climax: the final and most stable stage of a community succession

Community: a group of interacting populations in a particular habitat

Competition: the struggle for survival taking place between individuals of the same species and between individuals of different species

Conservation: the preservation of natural resources for use by future generations

Consumers: animals, feeding on plants or other animals

Decomposers: fungi and some bacteria that decompose organic matter in ecosystems, releasing water, CO_2 and mineral salts for recycling

Deme: a small, local subgroup within a population which can interbreed with individuals in other demes

Denitrification: the reduction of nitrate to nitrogen and its oxides

Density: the number of organisms of a species in a given unit of space

Detritus: semi-decomposed, granular organic matter

Diapause: a period of arrested development in the life cycle of insects

Ecology: the interactions between species and their environment

Ecosystem: a unit represented by all the interacting species, and all the environmental fators, in a particular locality

Edaphic: relating to conditions in the soil

Emigration: movement of individuals out of a population

Eutrophication: nutrient enrichment of water in rivers, ponds etc.

Food chain: a linear sequence of eating and being eaten

Food web: interconnected food chains

Genome: all the genes possessed by an individual

Habitat: the place where a species lives, grows and reproduces

Herbicide: a chemical weedkiller

Humus: semi-decomposed, gelatinous organic matter in soil

Immigration: movement of individuals into a population

Interspecific: interactions between individuals of different species

Intraspecific: interactions between individuals of the same species

Leaching: removal of mineral salts from a soil by water, mainly rain

Monoculture: a single crop plant grown over a large area

Mutation: a transmissable change in the structure of a gene or chromosome

Mycorrhiza: fungal hyphae that form a symbiotic association with the roots of flowering plants

Niche: an organism's role in an ecosystem, its habitat, limits of tolerance, interactions etc.

Nitrification: the oxidation of ammonia to nitrate, via nitrite

Nitrogen fixation: the reduction of atmospheric nitrogen to ammonia

Organic farming: growing crops without the aid of artificial fertilisers and other agrochemicals such as herbicides

Pioneer community: the first colonisers in plant or animal succession

Plankton: mostly microscopic floating aquatic plants (phytoplankton) and animals (zooplankton)

Pollution: the release of toxic, or otherwise harmful waste materials, into the environment

Population: a group of individuals of the same species occupying a given unit of space at a given time

Predation: catching and eating animals belonging to another species

Producers: green plants that produce food by photosynthesis

Productivity: the rate at which biomass is accumulated by a species

Quadrat: a square counting frame, often with 100 subdivisions, used to determine the distribution and density of herbs, algae, fungi etc.

Sere: the complete sequence of changes in a plant succession

Species: a group of populations of organisms, capable of interbreeding with one another

Stratification: the zonation of vegetation in a habitat

Succession: a progressive sequence of changes in the flora and fauna of a region, from pioneer to climax communities

Synecology: the ecology of communities and their interactions

Transect: a profile of changes in the distribution and density of plants along a line, or belt, of vegetation

Trophic level: a feeding level, such as producer and consumer, in a food chain

INDEX

ACKNOWLEDGEMENTS

Every effort has been made to trace and acknowledge ownership of copyright of photographs and figures. The publishers will be glad to make suitable arrangements with copyright holders whom it has not been possible to contact.

We are grateful to the following companies, institutions and individuals who give permission to reproduce photographs in this book.

Heather Angel (12 bottom left, 79); R A Beatty/Ecoscene (74); Biophoto Associates (11); John Buckingham/Swan Photographic Agency Ltd (1 – four pictures, 4 top left, 9 top left, 10 – three pictures, 15, 69 bottom, 73, 83, 89, 94 – two pictures, 107 bottom right); J Allan Cash Ltd (110, 111); Nigel Cattlin/Holt Studios Ltd (71, 77, 78, 87, 92); T G Coleman/Swan Photographic Agency Ltd (12 right, 91); Cooper/Ecoscene (81 left); Andrew J Davis/Swan Photographic Agency Ltd (84); Grant Demar/Swan Photographic Agency Ltd (9 right, 13); Greenpeace/Morgan (90); Hulme/Ecoscene (80); ICI Fertilizers (72); Sally Morgan/Ecoscene (18 top left and bottom left, 47, 81 right 107 top left); D Nicholls/Ecoscene (107 top right); Pearson/Ecoscene (46); Pickthall/Ecoscene (86); Popperfoto/Reuter (102 right); Popperfoto/UPI (102 left); Andrew Ruck/Swan Photographic Agency Ltd (4 top right); Mike Weston/Swan Photographic Agency Ltd (18 right); Don Withey/Swan Photographic Agency Ltd (12 top left, 37, 69 top).